Sociological Theory
and Philosophical Analysis

Other books by Dorothy Emmet

Whitehead's Philosophy of Organism

The Nature of Metaphysical Thinking

Function, Purpose and Powers

Rules, Roles and Relations

Space, Time and Deity (editor)

Sociological Theory
and Philosophical Analysis

A Collection Edited with an Introduction by

DOROTHY EMMET and
ALASDAIR MACINTYRE

Macmillan

First edition 1970
Reprinted 1972

Published by
THE MACMILLAN PRESS LTD
London and Basingstoke
Associated companies in New York Toronto
Dublin Melbourne Johannesburg and Madras

SBN 333 10521 4 (hard cover)
333 10522 2 (paper cover)

Printed in Great Britain by
ROBERT MACLEHOSE AND CO LTD
The University Press, Glasgow

Contents

v

Acknowledgements

Acknowledgements for permission to reprint the papers in this collection are made to the following:

For 'Concept and Theory Formation in the Social Sciences' and 'The Problems of Rationality in a Social World', to Martinus Nijhoff.

For 'Sociological Explanation' and 'Methodological Individualism Reconsidered', to Routledge and Kegan Paul (Publishers of The 'British Journal of Sociology'); also to Professor Tom Burns and Mr Steven Lukes respectively.

For 'Concepts and Society', to the International Sociological Association and to Professor Ernest Gellner.

For 'Knowledge and Interest', to the editor of 'Inquiry', the Norwegian Research Council and Professor Habermas.

For 'Is it a Science?', to the editor of 'Social Research' and to Professor Sidney Morgenbesser.

For 'Telstar and the Aborigines' to the editor of 'Annales' and to Dr Edmund Leach.

For 'Symbols in Ndembu Ritual', to the Aldine Publishing Company, to Professor Victor Turner and to Professor Max Gluckman.

For 'Groote Eylandt Totemism and *Le Totémisme aujourd'hui*', to Tavistock Publications Ltd, to Professor Peter Worsley, and to Dr Edmund Leach (editor); and to the Association of Social Anthropologists of the Commonwealth.

A full reference to the original provenance of each paper in this collection is given in a footnote to its title.

Introduction

The papers reprinted in this volume do in fact represent several distinct and distinctive philosophical traditions. But this is not at all because the editors felt any obligation to include differing viewpoints and it is not because of any editorial aspirations towards synthesis or eclecticism. The criterion for inclusion has rather been that a paper should seem to us to contribute to the clarification of and possibly to the solution of the philosophical and theoretical problems which arise for sociologists and anthropologists in the course of their own professional inquiries independently of any philosophical interests that they themselves may happen to possess. One advantage of this criterion is that it may avoid the suggestion, implicit in certain other anthologies, that *first,* one has to select some general philosophical standpoint — such as that of logical empiricism or phenomenology — on epistemological or other philosophical grounds, and then only *secondly* to apply the methods and insights of the chosen tradition to the problems of the philosophy of social science. This seems to us to get things the wrong way round. The value and relevance of any general philosophical standpoint to the philosophy of the social sciences can only be demonstrated by showing the contribution that it makes to the key problems.

We have also tried to avoid an approach which is sometimes connected with the tendency to approach the problems from a comprehensive philosophical standpoint, an approach which ties together a number of issues and suggests that where you stand on any one of these will entail a corresponding stance on all the others. Two of the papers in this collection are in fact specifically aimed at separating out questions that have been bundled together by others in this way. Professor Morgenbesser's 'Is it a Science?' (2) distinguishes the questions 'Are the methods and concepts of the social sciences similar to or dissimilar from those of the natural sciences?' 'Are the basic theories of the social sciences reducible to some suitable theory in the natural sciences?' and 'Is the aim of the social sciences to discover laws?' Mr Lukes's 'Methodological Individualism Reconsidered' (5) distinguishes four different theses which might be asserted by someone who wished to claim that facts about social institutions ought to be explained by reference to facts about individuals, theses which are logically independent of each other. To make this kind of distinction is obviously necessary if any progress at all is to be made in the philosophy of the social sciences and in particular any progress in directions which may be illuminating to social scientists themselves.

In placing such emphasis on the problems of the social scientists we have to be careful not to fall into another error. Social scientists are understandably and rightly intolerant of philosophical evaluations of their work which rest on a very partial knowledge and comprehension. But in insisting upon the need for wide-ranging and first-hand knowledge of any disciplines about which one may intend to philosophise social scientists may seek to canonise the present state of their own disciplines in a quite illegitimate way. An academic psychologist who reviewed Charles Taylor's book on the philosophy of psychology, *The Explanation of Behaviour*, complained in a somewhat shrill way that while philosophers accept the methods, concepts and theories actually employed by physicists as setting the standards for what physics ought to be, they refuse to treat the actual practices of psychologists as setting the standards for psychology. This complaint — apart from its ignoring of all too obvious differences between the present state of physics and that of psychology — seems to involve a misunderstanding of the philosophy of science.

What scientists actually do can never of itself provide a norm for what they ought to do, even in physics. The existence of 'German physics' under the Nazis — 'German physics' was, roughly speaking, physics *minus* those discoveries which had been made by Jews — and of 'German mathematics' is only the most striking example of the innumerable ways in which the scientific community may in part or in whole be led or misled away from the norms of scientific practice. But what are these norms? We would make a mistake here if we tried to articulate a body of rules which are abstract enough to have no reference to the specific subject-matter of any particular science and which taken together are such that to follow them is to satisfy the necessary and the sufficient conditions which are required if one's methods are to be scientific. Rules which constitute necessary conditions for this, certainly; but there are always in each specific well-developed science methods, procedures and concepts the justification for the use of which is only to be found in the prior decisions of that science. The very subject-matter appropriate to a given science comes to be identifiable only *via* the theories of that science.

Yet in saying this we have spoken of 'well-developed' sciences. Are the social sciences in this sense well-developed? One crucial point to be raised by anyone who wants to answer this question concerns the relationship of the different social sciences to each other. Economics is defined by its methods, not by its subject-matter. Political science is defined by its subject-matter and not by its methods. Psychology is defined partly by methods and partly by subject-matter. In the natural sciences there are of course similar contrasts to be found. But what there is no parallel to in the relations of the natural sciences to each other is the relationship of sociology to the other social sciences. For on the one hand sociology, using as it does a wide variety of methods, and approaching an even wider range of subject-matters, might seem to be almost a residual category, a rag-bag containing everything social and human not appropriated by economics, political science or psychology. But on the other hand, for precisely the same reasons, sociology may be taken to be the master science of the human sciences, raising questions about possible relationships to which the more limited inquiries may blind themselves by the very fact of their being limited.

The focus of the papers in this anthology is sociology in the wider rather than in the narrower sense. This means that some of them are concerned with problems that are of importance for all social science and indeed for all the human sciences. Others are concerned with problems of a more specific kind and some of the most interesting of these arise from the work of social anthropologists. We do not believe that it is possible any longer to treat social anthropology and sociology as separate disciplines. Accidents of academic history for too long kept apart the study of relatively primitive societies from the study of industrial societies and both from the study of all those societies betwixt and between whose life comprises a great part of human history. The methods which each discipline developed separately are now being fused with great profit and we have taken their mutual relevance for granted in this anthology.

The boundaries between such disciplines are not in fact based on what has been already discovered, as they are in the natural sciences, but there is a certain arbitrariness about them, a certain ambiguity. It is partly for this reason that questions of philosophical character arise for the social scientist himself and not merely for the philosophical observer of the social sciences. What some of these questions are can be suggested by considering some of the reasons which moved us to include this particular selection of papers.

Alfred Schutz, the only author represented in this collection by more than one paper, was in philosophy a follower of Husserl; but he resorted to Husserl's phenomenology precisely because he believed that he could find in it reasons to solve certain philosophical problems raised by the sociological theorising of Max Weber. Schutz has often been grouped with those, such as Dilthey and Rickert, who insisted on the existence of a fundamental rift between forms of understanding appropriate to the human sciences and the types of explanation produced by the natural sciences. But this is in some ways highly misleading, as is made clear in 'Concept and Theory Formation in the Social Sciences' (1). In this paper Schutz was commenting on papers contributed by Ernest Nagel and C. G. Hempel to an American Philosophical Association symposium with the same title. Nagel in particular had criticised Weber's notion of *Verstehen* on the grounds that Weber is committed by it to trying to explain human action in terms of the character of dubiously accessible inner states rather than of publicly observable behaviour. In replying to Nagel, Schutz emphasises his agreement with Nagel on the nature of the logical structure of theory in the social sciences and what the natural and the social sciences have in common in this respect. He further agrees with Nagel and Hempel that if *Verstehen*, as Weber understood it, were a matter of uncheckable intuitions of the private inner states of others, then it could have no legitimate place in scientific theory. But he cannot agree that Nagel has understood Weber correctly.

The core of Schutz's reply to Nagel is an argument in two stages. He interprets Weber's notion of *Verstehen** as being in essence the same as that of our everyday and indispensable notion of understanding each other. We ascribe to others — whatever philosophical difficulties there may be in understanding how it is possible for us to do this — emotions, motives, aims, and our own emotions, motives and aims presuppose our beliefs about those of others precisely because of their intentional (in the phenomenological sense) character. Schutz could have quoted in his support here Hume's remarking in his discussion of sympathy how much of the emotional life of each of us is a response to the emotions of others. We cannot simply equate the emotions, motives and aims of others with their behaviour or with certain features of their behaviour, because the same behaviour or behaviour exhibiting the same features may on different occasions be informed by very different emotions, motives and aims. We all do recognise this without difficulty in our everyday transactions in which we are neither behaviourists nor subjectivists, but 'experience the world we live in . . . not as a private but as an intersubjective one . . .'.

Weber's notion of *Verstehen* is, then, one to which we are committed, however we may at another level philosophise about it. The second stage of Schutz's argument is to the effect that what we learn from social science about human nature will only explain certain features of that nature and will omit others unless social science can explain why the character of our intersubjective experience of each other in social relationship is as it is. Schutz does not want to deny the possibility of theorising about the publicly observable (in the crudest sense) features of human life; it is just that there is more to be explained. If a theory can be developed on such principles, say in the form of ideally refined behaviourism —

* For the ancestry of this notion see the work by H. A. Hodges in the Bibliography.

and it is certainly possible to imagine this — then it will not tell us anything about social reality as experienced by men in everyday life.

Schutz unfortunately does seem to suppose that behaviourism is more in accordance with 'the principles of concept and theory formation prevailing in the natural sciences' than are non-behaviourist views, but he could only do so consistently if he agreed with the behaviourists as to the character of what is publicly accessible and observable; and we have already noticed that he does not. Hence Schutz unnecessarily weakens his own position by pointing to a contrast where none exists. Much more seriously, Schutz seems to us at best dangerously ambiguous when he insists that 'a theory which aims at explaining social reality' must not only explain but also 'agree with the commonsense experience of the social world'. If Schutz means by this no more than that there are certain truths which we all in our everyday lives learn about the character of those lives and that any theory inconsistent with those truths would necessarily be false, then what he says is true and obviously true. But if what he means entails that the commonsense view of the social world must be immune from correction and modification by the discoveries of social science then what he asserts is not only false but deprives the social sciences of part of their genuine importance. Our common-sense beliefs about society are not only often false, but are also sometimes incorrigible at the level of commonsense.

Nonetheless, Schutz's views on this point do not affect his claim that the notion of typicality can be used fruitfully in theory construction. Of course the vindication of Schutz's claim could in the end only be empirical: that theory employing such concepts did turn out to have explanatory and predictive power; but Schutz may perhaps prevent sociologists from supposing that there are *a priori* philosophical objections to constructing such theories. The phrase 'explanatory and predictive power' is not of course itself unproblematic. Professor Morgenbesser in his 'Is it a Science?' (2) makes two points about it which are perhaps even more crucial for the practice of social science than his paper itself suggests. The background to both points is his insistence that it is not merely the discovery of laws that is important to the social sciences, but the discovery of laws that can serve certain explanatory and predictive purposes. It might indeed be suggested that even when we believe ourselves to be in a position to assert generalisations which entail the truth of certain counterfactual conditions and not mere statements of *de facto* regularities we may hesitate to assign to them the status of laws unless they have a certain explanatory and predictive power.

But Professor Morgenbesser's point is that explanatory power and predictive power are not the same thing, and indeed that the degree of explanatory power possessed by a theory may be quite different from the degree of predictive power which it possesses, if by 'predictive power' we mean 'providing us with actual ability to predict'.

For it may be that at any given time the information that would be required if one was to make predictive use of a particular law is not available, although at some later time after the event the information that is required to make explanatory use of that same law will become available. Professor Morgenbesser does not himself emphasise one interesting corollary of this. It is that the laws the statement of which may be crucial to the development of a theory in a given area might well be laws whose predictive power, for the reason that he has given, is low. Hence the pursuit of predictive power as a goal for the social sciences could on occasion actually inhibit their theoretical development. When one considers that the funding of social science research is very often motivated by the wish of politicians and others to predict with a view to planning, it is clear that this is not a negligible consideration. It is part of the contemporary spirit to suppose that sciences suffer for lack of financial support; that they may also suffer intellectually because of the kind of financial support that they receive is worth remembering.

Professor Morgenbesser's second point that needs underlining is that in the natural sciences explanations are not all of one kind. Writers about social science often note the role of statistical generalisation in the natural sciences in a very general way without inquiring what different models the natural sciences offer them. Hence Professor Morgenbesser's brief but lucid questioning of the view that 'in a real science all real explanations and predictions are ... based on deterministic laws which, given information about the state of a system at t, allow us to deduce statements about future states of the system and also about its past states' has an importance out of all proportion to its brevity.

Professor Habermas's paper (3) is important for one minor reason as well as for some major ones. Like Schutz's work Habermas's springs from a tradition which Anglo-Saxon analytical philosophers all too often regard as one in which unclarity is endemic. Like Schutz Habermas provides an immediate refutation of this parochial view. Habermas's thesis is directed against those who suppose that the character and history of social orders can be explained without reference to the growth of knowledge and equally or even more against those who suppose that the growth of knowledge can be explained by some other feature of social orders or social interests. It is not just that it is a necessary precondition of the growth of knowledge that knowledge should free itself from too close a dependence on practical social interests. It is rather that the level of objective knowledge, undistorted by interest, that we possess determines what interests us and what effect our interests have upon us. So Habermas writes that 'the processes of cognition, which are inseparable from the creation of society cannot function only as a means of maintenance and reproduction of life; they serve equally to establish the very definitions of this life'.

Hence it is a corollary of Habermas's argument, just as it is of Morgenbesser's, that the aim of technical control may distort the development of science and of social science. Habermas has no doubts about the intimate relationship of explanation and prediction; he does also believe, like Schutz, that the natural sciences are to be understood in a positivistic way, so that they necessarily omit something that the social sciences have to grasp. Both Schutz and Habermas would agree in taking G. H. Mead's remark that behaviourism can explain only the observed and not the observer, even the behaviourist observer, as marking a contrast between natural and social science. For reasons we have already suggested we think this contrast to be a mistake and that one way to avoid at least one mistake is to learn from philosophers of natural science, such as Morgenbesser, both the danger of assimilating predictive power and explanatory power and the need, in natural as in social science, to introduce very different types of theoretical concept which stand in very different relationships to what is directly observed.

If one contrasts Morgenbesser's paper with Habermas's one point becomes clear: it is not that there are obscurities, or what will seem to the Anglo-Saxon reader obscurities, so much as the fact that these two papers come from two distinct philosophical and scientific traditions which have communicated insufficiently. Of English writers Habermas cites only Sir Karl Popper; of Continental writers Morgenbesser cites only in passing Comte, Gusdorf, Duverger and once again Sir Karl Popper (who belongs of course to both communities). Yet these papers provide clear evidence of a strong intellectual unity between these traditions.

Professor Burns's paper (4) views many of the same problems that we have raised in connection with the arguments of Schutz, Morgenbesser and Habermas, but from the standpoint of the sociologist. The importance of Professor Burns's paper seems to us at least twofold. Part of it arises from his argument that the explanations which the sociologists seek to advance are rival explanations to those which are actually employed in the cause of social life. When the sociologist explains why a given institution or practice functions as it does, his explanations may and often will entail the falsity of those explanations the giving of which are part of the normal functioning of the institute or practice which the sociologist is engaged in explaining. Burns gives us an example of this in Aubert's demonstration that variations in judicial sentencing in Norway are related to the social class of the accused person rather than to the avowed and overt principles relied upon by the judges.

What work like Aubert's achieves is of course only a preliminary to the task of explanation, and that for two reasons. First of all it tells us that there is more which needs to be explained than we had hitherto supposed. A new and disconcerting fact, the gap between what the judges take themselves to be doing and what others take them to be doing, on the one hand, and what they are actually doing, on the other hand, has been brought to our attention. Secondly in so far as Aubert has related type and severity of sentence to the social class of the accused it is still not at all clear what the relationship is and the unclarity involved has little to do with statistical imprecision. What is unclear is what causal generalisations, if any, we are or ought to be committed to by our acceptance of Aubert's contentions. Donald Davidson has pointed out that we may often know the truth of singular causal statements while unable to formulate the generalisations in virtue of which our assertion of the causal connection is warranted and to the assertion of which we are committed by our assertion of the singular statement. The importance of this may be brought to mind by considering another of Professor Burns's examples. He explains the juvenile delinquency in the Edinburgh district of Pilton in 1954 by citing the difficulty in exercising social control over and providing a social education for children who form a disproportionately large section of a population; and he explains the disproportionately large number of children in Pilton by citing the City of Edinburgh's housing policies in the 1930s. What is in question is not the correctness of Professor Burns's explanation; it is rather that it is not clear what the explanation he is advancing is and this is not because of any negligence on his part. How to formulate the precise generalisations on which he relies — on those towards which Aubert is moving — is unclear in the absence of any well-developed theory of delinquency. Indeed the type of generalisations which appear to be involved might make it questionable what a theory of delinquency or of sentencing would be.

We might also note that to emphasise — as Burns rightly does — the critical function of sociological explanation in exposing the falsity of the explanations actually used in social life may have under certain circumstances the same dangerous effects as an interest in predictive power. For those generalisations which are most important in their critical effect may not be those which it is most important to formulate in the interests of the intellectual development of sociological theory.

Mr Lukes's paper (5) links the abstract interests in explanation of a Schutz or a Morgenbesser to the concrete, substantive interests of a Burns. The effect of Mr Lukes's paper is to show that certain supposed *a priori* difficulties in the formulation of certain possible types of sociological theory are not in fact genuine. As against philosophers who have argued that all social phenomena must in the end be explained by the attitudes of individual human beings Mr Lukes contends that a wide variety of possibilities are open. It follows that whether individual behaviour is to be explained by reference to the characteristics of groups, social orders and institutions, or whether the characteristics of all these are instead to be explained by reference to the behaviour of individuals is an empirical and not a conceptual question. What answer we shall give will depend on the directions in which sociological theory develops. This is of course as uncomfortable a doctrine for those holistic theorists whom methodological individualists were criticising as it is for methodological individualists. (By 'holism' we intend to refer to any social theory which offers explanations in terms of collectivities.) There have been both overall holistic and overall individualistic social theories; but perhaps only holistic theories may turn out to be well-founded, perhaps only individualistic theories may turn out to be well-founded, or perhaps in some areas we shall require the one type of theory and in others the other. The moral of Mr Lukes's paper is that this type of issue cannot be settled by philosophy, but only by the progress of empirical inquiry.

Papers 7-10 are indicative of what may be a new stage in social anthropology. (We are thinking here in particular of social anthropology in Britain, the Commonwealth and the U.S.A. European anthropology has always been closely connected with philosophy, and indeed its anthropologists have often been trained in particular philosophical traditions: Durkheim in Comtean positivism; Weber in post-Kantian Idealism and Marxism; others such as Alfred Schutz in Husserlian phenomenology.) British anthropologists, for the last generation at any rate, have concentrated on field studies, using structural-functional concepts in order to see each society studied as a system of interrelated institutions. This has led to detailed particular studies, and also to caution in producing cross-cultural generalisations. Where there has been talk of general 'laws', this has been a programmatic hope rather than an actual attempt at formulating and testing such laws.

We are now seeing the end of what Professor Gellner (7) calls 'strong functionalism', the notion that each institution in a society is tightly fitted to its context, and uniquely suited to it. It was clear that this way of looking at societies, besides the problem it sets for generalisation, made societies appear as more stable and self-maintaining than the facts of conflict and crisis warrant, and also produced great difficulty over how to deal with social change. We have not included any papers directly representing this point of view, partly because in this 'strong' sense it is on the way out, and partly because the whole 'Functionalism' discussion is very fully documented in a volume of papers and extracts *System, Change and Conflict: A Reader on Contemporary Sociological Theory and the Debate over Functionalism.* * Two of the papers in this collection are especially worth noting: R. P. Dore's 'Function and Cause', for the kind of system and 'explanation' offered in functional views and the problem of their teleological overtones; and Ralph Dahrendorf's 'Out of Utopia', where the case is put for a 'conflict' model of society instead of consensus models centring on the notion of social 'equilibrium'.

Gellner's paper (7) brings out how 'strong functionalism' still gets applied in presenting people's beliefs and concepts. Here it can join hands with the Wittgensteinian view of 'language as a form of life'. This suggests that the meaning of a belief or a concept is to be found in its use in a particular culture-bound, indeed society-bound, context and this is all that need be said to justify it. There is no possibility of judging it by transcultural criteria of truth or rationality. Professor Peter Winch has been the main advocate of conceptual 'strong functionalism',† Gellner shows how this 'excessive charity' to concepts and beliefs does not even allow for the extent to which they may be ambiguous and questioned within their cultural context, and still less for the possibility of criticism to go on in developed societies where

* Ed. N. J. Demerath III and Richard A. Peterson (Free Press, New York, 1967).

† See his 'Understanding a Primitive Society', 'American Philosophical Quarterly', i (1964). The question of transcultural as well as culture-bound criteria of rationality is also discussed in a symposium between Steven Lukes, Martin Hollis, and John Torrance in *Archives européenes sociologiques*, viii (1967).

cross-cultural scientific ideas have had an impact and exist alongside of non-scientific ones, and in less developed ones where they are beginning to have an impact.

Abandoning 'strong functionalism' allows us to look at ways in which a belief or custom in the setting of one society may have its analogies elsewhere, and to return — cautiously — to attempts at transcultural generalisation. Professor Victor Turner's paper (8) is both a study in depth of certain symbols in Ndembu ritual, and presents a general hypothesis about the character of such symbols and how they work. Within a broadly structural-functional approach, in which he looks at performances of ritual as 'distinct phases in social processes whereby groups become adjusted to internal changes and adapted to their external environment', he distinguishes two 'poles of meaning': the ideological, where symbols refer to factors of social life and organisation, and through which they can be used as means of social control, and the 'sensory', where these same symbols are emotionally charged by association with processes and drives within the depths of the psyche. Turner's contribution in this paper is to show how these two aspects of a symbol may operate simultaneously. The 'sensory', especially as psycho-analytically interpreted, meaning of the symbol may show how it expresses ambivalent emotions and suppressed conflicts — hate and fear as well as love and trust. The 'ideological' meaning relates it to standards of ideal social harmony. Thus 'in the action situation of ritual . . . the ritual symbol effects an interchange of qualities between its poles of meaning. Norms and values, on the one hand, become saturated with emotion, while the gross and base emotions become ennobled through contact with social values. The irksomeness of moral constraint is transformed into the "love of virtue".' This essay is a sustained attempt to draw on psycho-analytic concepts as well as on sociological ones in interpreting ritual symbols, and to show that the effectiveness of a symbol in its social setting may depend on its emotional overtones (or undertones). But the 'synthesis' of the two kinds of concept, sociological and psycho-analytic or psychological, is given pragmatically, showing how in actual operation the effectiveness of the symbol is enhanced by its having these two 'poles of meaning'. This does not meet the theoretical problem of how both kinds of concept might be related in a more comprehensive kind of 'explanation', nor what would be the limitation of each kind of 'explanation' apart from the other. Nor does it meet the problems of whether there may be still other frames of reference within which the ritual symbol might be interpreted. Participants in a ritual may themselves believe that it is a way of responding to a cosmic, if not supernatural, environment and not only to a social one. Sociologists, as empirical scientists, have generally dismissed this as an overbelief, as perhaps it is. But to assume that it must be so, and that social realities must the the real referents, is to beg a metaphysical question.

A revival of interest, if not in 'Primitive Man as Philosopher',* at any rate in Primitive Man as Logician is being stirred up by the influential but very difficult work of Lévi-Strauss. Dr Edmund Leach's paper (9) in this collection is the original English version of an article published in French in the Paris journal *Annales*. It brings out in a clear, manageable way the main point Lévi-Strauss is making. Unlike Lévy-Bruhl, who believed that primitives did not operate with the principle of contradiction, Lévi-Strauss thinks that this is the fundamental principle of primitive thinking. Primitive thinking (which here stands for something which goes on in all of us) distinguishes subjects into pairs of contrasted opposites — whom you may marry/whom you mayn't; who belongs to your group/who doesn't; what is edible/what isn't; what is cooked/what is raw (these last being of great importance). These distinctions are remembered by the help of taxonomic devices which codify them, where there is no written language, by connecting them with things in the external world, and so with distinctions for ordering external nature: plant and animal totemism, as a classificatory language with which to think about social relations, is seen as such a taxonomic device. Professor Worsley (10) questions whether this simple and attractive theory stands up to the immense variety in totemic devices and their uses. He also suggests that being wedded to

* The title of a well-known book by an anthropologist of an older generation, Paul Radin.

'binary' notions can be 'numerology and fashion, not science'; and that primitive classification can proceed by methods other than that of contrasted opposites. All this is a field for the combined efforts of anthropologists, linguistic experts and logicians — a possibility of collaboration to which Lévi-Strauss has given a fresh impetus. As Leach says, binary discriminations of a yes/no kind may have been thought of as representing a crude level of thinking, but their use as the basis of programming codes in Communications Theory now shows how fundamental this simple basis is, and how it can be increasingly refined to convey messages of great subtlety and detail.

A connection between the thought system behind the satellite 'Telstar' and that of the 'aborigines' is a heady possibility suggested by Lévi-Strauss's views. A more particular problem is raised by the particular instances he gives of binary distinctions; some of these seem to be genuine contrasts (e.g. whom you may marry/whom you may not), while others are contrasts (e.g. mountain hunting/sea hunting) which need not be exhaustive classifications, and so do not lend themselves in the same way to binary coding.

Lévi-Strauss is often accused, as Professor Worsley accuses him (10), of 'formalism'. In a system of abstract logical relations if one element is transformed into its opposite throughout, another system can be produced which is its mirror image. Since the one can be derived from the other if one knows the rule, Lévi-Strauss says that they can be called the same system. A constant relationship between the elements has been preserved. Lévi-Strauss applies this principle to social structures, and in a paper 'The Bear and the Barber',* he plotted a caste system onto a totemic system by showing a logically inverted similarity between them: caste systems exchange women within the caste and occupational activities outside it; totemic systems exchange occupational activities inside the clan and women outside it (and there are further refinements on this basic inversion). This formal similarity does not mean of course that an actual caste society can be equated with a totemic one, but that the one system can be logically derived from the other. For Lévi-

* 'Journal of the Royal Anthropological Institute', xciii (1) 1-11.

Strauss the abstract level on which the social structure is codified is an artifact of the mind; it is the abstract model that people have of their society, and it need not correspond at all closely with what actually goes on in empirical reality. But, as Worsley says (10), distinctions of social groups are found preceding the dubbing of them by totemic classificatory labels. There are distinctions already there in social reality which the system classifies, albeit in artificial terms, and often no doubt by slurring over other distinctions. This process, started in rudimentary thinking, is carried further when sociologists produce more abstract categories, less tied to concrete analogies and so giving greater analytic power. So Lévi-Strauss's view of the methods of primitive classificatory thinking, as Leach explains them and Worsley criticises them in our last two papers, brings us back to the fundamental problem discussed by Schutz in our first and sixth papers: the construction of conceptual systems and their relation to an empirical subject-matter.

1 Concept and Theory Formation in the Social Sciences*

Alfred Schutz

The title of my paper refers intentionally to that of a Symposium held in December 1952, at the annual meeting of the American Philosophical Association.[1] Ernest Nagel and Carl G. Hempel contributed highly stimulating comments on the problem involved, formulated in the careful and lucid way so characteristic of these scholars. Their topic is a controversy which for more than half a century has split not only logicians and methodologists but also social scientists into two schools of thought. One of these holds that the methods of the natural sciences which have brought about such magnificent results are the only scientific ones and that they alone, therefore, have to be applied in their entirety to the study of human affairs. Failure to do so, it has been maintained, prevented the social sciences from developing systems of explanatory theory comparable in precision to those offered by the natural sciences and makes debatable the empirical work of theories developed in restricted domains such as economics.

The other school of thought feels that there is a basic difference in the structure of the social world and the world of nature. This feeling led to the other extreme, namely the conclusion that the methods of the social sciences are *toto coelo* different from those of the natural sciences. In order to support this position a variety of arguments was proffered. It has been maintained that the social sciences are ideographic, characterised by individualising conceptualisation and seeking singular assertory propositions, whereas the natural sciences are nomothetic, characterised by generalising conceptualisation and seeking general apodictic propositions. The latter

* 'Collected Papers', i 48-66, Ed. Maurice Natanson (Martinus Nijhoff, The Hague, 1962): presented at the Thirty-third Semi-Annual Meeting of the Conference on Methods in Philosophy and the Sciences, New York, 3 May 1953.

have to deal with constant relations of magnitude which can be measured and can perform experiments, whereas neither measurement nor experiment is practicable in the social sciences. In general, it is held that the natural sciences have to deal with material objects and processes, the social sciences, however, with psychological and intellectual ones and that, therefore, the method of the former consists in explaining, that of the latter in understanding.

Admittedly, most of these highly generalised statements are untenable under closer examination, and this for several reasons. Some proponents of the characterised arguments had a rather erroneous concept of the methods of the natural sciences. Others were inclined to identify the methodological situation in one particular social science with the method of the social sciences in general. Because history has to deal with unique and non-recurrent events, it was contended that all social sciences are restricted to singular assertory propositions. Because experiments are hardly possible in cultural anthropology, the fact was ignored that social psychologists can successfully use laboratory experiments at least to a certain extent. Finally, and this is the most important point, these arguments disregard the fact that a set of rules for scientific procedure is equally valid for all empirical sciences whether they deal with objects of nature or with human affairs. Here and there, the principles of controlled inference and verification by fellow scientists and the theoretical ideals of unity, simplicity, universality, and precision prevail.

This unsatisfactory state of affairs results chiefly from the fact that the development of the modern social sciences occurred during a period in which the science of logic was mostly concerned with the logic of the natural sciences. In a kind of monopolistic imperialism the methods of the latter were frequently declared to be the only scientific ones and the particular problems which social scientists encountered in their work were disregarded. Left without help and guidance in their revolt against this dogmatism, the students of human affairs had to develop their own conceptions of what they believed to be the methodology of the social sciences. They did it without sufficient philosophical knowledge and stopped their effort when they reached a level of generalisation which seemed to justify their deeply felt conviction

2

that the goal of their inquiry could not be reached by adopting the methods of the natural sciences without modification or implementation. No wonder that their arguments are frequently ill-founded, their formulations insufficient, and that many misunderstandings obfuscate the controversy. Not what social scientists *said* but what they *meant* is therefore our main concern in the following.

The writings of the late Felix Kaufmann[2] and the more recent contributions by Nagel[3] and Hempel[4] have criticised many fallacies in the arguments proposed by social scientists and prepared the ground for another approach to the problem. I shall here concentrate on Professor Nagel's criticism of the claim made by Max Weber and his school that the social sciences seek to 'understand' social phenomena in terms of 'meaningful' categories of human experience and that, therefore, the 'causal functional' approach of the natural sciences is not applicable in social inquiry. This school, as Dr Nagel sees it, maintains that all socially significant human behaviour is an expression of motivated psychic states, that in consequence the social scientist cannot be satisfied with viewing social processes simply as concatenations of 'externally related' events, and that the establishment of correlations or even of universal relations of concomitance cannot be his ultimate goal. On the contrary, he must construct 'ideal types' or 'models of motivations' in terms of which he seeks to 'understand' overt social behaviour by imputing springs of action to the actors involved in it. If I understand Professor Nagel's criticism correctly, he maintains:

1. That these springs of action are not accessible to sensory observation. It follows and has frequently been stated that the social scientist must imaginatively identify himself with the participants and view the situation which they face as the actors themselves view it. Surely, however, we need not undergo other men's psychic experiences in order to know that they have them or in order to predict their overt behaviour.

2. That the imputation of emotions, attitudes, and purposes as an explanation of overt behaviour is a twofold hypothesis: it assumes that the agents participating in some social phenomenon are in certain psychological states; and it

3

assumes also definite relations of concomitance between such states, and between such states and overt behaviour. Yet none of the psychological states which we imagine the subjects of our study to possess may in reality be theirs, and even if our imputations should be correct none of the overt actions which allegedly issue from those states may appear to us understandable or reasonable.

3. That we do not 'understand' the nature and operations of human motives and their issuance in overt behaviour more adequately than the 'external' causal relations. If by meaningful explanation we assert merely that a particular action is an instance of a pattern of behaviour which human beings exhibit under a variety of circumstances and that, since some of the relevant circumstances are realised in the given situation, a person can be expected to manifest a certain form of that pattern, then there is no sharp gulf separating such explanations from those involving merely 'external' knowledge of causal connections. It is possible to gain knowledge of the actions of men on the evidence supplied by their overt behaviour just as it is possible to discover and know the atomic constitution of water on the evidence supplied by the physical and chemical behaviour of that substance. Hence the rejection of a purely 'objective' or 'behaviouristic' social science by the proponents of 'meaningful connections' as the goal of social sciences is unwarranted.

Since I shall have to disagree with Nagel's and Hempel's findings on several questions of a fundamental nature, I might be permitted to start with a brief summary of the no less important points on which I find myself happily in full agreement with them. I agree with Professor Nagel that all empirical knowledge involves discovery through processes of controlled inference, and that it must be statable in propositional form and capable of being verified by anyone who is prepared to make the effort to do so through observation[5] — although I do not believe, as Professor Nagel does, that this observation has to be sensory in the precise meaning of this term. Moreover, I agree with him that 'theory' means in all empirical sciences the explicit formulation of determinate relations between a set of variables in terms of which a fairly extensive class of empirically ascertainable regu-

4

larities can be explained.[6] Furthermore, I agree whole-heartedly with his statement that neither the fact that these regularities have in the social sciences a rather narrowly restricted universality, nor the fact that they permit prediction only to a rather limited extent, constitutes a basic difference between the social and the natural sciences, since many branches of the latter show the same features.[7] As I shall try to show later on, it seems to me that Professor Nagel misunderstands Max Weber's postulate of subjective interpretation. Nevertheless, he is right in stating that method which would require that the individual scientific observer identify himself with the social agent observed in order to understand the motives of the latter, or a method which would refer the selection of the facts observed and their interpretation to the private value system of the particular observer, would merely lead to an uncontrollable private and subjective image in the mind of this particular student of human affairs, but never to a scientific theory.[8] But I do not know of any social scientist of stature who ever advocated such a concept of subjectivity as that criticised by Professor Nagel. Most certainly this was not the position of Max Weber.

I also think that our authors are prevented from grasping the point of vital concern to social scientists by their basic philosophy of sensationalistic empiricism or logical positivism, which identifies experience with sensory observation and which assumes that the only alternative to controllable and, therefore, objective sensory observation is that of subjective and, therefore, uncontrollable and unverifiable introspection. This is certainly not the place to renew the age-old controversy relating to the hidden presuppositions and implied metaphysical assumptions of this basic philosophy. On the other hand, in order to account for my own position, I should have to treat at length certain principles of phenomenology. Instead of doing so, I propose to defend a few rather simple propostions:

1. The primary goal of the social sciences is to obtain organised knowledge of social reality. By the term 'social reality' I wish to be understood the sum total of objects and occurrences within the social cultural world as experienced by the commonsense thinking of men living their daily lives among their fellow-men, connected with them in manifold

5

relations of interaction. It is the world of cultural objects and social institutions into which we are all born, within which we have to find our bearings, and with which we have to come to terms. From the outset, we, the actors on the social scene, experience the world we live in as a world both of nature and of culture, not as a private but as an inter-subjective one, that is, as a world common to all of us, either actually given or potentially accessible to everyone; and this involves intercommunication and language.

2. All forms of naturalism and logical empiricism simply take for granted this social reality, which is the proper object of the social sciences. Intersubjectivity, interaction, inter-communication and language are simply presupposed as the unclarified foundation of these theories. They assume, as it were, that the social scientist has already solved his fundamental problem, before scientific enquiry starts. To be sure, Dewey emphasised, with a clarity worthy of this eminent philosopher, that all inquiry starts and ends within the social cultural matrix; to be sure, Professor Nagel is fully aware of the fact that science and its self-correcting process is a social enterprise.[9] But the postulate of describing and explaining human behaviour in terms of controllable sensory observation stops short before the description and ex-planation of the process by which scientist B controls and verifies the observational findings of scientist A and the conclusions drawn by him. In order to do so, B has to know what A has observed, what the goal of his inquiry is, why he thought the observed fact worthy of being observed, i.e. relevant to the scientific problem at hand, etc. This know-ledge is commonly called understanding. The explanation of how such a mutual understanding of human beings might occur is apparently left to the social scientist. But whatever his explanation might be, one thing is sure, namely, that such an intersubjective understanding between scientist B and scientist A occurs neither by scientist B's observations of scientist A's overt behaviour, nor by introspection performed by B, nor by identification of B with A. To translate this argument into the language dear to logical positivism, this means, as Felix Kaufmann[10] has shown, that so-called protocol propositions about the physical world are of an entirely different kind from protocol propositions about the

6

psycho-physical world.

3. The identification of experience with sensory observation in general and of the experience of overt action in particular (and that is what Nagel proposes) excludes several dimensions of social reality from all possible inquiry.

(a) Even an ideally refined behaviourism can, as has been pointed out for instance by George H. Mead,[11] merely explain the behaviour of the observed, not of the observing behaviourist.

(b) The same overt behaviour (say a tribal pageant as it can be captured by the movie camera) may have an entirely different meaning to the performers. What interests the social scientist is merely whether it is a war dance, a barter trade, the reception of a friendly ambassador, or something else of this sort.

(c) Moreover the concept of human action in terms of commonsense thinking and of the social sciences includes what may be called 'negative actions', i.e. intentional refraining from acting,[12] which, of course, escapes sensory observation. Not to sell certain merchandise at a given price is doubtless as economic an action as to sell it.

(d) Furthermore, as W. I. Thomas has shown,[13] social reality contains elements of beliefs and convictions which are real because they are so defined by the participants and which escape sensory observation. To the inhabitants of Salem in the seventeenth century, witchcraft was not a delusion but an element of their social reality and is as such open to investigation by the social scientist.

(e) Finally, and this is the most important point, the postulate of sensory observation of overt human behaviour takes as a model a particular and relatively small sector of the social world, namely, situations in which the acting individual is given to the observer in what is commonly called a face-to-face relationship. But there are many other dimensions of the social world in which situations of this kind do not prevail. If we put a letter in the mail box we assume that anonymous fellow-men, called postmen, will perform a series of manipulations, unknown and unobservable to us, with the effect that the addressee, possibly also unkown to us, will receive the message and react in a way which also escapes our sensory observation; and the result of all this is that we receive the book we have ordered. Or if I read an editorial stating that France fears the rearmament of Germany, I know perfectly well what this statement means without knowing the editorialist and even without knowing a Frenchman or a German, let alone without observing their overt behaviour.

In terms of commonsense thinking in everyday life men have knowledge of these various dimensions of the social world in which they live. To be sure, this knowledge is not only fragmentary since it is restricted principally to certain sectors of this world, it is also frequently inconsistent in itself and shows all degrees of clarity and distinctness from full insight or 'knowledge-about,' as James[14] called it, through 'knowledge of acquaintance' or mere familiarity, to blind belief in things just taken for granted. In this respect there are considerable differences from individual to individual and from social group to social group. Yet, in spite of all these inadequacies, commonsense knowledge of everyday life is sufficient for coming to terms with fellow-men, cultural objects, social institutions — in brief, with social reality. This is so, because the world (the natural and the social one) is from the outset an intersubjective world and because, as shall be pointed out later on, our knowledge of it is in various ways socialised. Moreover, the social world is experienced from the outset as a meaningful one. The Other's body is not experienced as an organism but as a fellow-man, its overt behaviour not as an occurrence in the time of the outer-world, but as our fellow-man's action. We normally 'know' what the Other does, for what reason he does it, why he does it at this particular time and in these particular circum-stances. That means that we experience our fellow-man's action in terms of his motives and goals. And in the same way, we experience cultural objects in terms of the human action of which they are the result. A tool, for example, is not experienced as a thing in the outer world (which of course it is also) but in terms of the purpose for which it was designed by more or less anonymous fellow-men and its possible use by others.

The fact that in commonsense thinking we take for granted our actual or potential knowledge of the meaning of human actions and their products, is, I suggest, precisely what social scientists want to express if they speak of under-

8

standing or *Verstehen* as a technique of dealing with human affairs. *Verstehen* is, thus, primarily not a method used by the social scientist, but the particular experiential form in which commonsense thinking takes cognisance of the social cultural world. It has nothing to do with introspection; it is a result of processes of learning or acculturation in the same way as the commonsense experience of the so-called natural world. *Verstehen* is, moreover, by no means a private affair of the observer which cannot be controlled by the experiences of other observers. It is controllable at least to the same extent to which the private sensory perceptions of an individual are controllable by any other individual under certain conditions. You have just to think of the discussion by a trial jury of whether the defendant has shown 'premeditated malice' or 'intent' in killing a person, whether he was capable of knowing the consequences of his deed, etc. Here we even have certain 'rules of procedure' furnished by the 'rules of evidence' in the juridical sense and a kind of verification of the findings resulting from processes of *Verstehen* by the Appellate Court, etc. Moreover, predictions based on *Verstehen* are continuously made in commonsense thinking with high success. There is more than a fair chance that a duly stamped and addressed letter put in a New York mailbox will reach the addressee in Chicago.

Nevertheless, both defenders and critics of the process of *Verstehen* maintain, and with good reason, that *Verstehen* is 'subjective'. Unfortunately, however, this term is used by each party in a different sense. The critics of understanding call it subjective, because they hold that understanding the motives of another man's action depends upon the private, uncontrollable, and unverifiable intuition of the observer or refers to his private value system. The social scientists such as Max Weber, however, call *Verstehen* subjective because its goal is to find out what the actor 'means' in his action, in contrast to the meaning which this action has for the actor's partner or a neutral observer. This is the origin of Max Weber's famous postulate of subjective interpretation, of which more will have to be said in what follows. The whole discussion suffers from the failure to distinguish clearly between *Verstehen* (1) as the experiential form of common-sense knowledge of human affairs, (2) as an epistemological problem, and (3) as a method peculiar to the social sciences.

So far we have concentrated on *Verstehen* as the way in which commonsense thinking finds its bearing within the social world and comes to terms with it. As to the epistemological question: 'How is such understanding or *Verstehen* possible?', alluding to a statement Kant made in another context, I suggest that it is a 'scandal of philosophy' that so far a satisfactory solution to the problem of our knowledge of other minds and, in connection therewith, of the intersubjectivity of our experience of the natural as well as the socio-cultural world has not been found and that, until rather recent times, this problem has even escaped the attention of philosophers. But the solution of this most difficult problem of philosophical interpretation is one of the first things taken for granted in our commonsense thinking and practically solved without any difficulty in each of our everyday actions. And since human beings are born of mothers and not concocted in retorts, the experience of the existence of other human beings and of the meaning of their actions is certainly the first and most original empirical observation man makes.

On the other hand, philosophers as different as James, Bergson, Dewey, Husserl, and Whitehead agree that the commonsense knowledge of everyday life is the unquestioned but always questionable background within which enquiry starts and within which alone it can be carried out. It is this *Lebenswelt*, as Husserl calls it, within which, according to him, all scientific and even logical concepts originate; it is the social matrix within which, according to Dewey, unclarified situations emerge, which have to be transformed by the process of inquiry into warranted assertability; and Whitehead has pointed out that it is the aim of science to produce a theory which agrees with experience by explaining the thought objects constructed by common sense through the mental constructs or thought objects of science. For all these thinkers agree that any knowledge of the world, in commonsense thinking as well as in science, involves mental constructs, syntheses, generalisations, formalisations, idealisations specific to the respective level of thought organisation. The concept of Nature, for instance, with which the natural sciences have to deal is, as Husserl has shown, an

10

idealising abstraction from the *Lebenswelt*, and abstraction which, on principle and of course legitimately, excludes persons with their personal life and all objects of culture which originate as such in practical human activity. Exactly this layer of the *Lebenswelt*, however, from which the natural sciences have to abstract, is the social reality which the social sciences have to investigate.

This insight sheds a light on certain methodological problems peculiar to the social sciences. To begin with, it appears that the assumption that the strict adoption of the principles of concept and theory formation prevailing in the natural sciences will lead to reliable knowledge of social reality is inconsistent in itself. If a theory can be developed on such principles, say in the form of an ideally refined behaviourism — and it is certainly possible to imagine this — then it will not tell us anything about social reality as experienced by men in everyday life. As Professor Nagel himself admits,[15] it will be highly abstract, and its concepts will apparently be remote from the obvious and familiar traits found in any society. On the other hand, a theory which aims at explaining social reality has to develop particular devices foreign to the natural sciences in order to agree with the commonsense experience of the social world. This is indeed what all theoretical sciences of human affairs — economics, sociology, the sciences of law, linguistics, cultural anthropology, etc. — have done.

This state of affairs is founded on the fact that there is an essential difference in the structure of the thought objects or mental constructs formed by the social sciences and those formed by the natural sciences.[16] It is up to the natural scientist and to him alone to define, in accordance with the procedural rules of his science, his observational field, and to determine the facts, data and events within it which are relevant for his problem or scientific purpose at hand. Neither are those facts and events preselected, nor is the observational field preinterpreted. The world of nature, as explored by the natural scientist, does not 'mean' anything to molecules, atoms and electrons. But the observational field of the social scientist — social reality — has a specific meaning and relevance structure for the human beings living, acting and thinking within it. By a series of commonsense con-

11

structs they have preselected and preinterpreted this world which they experience as the reality of their daily lives. It is these thought objects of theirs which determine their behaviour by motivating it. The thought objects constructed by the social scientist, in order to grasp this social reality, have to be founded upon the thought objects constructed by the commonsense thinking of men, living their daily life within their social world. Thus, the constructs of the social sciences are, so to speak, constructs of the second degree, that is, constructs of the constructs made by the actors on the social scene, whose behaviour the social scientist has to observe and to explain in accordance with the procedural rules of his science.

Thus, the exploration of the general principles according to which man in daily life organises his experiences, and especially those of the social world, is the first task of the methodology of the social sciences. This is not the place to outline the procedures of a phenomenological analysis of the so-called natural attitude by which this can be done. We shall briefly mention only a few problems involved.

The world, as has been shown by Husserl, is from the outset experienced in the pre-scientific thinking of everyday life in the mode of typicality. The unique objects and events given to us in a unique aspect are unique within a horizon of typical familiarity and pre-acquaintanceship. There are mountains, trees, animals, dogs — in particular Irish setters and among them my Irish setter, Rover. Now I may look at Rover either as this unique individual, my irreplaceable friend and comrade, or just as a typical example of 'Irish setter', 'dog', 'mammal', 'animal', 'organism' or 'object of the outer world'. Starting from here, it can be shown that whether I do one or the other, and also which traits or qualities of a given object or event I consider as individually unique and which as typical, depends upon my actual interest and the system of relevances involved — briefly, upon my practical or theoretical 'problem at hand'. This 'problem at hand', in turn, originates in the circumstances within which I find myself at any moment of my daily life and which I propose to call my biographically determined situation. Thus, typification depends upon my problem at hand for the definition and solution of which the type has been formed. It

12

can be further shown that at least one aspect of the bio-graphically and situationally determined systems of interest and relevances is subjectively experienced in the thinking of everyday life as systems of motives for action, of choices to be made, of projects to be carried out, of goals to be reached. It is this insight of the actor into the dependencies of the motives and goals of his actions upon his biographically determined situation which social scientists have in view when speaking of the subjective meaning which the actor 'bestows upon' or 'connects with' his action. This implies that, strictly speaking, the actor and he alone knows what he does, why he does it, and when and where his action starts and ends.

But the world of everyday life is from the outset also a social cultural world in which I am interrelated in manifold ways of interaction with fellow-men known to me in varying degrees of intimacy and anonymity. To a certain extent, sufficient for many practical purposes, I understand their behaviour, if I understand their motives, goals, choices and plans originating in *their* biographically determined circum-stances. Yet only in particular situations, and then only fragmentarily, can I experience the Other's motives, goals, etc. — briefly, the subjective meanings they bestow upon their actions, in their uniqueness. I can, however, experience them in their typicality. In order to do so I construct typical patterns of the actors' motives and ends, even of their attitudes and personalities, of which their actual conduct is just an instance or example. These typified patterns of the Others' behaviour become in turn motives of my own actions, and this leads to the phenomenon of self-typification well known to social scientists under various names.

Here, I submit, in the commonsense thinking of everyday life, is the origin of the so-called constructive or ideal types, a concept which as a tool of the social sciences has been analysed by Professor Hempel in such a lucid way. But at least at the commonsense level the formation of these types involves neither intuition nor a theory, if we understand these terms in the sense of Hempel's statements.[17] As we shall see, there are also other kinds of ideal or constructive types, those formed by the social scientist, which are of a quite different structure and indeed involve theory. But

Hempel has not distinguished between the two.

Next we have to consider that the commonsense knowledge of everyday life is from the outset socialised in many respects.

It is, first, structurally socialised, since it is based on the fundamental idealisation that if I were to change places with my fellow-man I would experience the same sector of the world in substantially the same perspectives as he does, our particular biographical circumstances becoming for all practical purposes at hand irrelevant. I propose to call this idealisation that of the reciprocity of perspectives.*

It is, second, genetically socialised, because the greater part of our knowledge, as to its content and the particular forms of typification under which it is organised, is socially derived, and this in socially approved terms.

It is, third, socialised in the sense of social distribution of knowledge, each individual knowing merely a sector of the world and common knowledge of the same sector varying individually as to its degree of distinctness, clarity, acquaintanceship or mere belief.

These principles of socialisation of commonsense knowledge, and especially that of the social distribution of knowledge, explain at least partially what the social scientist has in mind in speaking of the functional structural approach to studies of human affairs. The concept of functionalism — at least in the modern social sciences — is not derived from the biological concept of the functioning of an organism, as Nagel holds. It refers to the socially distributed constructs of patterns of typical motives, goals, attitudes, personalities, which are supposed to be invariant and are then interpreted as the function or structure of the social system itself. The more these interlocked behaviour patterns are standardised and institutionalised, that is, the more their typicality is socially approved by laws, folkways, mores, and habits, the greater is their usefulness in commonsense and scientific thinking as a scheme of interpretation of human behaviour.

These are, very roughly, the outlines of a few major features of the constructs involved in commonsense

* See 'Common-Sense and Scientific Interpretation of Human Action', 'Collected Papers', i 11 f. [M.N.]

14

experience of the intersubjective world in daily life, which is called *Verstehen*. As explained before, they are the first-level constructs upon which the second-level constructs of the social sciences have to be erected. But here a major problem emerges. On the one hand, it has been shown that the constructs on the first level, the commonsense constructs, refer to subjective elements, namely the *Verstehen* of the actor's action from his, the actor's, point of view. Consequently, if the social sciences aim indeed at explaining social reality, then the scientific constructs on the second level, too, must include a reference to the subjective meaning an action has for the actor. This is, I think, what Max Weber understood by his famous postulate of subjective interpretation, which has, indeed, been observed so far in the theory formation of all social sciences. The postulate of subjective interpretation has to be understood in the sense that all scientific explanations of the social world *can*, and for certain purposes *must*, refer to the subjective meaning of the actions of human beings from which social reality originates.

On the other hand, I agree with Professor Nagel's statement that the social sciences, like all empirical sciences, have to be objective in the sense that their propositions are subjected to controlled verification and must not refer to private uncontrollable experience.

How is it possible to reconcile these seemingly contradictory principles? Indeed, the most serious question which the methodology of the social sciences has to answer is: How is it possible to form objective concepts and an objectively verifiable theory of subjective meaning-structures? The basic insight that the concepts formed by the social scientist are constructs of the constructs formed in commonsense thinking by the actors on the social scene offers an answer. The scientific constructs formed on the second level, in accordance with the procedural rules valid for all empirical sciences, are objective ideal typical constructs and, as such, of a different kind from those developed on the first level of commonsense thinking which they have to supersede. They are theoretical systems embodying general hypotheses in the sense of Professor Hempel's definition.[18] This device has been used by social scientists concerned with theory long before this concept was formulated by Max Weber and

15

developed by his school.

Before describing a few features of these scientific constructs, let us briefly consider the particular attitudes of the theoretical social scientist to the social world, in contradistinction to that of the actor on the social scene. The theoretical scientist — *qua* scientist, not *qua* human being (which he is, too) — is not involved in the observed situation, which is to him not of practical but merely of cognitive interest. The system of relevances governing commonsense interpretation in daily life originates in the biographical situation of the observer. By making up his mind to become a scientist, the social scientist has replaced his personal biographical situation by what I shall call, following Felix Kaufmann,[19] a scientific situation. The problems with which he has to deal might be quite unproblematic for the human being within the world and vice versa. Any scientific problem is determined by the actual state of the respective science, and its solution has to be achieved in accordance with the procedural rules governing this science, which among other things warrant the control and verification of the solution offered. The scientific problem, once established, alone determines what is relevant for the scientist as well as the conceptual frame of reference to be used by him. This and nothing else, it seems to me, is what Max Weber means when he postulates the objectivity of the social sciences, their detachment from value patterns which govern or might govern the behaviour of the actors on the social scene.

How does the social scientist proceed? He observes certain facts and events within social reality which refer to human action and he constructs typical behaviour or course-of-action patterns from what he has observed. Thereupon he co-ordinates to these typical course-of-action patterns models of an ideal actor or actors, whom he imagines as being gifted with consciousness. Yet it is a consciousness restricted so as to contain nothing but the elements relevant to the performing of the course-of-action patterns observed. He thus ascribes to this fictitious consciousness a set of typical notions, purposes, goals, which are assumed to be invariant in the specious consciousness of the imaginary actor-model. This homunculus or puppet is supposed to be interrelated in interaction patterns to other homunculi or puppets con-

16

structed in a similar way. Among these homunculi with which the social scientist populates his model of the social world of everyday life, sets of motives, goals, roles — in general, systems of relevances — are distributed in such a way as the scientific problems under scrutiny require. Yet — and this is the main point — these constructs are by no means arbitrary. They are subject to the postulate of logical consistency and to the postulate of adequacy. The latter means that each term in such a scientific model of human action must be constructed in such a way that a human act performed within the real world by an individual actor as indicated by the typical construct would be understandable to the actor himself as well as to his fellow-men in terms of commonsense interpretation of everyday life. Compliance with the postulate of logical consistency warrants the objective validity of the thought objects constructed by the social scientist; compliance with the postulate of adequacy warrants their compatibility with the constructs of everyday life.*

As the next step, the circumstances within which such a model operates may be varied, that is, the situation which the homunculi have to meet may be imagined as changed, but not the set of motives and relevances assumed to be the sole content of their consciousness. I may, for example, construct a model of a producer acting under conditions of unregulated competitions and another of a producer acting under cartel restrictions, and then compare the output of the same commodity of the same firm in the two models.[20] In this way, it is possible to predict how such a puppet or system of puppets might behave under certain conditions and to discover certain 'determinate relations between a set of variables, in terms of which . . . empirically ascertainable regularities . . . can be explained'. This, however, is Professor Nagel's definition of a theory.[21] It can easily be seen that each step involved in the construction and use of the scientific model can be verified by empirical observation, provided that we do not restrict this term to sensory perceptions of objects and events in the outer world but include the experiential form, by which commonsense thinking in everyday life understands human actions and their outcome

* See 'Common-Sense and Scientific Interpretation of Human Action', 'Collected Papers' i 43 f. [M.N.]

17

in terms of their underlying motives and goals.

Two brief concluding remarks may be permitted. First, a key concept of the basic philosophic position of naturalism is the so-called principle of continuity, although it is under discussion whether this principle means continuity of existence, or of analysis, or of an intellectual criterion of pertinent checks upon the methods employed.[22] It seems to me that this principle of continuity in each of these various interpretations is fulfilled by the characterised device of the social sciences, which even establishes continuity between the practice of everyday life and the conceptualisation of the social sciences.

Second, a word on the problem of the methodological unity of the empirical sciences. It seems to me that the social scientist can agree with the statement that the principal differences between the social and the natural sciences do not have to be looked for in a different logic governing each branch of knowledge. But this does not involve the admission that the social sciences have to abandon the particular devices they use for exploring social reality for the sake of an ideal unity of methods which is founded on the entirely unwarranted assumption that only methods used by the natural sciences, and especially by physics, are scientific ones. So far as I know, no serious attempt has ever been made by the proponents of the 'unity of science' movement to answer or even to ask the question whether the methodological problem of the natural sciences in their present state is not merely a special case of the more general, still unexplored, problem how scientific knowledge is possible at all and what its logical and methodological presuppositions are. It is my personal conviction that phenomenological philosophy has prepared the ground for such an investigation. Its outcome might quite possibly show that the particular methodological devices developed by the social sciences in order to grasp social reality are better suited than those of the natural sciences to lead to the discovery of the general principles which govern all human knowledge.

NOTES

1. Published in the volume 'Science, Language and Human Rights' (American Philosophical Association, Eastern Division, i, Philadelphia, 1952) pp. 43-86 (referred to as 'SLH').
2. Especially his 'Methodology of the Social Sciences' (New York, 1941).
3. 'Science, Language and Human Rights', pp. 43, 64 (after referred to as 'SLH').
4. 'SLH', pp. 65-86.
5. 'SLH', p. 56.
6. 'SLH', p. 46.
7. 'SLH', pp. 60 ff.
8. 'SLH', pp. 55-57.
9. 'SLH', p. 53.
10. 'Methodology of the Social Sciences', p. 126.
11. 'Mind, Self and Society' (Chicago, 1937).
12. See Max Weber, 'The Theory of Social and Economic Organisation', trans. A. M. Henderson and Talcott Parsons (New York, 1947) p. 88.
13. See W. I. Thomas, 'Social Behaviour and Personality', ed. E. H. Volkart (New York, 1951) p. 81.
14. 'Principles of Psychology', i 221 f.
15. 'SLH', p. 63.
16. Some of the points dealt with in the following are presented more elaborately in 'Common-Sense and Scientific Interpretation of Human Action', 'Collected Papers', i.
17. 'SLH', pp. 76 ff. and 81.
18. 'SLH', pp. 77 ff.
19. 'Methodology of the Social Sciences', pp. 52 and 251.
20. See Fritz Machlup, 'The Economics of Seller's Competition: Model Analysis of Seller's Conduct' (Baltimore, 1952) pp. 9 ff.
21. 'SLH', p. 46; see also pp. 4-5 above.
22. See Thelma Z. Lavine, 'Note to Naturalists on the Human Spirit', 'Journal of Philosophy', l (1953) 145-54, and Ernest Nagel's answer, ibid., pp. 154-7.

2 Is it a Science?*

Sidney Morgenbesser

The controversies over the thesis of the unity of the natural and social sciences and its kin, social scientific naturalism, which are conventionally but misleadingly dated as having begun with A. Comte,[1] are still very much with us. And for good reason. Throughout the history of these controversies many important issues about the social sciences were raised, some of which are still unsettled and which deserve review. I propose to consider some of them and to criticise some assumptions which were supported both by social scientific naturalists and their opponents (whom we may label anti-social scientific naturalists) about and in the course of the controversies.

It is comparatively easy to dismiss the entire issue thus. It appears that a social scientific naturalist who is committed to the unity of the social and natural sciences must defend either the thesis that the social sciences are or ought to be identical with the natural, or the one that they are or ought to be similar. In either case, then, the social scientific naturalist is doomed, forced to defend either a false or a trivial thesis. And of course it is equally easy to dismiss the anti-social scientific naturalist by attributing to him either the needless thesis that there are differences, indeed important differences, between the natural and social sciences, or the ridiculous one that they are totally dissimilar and have nothing in common.[2] But these formulations are not historically happy ones. Philosophers and social scientists like Comte, Mill, Dewey, Nagel, Skinner, Merton knew that it was silly to argue that the aims, methods, concepts and theories of the social sciences are identical with the natural sciences, and also knew that it was unnecessary to insist that they are similar to, or ought to resemble, each other. Rather, they attempted to specify the similarities which they thought

* Reprinted from 'Social Research', xxxiii 2 (summer 1966).

the social and natural sciences ought to have, and hence offered specific normative theses. Note however that the specific theses they did offer were not entailed by a general naturalistic thesis and that the specific thesis offered by one social scientific naturalist was not always compatible with those offered by another.[3] It is vain therefore to seek a general formulation of social scientific naturalism which is worthy of debate and which was also accepted by all who have called themselves social scientific naturalists. But if we drop the last requirement, the way is open to us to construct an ideal type of social scientific naturalism and to consider it. I propose to take that way, and specifically, to consider a canonical version of teleological social scientific naturalism which accepts the plausible thesis that it is the major aim of the sciences to discover general laws and theories and to use them for explanatory and predictive purposes, and the more debatable view, that it is the major aim of any given science S to discover and confirm S types of laws which can be used for explanatory and predictive purposes. Indeed it goes further and accepts the definitional schema that a given discipline S is a science at time t if and only if there are S-type laws available at given time t and also sundry subsidiary theses about the aims and purposes of specific theories — among them, the popular one that it is the major aim of any theory to explain and predict, or more bluntly, to predict. These four theses and theses schemata are about the social sciences taken distributively. About the social sciences taken collectively, the canonical version of social scientific naturalism maintains that all the basic theories of the social sciences, or perhaps more distinctly of psychology, are reducible to some suitable theory in the natural sciences. It is the last thesis which articulates a vision of the unity of the sciences, a unification in principle, via reduction of the theories of all the social sciences or at least of the basic one to the theories of the natural sciences.

Remember that we have specified an ideal type of naturalism which many of the social scientific naturalists do not accept. Thus Popper,[4] though he considers himself a social scientific naturalist, dissents from the thesis that it is the aim of the social sciences to discover general laws and theories which can be used both for explanatory and pre-

21

dictive purposes. Again, a social scientific naturalist like Nagel,[5] who identifies the thesis of the unity of the natural and social sciences primarily with the one that the criteria for the acceptance of theories as worthy of belief are the same in the natural and social sciences, and may be characterised as a methodological naturalist, doubts whether anyone can definitively specify the aims for the social sciences.

Conversely, a canonical social scientific naturalist need not accept all theses which have been labelled naturalistic and in particular need not accept structural naturalistic theses which attempt to specify the content of social scientific theories.[6] Specifically, the canonical naturalist who insists that the laws of psychology are reducible to theories in the natural sciences need not insist that the former are behaviouristic ones or show that all human action is caused by environmental and natural factors alone. Hence recent critics of behaviourism[7] and kindred theses may here be bypassed; all to the good, since I think the importance of the fight over behaviourism has been exaggerated.[8] More generally the social scientific naturalist is not denying the obvious fact that there are differences in the subject-matter and hence theories of the natural and social sciences, and therefore he need not be nettled by the observations of the fine anthropologist, Evans-Pritchard, who writes, 'The thesis I put before you implies that social anthropology studies societies as moral, not as natural systems, and that it therefore seeks patterns, not scientific laws. The concepts of the natural system and the natural law modeled on the constructs of the natural sciences have dominated anthropology from the beginning and we can see that they have been responsible for false scholasticism which has led to one rigid formulation after the other.'[9]

Evans-Pritchard seems to believe that a social scientific naturalist who argues that it is the aim both of the social sciences and the natural sciences to discover general laws and theories must maintain that societies are natural systems and deny that they are moral ones. But here Evans-Pritchard is, I think, in error. A social scientific naturalist could agree that societies are not natural systems but add that neither are bridges or buildings; that they too are on the face of the earth because of human decision and effort. But this is a relatively glib answer. A fuller one must be indicated. The

22

naturalist of course need not deny the familiar stories that bridges do not try to accomplish certain ends, and cannot change the laws that describe their behaviour, and that societies, or at least their members, do try to accomplish certain ends in accord with rules which they can, and often do, change. The naturalist would add, that the conclusion that a social scientist studies rules and the natural scientist studies laws is misleading. To support this claim he would emphasise the obvious point that the social scientist wants to know not merely that someone obeys a law but also why he does, and add that the social scientist is afforded no explanation of why a given person does obey a rule by the observation that there is a rule to be followed. Once we know the rules we may perhaps know that they will for the most part be obeyed, but only because we tacitly accept some general law about human behaviour. Adding some obvious subsidiary premises the naturalist ends with the definitional schema proposed above, and which I shall label A. But of course not he alone; A can be accepted by an anti-social naturalist as well. Let us turn to it, and hence to a thesis shared by the naturalist and the anti-naturalist alike.

A, it will be recalled, reads that a given discipline S is a science at time t if at that time there are S-type laws available and it is best interpreted as maintaining that at a given time t a discipline S is a science if and only if there are S-type lawful statements available which have been confirmed by members of S. Interpreted in this manner we may avoid certain worries about the possible application of A, concern occasioned by epistemological doubts about our possible knowledge of laws. The original formulation required that we know that a given lawlike statement, a completely general statement, is true. In the interpretation, all that is required is that we know that a given lawlike statement is well confirmed, and well confirmed by the members of a given discipline. The latter addition is, I think, a satisfactory one. We would not want to credit a social science with being a social science simply on the grounds that we know certain lawlike statements to be well confirmed. For example, that we know that all men who have reached their twenty-first birthday have had at least one meal, or that all men have sought happiness at least once in their lives, or that all men have touched the ground at least once. Such generalisations are too commonplace to be credited to any given specific social science.

A appears plausible, but there is a slightly unhappy consequence about its acceptance which deserves to be noticed. Imagine that a given discipline (example: economics) has certain lawful statements available at a given time and that these lawful statements are falsified, disconfirmed at some later time. Applying our criteria then, we must say that the discipline economics was a science at a time when it had 'faulty' knowledge, and that with increased knowledge it lost its status as a science. Of course, defenders of A need not balk at this consequence, for they may add that economics has not lost its status as being scientific, only its status as a science. But all is not well, neither with the answer nor indeed with the original question, for both presuppose that we know when a given generalisation is one that really belongs either to economics or to psychology or sociology, and though in many cases it is clear how to classify a given statement, I doubt whether we have criteria which enable us in most cases to decide whether a given statement belongs to one rather than to another social science. This is not a minor difficulty with A, but even if we waive it, A is not completely acceptable. As it stands, it is mute about numbers, and hence, may be understood as granting that a given discipline S is a science at t if at t there are some lawful statements which have been confirmed by members of it, possibly even one. So understood, it grants that psychology is a science if, let us say, Emmett's law is highly confirmed, economics is a science if it is true that there are no exceptions to what Marshall called 'the law of demand',[10] and that political science is a science if we accept Duverger's law.[11] The difficulty therefore is that A is too liberal and allows us to consider a given discipline S to be a science no matter how few and far between its triumphs may be, and no matter how unsettled the state of the discipline may be.

It is therefore, I think, apparent that A needs emendation. But before we turn to consider some possible candidates, let us observe that the limitations and the unclarities of A are shared by many discussions of the nature and aims of the social sciences to which we have already alluded and which seem to presuppose A or some one of its alternates. Thus

24

many social scientists who have been opposed to naturalism and who seem to insist that the social sciences cannot be sciences on the grounds that there are no social scientific laws to be discovered, may be right if they mean the term 'law' strictly; it may be true that any lawful statement discovered by the social scientist and confirmed at t may be known to be false later. But this thesis is not of unique interest to the social sciences; any lawful statement discovered by a natural scientist may be disconfirmed in later inquiry. However, if the anti-social scientific naturalist means that at no time t will a social scientist discover any well-confirmed lawlike statement, then his thesis seems to be false; as we have indicated, the social scientist seems to have discovered some lawful sentences. Conversely, the social scientific naturalist who insists that the social sciences can be sciences because some laws can be discovered, is vindicated, but his vindication is of slight moment. Upon reflection, both he and the anti-social scientific naturalist might want to offer a slightly strengthened version of A in order to rule out the cases we have considered, disciplines which have one or two lawful sentences and very little to say about the other aspects of their subject-matter. The more general point is this: to say that a given discipline is a science is to commend it; to say that it has laws is not necessarily to do so. Again it may very well be that a given science cannot really accomplish its tasks unless it has laws; it does not follow that it can accomplish its tasks once it has laws. The social sciences may be replete with such lawlike and perhaps true statements as 'All men seek happiness', and 'Supply is an increasing function of price', which are not useful enough for the tasks which a social scientist faces, e.g. of making refined predictions and explanations. The problem, therefore, is not whether the social sciences *can* contain laws but whether they can contain enough laws *or* theories to enable them to be used for certain tasks. Let us therefore change our focus and begin by assuming that every discipline S can at least *prima facie* be identified as being concerned to deal with L_1 — n types of phenomena — psychology with learning, forgetting, perception; sociology with actions and behaviour of members of small groups and organised communities, and so forth. Now we might say that a given discipline S is not a science at t, if at t it has some laws, but only that a given discipline S is a science at t if and only if at t it has enough laws to enable it to explain and predict n-type phenomena with which it is identified. Let us label this B.

B appears to be an improvement over A. It emphasises the subject-matter of B and also that scientists seek general laws not for their own sake but in order to employ them for explanatory and predictive purposes. But though an improvement over A in some respects, it shares some of A's limitations and has an additional important difficulty of its own. It would not do to suggest that a given discipline S is a science if at t it is able to explain and predict *all* its intended subject-matter; then a discipline would be a science only at the end of its creative days. And I presume by now that there is no need to repeat the lesson we have learned when discussing A, and hence to repeat the difficulties that we would encounter if we assert that a discipline S is a science at t, if at t its members are able to explain *some* of its L_1 — n-type of phenomena. At best B is acceptable if it is amended to read, 'S is a science at t if and only if at t it contains enough lawlike laws to explain enough of its subject-matter.' But this of course is not a helpful definition but at best a sketch of one, which seems to defy completion since there appears to be no non-question-begging way of specifying what the term 'enough' might mean in this context. But even as a sketch B is deficient. The intent of B is that a discipline S is a science at t if and only if there are enough type laws which will enable members of S to explain and predict their subject-matter, but it adds that the work is to be done by S-type laws. But so understood, it is clearly wrong or at least begs an important issue. No one thinks that accidents are explained by accidental laws, that snow is predicted or explained by snow laws. Why then should sociologists have to explain the behaviour of a small group by looking for small group laws, or political behaviour by looking for political laws, or crime by looking for laws of crime? Even if one assumes that no scientist can explain or predict in a scientific manner except by appealing to laws, it does not at all follow that a scientist must explain the phenomena L_1 by looking for L_1-type laws. This latter difficulty is of no minor importance. It affects not merely B but many alternatives which might be suggested as

26

an improvement over it. Consider for example the proposed definition C: S is a science at t if and only if at t, S has not only laws which enable it to explain and predict its L-type phenomena but also S theories to explain the S-type laws. C might be claimed to be superior over B since it emphasises the important point that scientists do not merely present lists of laws but theories which systematise them. But as with B, so with C. There is no need to think that an S-type theory or one of discipline S will be needed to explain the S-type laws; laws and theories of another discipline may be required. Thus it may transpire that generalisations or laws of biology will be explained not by biological theories but by theories of physical chemistry. And it very well may be the case that various laws of psychology will be ultimately explained by physiological laws. C therefore inherits the difficulties of B and obviously gives birth to some of its own.

At this point we might suggest that we try to define the phrase 'is a science' not by reference to what its members have achieved but it terms of their procedures and collective aims. The emphasis on collective is appropriate. Modern science is distinguished by co-operative and shared work or at least by institutionalised methods of communication of results and criticism, methods which have resulted not in chaos, but in the miracle of modern science; men building on the labour of others. It is therefore all to the good that we shall try to specify our rules for the use of the phrase 'is a science' by reference to the shared aims and collective research of scientists.[1][2]

Unfortunately, it is not easy to fulfil the programme; to provide an adequate definition which refers to collective shared aims. We have already noted that Evans-Pritchard dissents from the programme of seeking laws which is accepted by other anthropologists; we need only to remind ourselves of the difference in programmes between psychologists like Skinner[13] and Allport,[14] and sociologists like Lazarsfeld[15] and C. Wright Mills.[16] But these differences only in part count against the canonical form of social scientific naturalism, a programme which is partly normative, and not simply descriptive. It is open to a defender of social scientific naturalism to specify aims for a given science, and only in part to justify such specification by reference to the

27

actual commitments of the scientist. What then are the aims? Fortunately the version of social scientific naturalism is not silent about this matter and maintains, it will be recalled, that science in general ought to attempt to discover general laws and theories and that any given science S ought to attempt to discover S-type laws which it can use for explanatory and predictive purposes. But even if we overlook the obvious difficulties which appeal to S-type laws, other problems remain with the attempt to transform this thesis into a definition of 'is a science'. The suggestion that S is a science if at least some members of S try to discover some or use some laws to deal with L_1 — n-type phenomena is faulty; it is too liberal. For of any discipline it may be true that some of its members try to use some laws on some occasions to explain some phenomena with which they are concerned. And I think it would not at all do, at least at this stage of inquiry, to insist that S is a science if and only if its members try to find laws to explain and predict every event with which they are concerned, and try to do so under every refined true description of that event. Construed this way, social scientific naturalism insists that S is a science only if its members accept a very strong version of determinism — a version which may be challenged by the very findings of this discipline; it is sufficient to remind ourselves of the twentieth-century development in physics and philosophy.[17]

Still we might insist that scientists ought to accept determinism interpreted as a rule of procedure, and hence ought to seek general laws and theories to explain and predict all the phenomena with which they are concerned, unless there is evidence for a theory that shows the rule to be unwise. But even so, we are far from our goal. To specify a science in terms of aims it will not do merely to say that its members, among other things, try to discover general laws and theories to explain and predict every event with which they are concerned, for at least two other types of problems remain. We must examine the relationships between these aims and others and try to specify the interrelationships between ends and actions. Obviously scientists do not or should not try only to discover general laws and theories which are useful for explanatory and predictive purposes. They do and ought to attempt to add to our knowledge

28

about the past, to offer descriptions of the state of contemporary and other societies, to help us make rational decisions;[18] aims which seem to me plausible ones for science in general and which are only indirectly related to the end of finding general laws and theories. Moreover, even if we agree that scientists should only seek general laws and theories which can be used for explanatory and predictive purposes, it does not follow that we have provided them with a method of procedure. This for at least three reasons. Assume that theory T is useful for explanatory purposes, and theory S for predictive ones. Which one shall a scientist try to confirm? Again, assume that theory T^1 is useful for the explanation of U-type of phenomena, and T^2 for V-type, and that we are more interested for whatever reason in U- rather than V-type phenomena, which theory shall scientists try to confirm?[19] Finally, assume that S^1 is more general than S^2 but that the chances of confirming S^1 are greater than the chances of confirming S^2. Shall a scientist try to confirm S^1 rather than S^2? Of course, all these problems disappear if we assume that a theory T which is useful for explanatory purposes is *ipso facto* useful for predictive purposes, or assume that scientists are not, as scientists, allowed to show preference for knowledge about one type of phenomenon rather than another, or assume with Popper's students if not Popper himself that scientists are primarily interested in testing the more general lawlike sentence and not primarily in adding to our knowledge. But all of these assumptions are dubious and although they cannot be completely discussed, a word about the first may be in order. Much of economic theory of demand may be useful for explanatory purposes, but it is not as obviously useful for predictive ones.[20] That is, it is not as useful if we want to use the theory of a given time t to predict the demand of a group or a person at some time t^1 later than t. Note that we are here using 'predict' in what may be called its pragmatic sense, one in which it makes sense to say that a man predicts, and does not make sense to say that a theory does. In this sense, to predict is to do something, to perform an act, a linguistic one or at least one in which symbols are employed. Patently there is another sense of 'predict' — a semantic one in which it does make perfectly good sense to say that a theory predicts. Observe,

29

however, that 'predict' is now used interchangeably with 'entails' or with some suitable converse of 'is deducible from'; for to say in the semantic sense that a theory T predicts $S^1 - n$ is to say that from T 'S' 'S_n' (sentences describing the phenomena $S^1 - n$) are deducible. In sum, 'predicts' is therefore used in at least two ways, semantically and pragmatically; it is employed in the former way to talk about a relationship between bodies of sentences; it is employed in the latter to attribute an action to a person. Of course when we approve of a given prediction made by a scientist, we frequently make tacit reference to one or more laws and theories, plus subsidiary information about initial conditions that are available to the scientist, and from which he may have deduced his predictive utterance. But it would not do to claim that every time scientists have laws and theories which can be used to 'predict' the events (that is, theories from which the sentences describing the events are in principle deducible), the scientist can predict those events. He may not be able to do so, if for no other reason than the obvious one that the information may not be available. Moreover, I may make a perfectly acceptable prediction based on a simple law or theory and not use that law or theory to explain the event which I have predicted. Thus I may predict that President Johnson will address the nation on the basis of information I read in *The New York Times*, but I will not explain President Johnson's talking to the nation by reference to the lawful statement '*The New York Times* always prints the news that it is fitting to believe', which I tacitly used to predict.

We are still not home free, for the term 'or predicts' is used in still another sense, which may be called the epistemological one. Examine, for instance, the following passage by Professor Friedman:

'To avoid confusion, it should perhaps be noted explicitly that the "predictions" by which the validity of a hypothesis is tested need not be about phenomena that have not yet occurred, that is, need not be forecasts of future events; they may be about phenomena that have occurred but observations on which have not yet been made or are not known to the person making the prediction.'[2][1]

Here Professor Friedman seems to be saying that a scientist uses theory P predictively about E at t, if he presents the theory at t, and does not know at t whether E is true or false, and E is deducible from P, or at least E and P are compatible. There is nothing amiss with this usage, but notice that it is at best a partial explication of the converse of 'is confirmed by'. There is need for the 'at best'. Professor Friedman would not, I think, want to say that a given theory is confirmed by an event or a regularity only if the scientist did not know about the event or regularity when he first constructed his theory. I presume that Professor Friedman grants that a theory about the depression of 1929 is confirmable even if presented in the 1960s by one who lived through the bad years. But even if it were the case that S predicts E if and only if S is confirmed by E, it would not be the case that S explains E if and only if S is confirmed by E. The statement 'I have a left hand and I have a right hand' is confirmed by my having a right hand, but cannot be used to explain it, at least not alone. And once again we have asymmetry between explanation and prediction.

Still it may be argued that in a real science all real explanations and predictions are isomorphic, for both are based on deterministic laws which, given information about the state of a system at t, allow us to deduce statements about future states of the system and also about its past states. This view is not a silly one, and is indeed widely accepted. Nevertheless, it is debatable for at least three reasons. Many acceptable explanations are not based on deterministic dynamic laws of the type here contemplated, e.g. explanations based on conservation or symmetry principles. Again, as the repeated arguments about action at a distance show, the mere availability of deterministic laws does not show that they present us with acceptable explanations of the past states they retrodict. Finally, there seem to be clear counter-examples, even in classical physics, to the analysis of deterministic laws which this view seems to presuppose. Consider, for example, the following: '. . . the solution of a dynamical problem with a finite number of degrees of freedom is a solution valid for all values of t, both subsequent and antecedent to the instant t_0, whereas in radiation problems we cannot trace the radiation back beyond the instant when it issued from the source. The formulae which will be useful in the practical applications of

Huygens' principle will generally be formulae which are valid only at instants t subsequent to some initial instant t_0; the results obtained by substituting values of t less than t_0 need bear no relation whatever to the actual phenomenon.'[2]

I add that if we say that a theory T is deterministic if it can be used to predict, in the pragmatic sense specified above, all states of all systems with which it deals, then even classical mechanics is not deterministic.[23]

In sum, the naturalistic theses that all sciences of type P should seek P-type laws, that all laws are useful both for explanation and prediction, that explanation and prediction are isomorphic, are dubious. And the thesis that science is committed to determinism is acceptable only if qualified.

These problems indicate not the falseness of the canonical version of social scientific naturalism, but its incompleteness. But here the anti-naturalist should not exult, for the argument may also be turned around to show the inconclusiveness of some of his claims, and especially claims akin to those with which we began and which are intended to show that the social sciences cannot be or should not be sciences. Let us, benefiting from the discussion of A, B, C, try to capture the intent of the anti-naturalist and begin by assuming that for every discipline S there are some $L_1 \ldots$ n-type phenomena which are the subject matter of S and which members of S attempt to deal with by law and theory. We will then say S is a science at t if at t there are some laws and theories (not necessarily laws and theories of S) which the members of S can use to explain and predict at least some $L_1 \ldots$ n-type phenomena, and further that at t there is no good reason to deny that all $L_1 \ldots$ n-type of phenomena can be explained and predicted by law. Given this definition, which I assume an anti-naturalist accepts, a given discipline fails to be a science of L once it is known that it cannot discover laws and theories to deal with all $L_1 \ldots$ n-type phenomena (of course it may still be able to deal lawfully with $L_1 \ldots$ n-l types). Applying this definition, the anti-social scientific naturalist argues that the social sciences cannot be sciences of their subject-matter, sciences that will explain and predict via law all the phenomena with which they are concerned.

But if this is his main point, then it is an embarrassing one, for it is not evident how the anti-social scientific naturalist can establish it. He may argue on general metaphysical grounds that human agents have free will, but then the naturalist need not grant that he has given a good reason for his position. Of course, he may give a good empirical reason, but then he would appeal to laws and theories and argue in a manner analogous to the one used by physicists who argue from the truth of quantum mechanics to the falsity of determinism. And so he would have no type of argument of unique relevance to the understanding of the human condition.

NOTES

1. There is much important historical information contained in George Gusdorf's 'Introduction aux Sciences Humaines (Publication de la Faculté des Lettres de l'Université de Strasbourg, Paris, 1960).

2. But this is overlooked by some anti-naturalists, e.g. by Maurice Natanson in 'Philosophy of the Social Sciences: A Reader,' on pp. 186, 274, 275. E.g. p. 274: 'In other words, the naturalist is suggesting that the concepts of the social sciences, as well as the theoretical matrix for those concepts, are identical with those of the natural sciences.'

3. Read for example the discussion on 'Scientific Change' in the article by T. S. Kuhn, 'The Function of Dogma in Scientific Research', pp. 347-75, ed. A. C. Crombie (Heinemann, London, 1963).

For controversies between naturalists read Dewey on Mill in 'Dewey's Logic' (passim) and Popper, on other naturalists, essay: 'Three Views Concerning Human Knowledge', in 'Contemporary British Philosophy', 3rd series, ed. H. D. Lewis.

4. In Popper, see 'Conjectures and Refutations: Growth of Scientific Knowledge' (Basic Books, 1962) and 'Predictions and Prophecy in the Social Sciences', pp. 336-47. Also 'The Critical Approach to Science and Philosophy' (Basic Books, 1964) ed. M. Bunge (essays in honour of Karl R. Popper) and the article by Hans Albert in 'Social Science and Moral Philosophy', pp. 385-410.

5. See 'Logic Without Metaphysics' (Free Press, Glencoe, Ill.) especially the chapter on 'The Logic of Social Science', pp. 367-8. Also the article 'Problems of Concept and Theory Formation in the Social Sciences', reprinted in Natanson, 'Philosophy of the Social Sciences, pp. 189-90.

6. More fully they provide sketches of the lawlike statements, and do so by specifying either the terms or type of terms that will appear in such laws, according to the naturalist. It is important to observe that the methodological naturalist generally has no commitments to forms

33

of structural naturalism. The reason: he thinks that inquiry must decide what type of laws are needed. As a consequence, he denies the oft-repeated thesis that explanations in the social sciences must be motivational ones or based on understanding. Alexander Gerschenkron's article 'Reflections on Ideology as a Methodological and Historical Problem', in 'Money Growth, and Methodology' in honour of Johan Akerman, ed. H. Hegeland (Cwk. Gleerup, Sweden, 1961); esp. pp. 181-2.

7. One of the limitations of phenomenological approaches to the social sciences is that they are often presented as contrasts to behaviourism and only to it. This, in the main, is true of S. Strasse's 'Phenomenology and the Human Sciences', esp. ch. 3, pp. 21-7, and Erwin Strauss's 'The Primary World of the Senses'.

8. See the article by Paul Ziff, 'About Behaviourism', pp. 147-51, reprinted in 'The Philosophy of Mind', ed. V. Chappell. Also Noam Chomsky's critique of Skinner, 'A Review of B. F. Skinner's Verbal Behaviour', reprinted in 'The Structure of Language', ed. J. A. Fodor and J. Katz, pp. 547-79.

9. E. Evans-Pritchard, 'Social Anthropology and Other Essays' (Free Press) p. 162.

10. Stigler, 'Essays in the History of Economics' (University of Chicago Press) Chapter 14 (note on 'The History of the Giffen Paradox', p. 374).

11. Maurice Duverger and John Wily, 'Political Parties' (1954) p. 217. For discussion of a much more interesting lawlike statement, see 'Decision Making and the Theory of Learning' by Robert Radlow, p. 267, and 'Individual Choice and Strategy Behaviour' by H. H. Killy, p. 240, in 'Decision and Choice', contribution of Sydney Siegel, ed. Samuel Messik and A. H. Brayfield (1964).

For a cogent defence of some social scientific generalisations on laws, especially of the statement 'All societies taboo incest', see G. P. Murdock, 'Social Structure', esp. pp. 260-3. Also E. Sapir on the status of phonetic laws in 'The Concept of Phonetic Law as Treated in Primitive Tribes' by Leonard Bloomfield, 'Methods in Social Sciences', ed. S. Rice (University of Chicago Press, 1931) p. 297.

12. Read the fascinating article by L. Edelstein, 'Recent Trends in the Interpretation of Ancient Science', in 'Roots of Scientific Thought', ed. P. P. Wiener and Aaron Noland. See esp. pp. 90, 118.

13. For Skinner see the article 'Is a Science of Human Behaviour Possible?' in 'Philosophical Problems of the Social Sciences', ed. D. Braybrooke. For criticism, see W. S. Verplank, 'Modern Learning Theory' (Estes and others) (Appleton-Century Crofts, 1964) esp. pp. 268-72, 305.

14. For Allport's position, see 'Pattern and Growth in Personality' (Holt, Rinehart & Winston, 1961) esp. pp. 555-67.

15. For a more complete statement of Lazarsfeld's position, see his article 'Philosophy of Science and Empirical Social Research', p. 463, in 'Logic, Methodology and Philosophy of Science', ed. E. Nagel, P. Suppes, A. Tarski.

16. For Mills's position as presented and defended by his students, see 'The New Sociology', ed. Irwin Louis Horowitz, esp. ch. 5, 'Mills and the Profession of Sociology' by Ron Golden. See also the article 'Anti-Minotaur: Myth of a Value-Free Sociology' by A. Gouldner, pp. 35-52 in 'Sociology on Trial', ed. Maurice Stein and A. Vidich.

17. See especially the discussion in 'Quantum Mechanics of Particles and Wave Fields' by A. March, ch. 1.

18. Even for minor decisions. It is therefore desirable that a theory of test construction and use consider how tests can best serve in making decisions! 'Psychological Test and Personnel Decision', Lee J. Cronbach and G. C. Gleser, pp. 1, 121-4.

19. For some of the problems related to specific theories see 'The Choice of Choice Theories', R. P. Abelson, pp. 257-67, in 'Decision and Choice'. See also 'Science of Culture', Leslie White, ch. v: 'Expansion of Culture' (Grove Press, N.Y., 1949). Of course the issue is a deep one and concerns the time-honoured problem of the use of knowledge. On this point see M. R. Cohen, 'Reason and Nature', p. 249.

20. See the interesting discussion in 'The Predictive Accuracy of Empirical Demand Analysis', M. B. Shupack, pp. 550-76, in 'The Economic Journal' (Sept. 1962).

21. Milton Friedman, 'Essays in Positive Economics' (University of Chicago Press, 1953) p. 9.

22. B. B. Baker and E. T. Copson, 'The Mathematical Theory of Huygens' Principle', p. 6. See E. Hill, 'Function Analysis and Semi-Groups', ch. xx.

23. See the essay 'Is Classical Mechanics in Fact Deterministic?' by Max Born, in 'Physics in My Generation' (Pergamon Press, New York, 1956) p. 164.

3 Knowledge and Interest*

Jürgen Habermas

Husserl saw as a reason for the crisis of a positivistic science its dissociation from practical interests. His remedy was to institute a purely contemplative attitude which should not only release the sciences from the grip of the illusion that the world is a ready-made universe of facts to be grasped in purely descriptive terms, but also by its own therapeutic powers, lead to 'a new kind of practice'. In adhering to this traditional concept of the relation of knowledge to interest Husserl misconceived the scientific crisis. Even though phenomenological description would effectively dispel the illusion of objectivism, objectivism in no way prevents science from influencing practice; what was needed was not to restore the practical significance of the sciences by making them finally break with interest, but rather to reveal the true relationship of knowledge and interest which the objectivistic attitude conceals. After outlining the fundamental interests guiding the respective scientific enterprises, the author summarises in five theses what he takes to be the basic aspects of the relationship between knowledge and interest.[1]

I

During the summer term of 1802 in Jena, Schelling gave his lectures on the method of academic study. In the language of German Idealism he restored and emphasised the concept of theory which had prevailed in the philosophical tradition from its beginning: 'Timidity in speculation, the ostensible taking refuge from the theoretical in the merely practical, necessarily gives to action the same shallowness as it does to knowledge. The study of a strictly theoretical philosophy

* 'Inquiry', ix (1966). This article was translated from the German by Guttorm Flöistad.

makes us, in the most immediate way, familiar with ideas, and ideas alone lend firmness and moral significance to action.'[2] Only knowledge which has been freed from mere practical concerns and has been centred around ideas, which has, in other words, acquired a theoretical basis, is able to provide the right setting for action.

The word 'theory' has a religious etymology. *Theoros* was the name for the holy representative sent to the public festivals by the Greek cities.[3] In *theoria*, that is, in the role of impersonal onlooker, he witnessed the sacred proceedings. In philosophical terminology Theoria has come to mean the contemplation of the cosmos. In this context, theory pre-supposes the distinction between Being and Time, a distinction underlying Ontology, first occurring in the poem of Parmenides and re-occurring in Plato's *Timaeus*. Theory sets aside Being for the Logos as an entity purged of in-constancy and uncertainty, leaving the realm of the transitory to Doxa. The philosopher regarding the eternal order is forced to adjust himself to the cosmos, to reproduce its order in himself. Through mimesis he recreates in himself those proportions which he observes in the workings of nature, and which can also be found in the harmonic pro-gressions of music. In this way theory extends over into the practical life by means of an adjustment or adaptation of the soul to the ordered movement of the cosmos: theory imprints its form on life and, in the ethos, is reflected in the attitude of the person who subjugates himself to its dis-cipline.

This notion of theory and of a life lived according to theory has influenced philosophical thought from the very beginning. We can pick up the thread in an inquiry by Husserl[4] where he takes as his guide just that notion of theory. Husserl is dealing not with crises *within* the sciences, but with the crisis of science *as science*, for 'in the afflictions of our daily life this science has nothing to say to us'.[5] Husserl, like most philosophers before him, uncritically adopts as a *standard* of criticism an idea of knowledge which preserves the Platonic link between pure theory and practical life. According to this idea it is not the information con-tained in the theories, but rather the formation of a considered and enlightened way of life among the theoreticians themselves which finally gives rise to a scientific culture. To Husserl the European spirit had seemed to be headed towards the creation of just such a scientific culture, but after 1933 this historical tendency seemed to him to be in danger, and he became convinced that this danger did not threaten from outside, but was inherent in the scientific enterprise itself. The cause of this crisis he understood as being the dissociation of the most advanced scientific disciplines, chiefly physics, from what could properly be called theory — in the old sense.

II

Let us consider what the position really is here. There may indeed be some connection between the positivistic self-image of the sciences and the old Ontology; the way in which, or the framework within which, the sciences develop their theories can, without undue strain, be seen to form a continuity with the beginnings of philosophical thought. In both cases there is a commitment to a theoretical attitude, with its function of freeing them from dogmatism and the irritating influence of practical concerns, and both find themselves part of the cosmological intention to describe the universe in its regulated order. It is less easy to trace a continuity in the case of the historical and interpretative sciences, since dealing with the sphere of transitory phenomena and the mere occurrence of opinion, they have nothing to do with cosmology. Yet they too created a scientistic consciousness as soon as they orientated themselves towards the model of the natural sciences; even the patterns of meaning inherited from the past seem to lend themselves to simultaneous combination into a cosmos of facts. However much the hermeneutic sciences (*Geisteswissenschaften*) postulate a special access via understanding, and however little they may be concerned with the discovery of general laws, they nevertheless share with strict science a methodological awareness — of the importance of the theoretical attitude, and of describing a structured reality from a theoretical point of view. In effect nineteenth-century historicism has become the positivism of the non-natural sciences.

This positivistic influence has also maintained itself in the social sciences, irrespective of whether they conform to the methodological requirements of an empirical analytical behavioural science, like psychology, or orientate themselves to the pattern of the normative analytical sciences, pre-supposing maxims for actions, like economic theory.[6] Under the title of *Wertfreiheit* the code has simply been confirmed once more in this field of investigation, a code which modern science would like to attribute to the beginnings of theor-etical thought in Greek philosophy: psychologically the unconditional commitment to theory, and epistemologically the separation of knowledge from practical concern (*Interesse*). Corresponding to this on the logical level is the differentiation between normative and descriptive state-ments — making the isolation of the purely emotive content from the cognitive a requirement even of grammar.

And yet the expression 'freedom from value' itself reminds us that the implied assumptions cannot be reconciled with the classical sense of theory. When they are separated from facts, values constitute an abstract 'should' in opposition to a pure 'is'. Values are the nominalistic by-product of a centuries-old criticism of that emphatic concept of Being towards which theory was once exclusively directed. The very name 'values', deriving from neo-Kantianism and implying something in respect of which science is supposed to remain neutral, denies the unity (*Zusammenhang*) once intended by theory.

Thus, although the positivistic sciences share their notion of theory with the tradition of philosophy hitherto, they nevertheless destroy its claim to classicism. They borrow two factors from the philosophical heritage: first, the idea that the theoretical attitude is important as a method, and secondly, the basic ontological assumption of a universal structure existing independently of the knower. But on the other hand, the connection between *theoria* and *kosmos* and between *mimesis* and *bios theoretikos*, which underlies philosophy from Plato up to Husserl, is lost. What was once meant to form the practical functioning of theory is now

39

But just for this reason Husserl ought not to expect educational processes to emerge from a phenomenology which has transcendentally purged the old theory of its cosmological content, and which consequently merely sticks to something like a theoretical attitude in an abstract kind of way. What was needed was not a re-alliance of knowledge with interest by an extension of the influence of theory into practical life; on the contrary, theory through the very concealment of its true interest had acquired a pseudo-normative power of its own. Though criticising the uncritical objectivism of the sciences, Husserl succumbs to another objectivism, and one which had always been latent in the traditional concept of theory.

IV

In the old Greek tradition those same forces which in philosophy were reduced to powers of the mind still appeared as gods and superhuman forces. Philosophy, however, had domesticated them and forced them into the domain of the mind as inwardly active demons. But when the instincts and passions, through which man becomes subjected to the full range of interests which govern his inconstant and variable activity, are conceived from this point of view, the purely theoretical attitude acquires a new significance: it promises a purification from these passions. In this way a standpoint freed from interests obviously does mean emancipation. Thus, the purpose of freeing knowledge from interest was not to rid theory of the blurrings of subjectivity, as it were, but on the contrary, to submit the subject himself to an ecstatic expurgation from the passions. The fact that catharsis at this point was no longer achieved by means of mystic cults, but became annexed to the will of the individual through theory, merely indicates the new stage of emancipation. The individualisation of each human being is, to the extent of communication made possible by the city-state, advanced to such a degree that the identity of every single I, as a fixed entity, can only be brought into existence through an identification with the abstract laws of the cosmic order. Consciousness, emancipated from the original forces,

42

now finds its hold in the unity of a cosmos resting in itself, and in the identity of a never-changing Being.

At one time, then, it was only through the ontological distinction that theory gave evidence of a freed world in which all demons were cast out. At the same time the seeming objectivity of a cosmos, according to pure theory, prevented a reversion to a stage already overcome. If the identity of a pure Being had come to be seen as an objectivistic illusion, then the identity of the I could not have formed itself on it. The repression of the interest in emancipation was, then, part of the interest itself.

But if this is so, then the two most powerful elements of the Greek tradition, the theoretical attitude and the basic ontological assumption of a structured world existing in itself, are assumed to enter into that very relationship which they themselves prohibit: a relationship between knowledge and interest. We return therefore to Husserl's criticism of the objectivism of the sciences. Now, however, the argument is turned against Husserl: it is not, as Husserl thought, because the sciences have *detached* themselves from the classical concept of theory that we assume for them a hidden connection of knowledge and interest, but because they have *not finally liberated* themselves from that concept. The suspicion of objectivism subsists on account of the ontological hypostasis of pure theory which the sciences, once educational elements have been removed, still share misleadingly with the philosophical tradition.

Following Husserl we call an attitude objectivistic which naïvely relates theoretical statements to reality. Such an attitude turns the relations between empirical entities, as they are presented in theoretical statements, into things that exist in themselves, and at the same time neglects the transcendental frame upon which the meaning of such statements primarily depends. As soon as the statements are understood relative to the *a priori (mitgesetzt)* frame of reference *(Bezugssystem)* the objectivistic illusion breaks down and attention is drawn to fundamental interests guiding the cognition. A specific connection between logical rules of procedure and the interests guiding cognition can be shown to hold for three categories of research. This is the task of a critical theory of science, which avoids the pitfalls of

43

positivism.[8] Into the assessment of the strict sciences, there enters a technical interest in cognition, an interest which in the case of the hermeneutic sciences is practical and in the case of the critically orientated sciences emancipatory. It is this interest which, as we saw, lay at the root of the traditional theories without the fact actually being admitted. I should like to explain this thesis by means of a few paradigm examples.

V

In the *empirical analytical sciences* the transcendental frame of reference determining the meaning of the validity of possible statements lays down rules both for the construction of theories and for their critical testing *(Überprüfung)*.[9] Hypothetico-deductive systems of statements which permit the derivation of lawlike hypotheses *(Gesetzeshypothesen)* with empirical content can be used as theories. These may be interpreted as statements about the covariance of observable events; under given initial conditions they make predictions possible. Thus empirical analytical knowledge is predictive knowledge. It is to be noted, however, that the general meaning of such predictions, that is, their technical applicability *(Verwertbarkeit)*, only becomes clear in view of the rules according to which we apply theories to reality.

In controlled observation, which frequently takes the form of experiments, we produce the initial conditions and measure the success of the operations thus performed. Empiricism tends now to hypostatise the observations expressed in the basic statements, for it seems that in these observations something evident and immediate can be relied upon to appear, without any subjective interference. The basic statements, however, do not picture the facts as such; rather, they express the successes or failures of our operations. We may say, of course, that the facts and the relations between them are descriptively recorded, but we should not allow this way of putting it to conceal that the empirical and scientifically relevant facts as such primarily constitute themselves through a prior organisation of our

44

experience within the range of the function of instrumental action.

Both elements taken together, the logical construction of reliable systems of statements and the type of test-conditions, suggest the following interpretation: that in inferring the nature of reality, empirical scientific theories are guided by a concern for certainty combined with informativeness, pertaining to purposive actions which might be controlled by their success. This is the cognitive interest involved in keeping objectified processes under technical control.

The *historical interpretative* sciences derive their knowledge from another methodological frame. Here the system of reference which establishes the meaning of the validity of possible statements is not determined by the requirements of manipulation. The levels of formalised language and objectified experience are not yet separated *(auseinandergetreten)*. For it is neither the case that the theories are constructed deductively, nor that experience itself is organised with a view to operational success. Here it is the understanding of meaning, and not controlled observation, which provides access to the facts. Corresponding to the systematic testing of lawlike assumptions in the empirical analytical sciences we have here the interpretation of texts. Thus the rules of hermeneutic procedure determine the general meaning of interpretations in the non-natural sciences.[10]

To this understanding of meaning, for which the facts of the mind are held to be evidently given, historicism has attached the illusion of objectivity according to pure theory. It seems as if the interpreter simply places himself within the horizon of the world or language from which a given historical fact derives its meaning. In this case too, however, the facts constitute themselves only in relation to the standards by which they have been stated *(Feststellung)*. Just as the positivistic way in which the empirical analytical sciences understand themselves does not explicitly acknowledge the connection of basic sentences with measuring operations, so too the hermeneutic sciences neglect to account for the prior understanding of the interpreter, which is inherent in his vantage point and through which inter-

45

pretative knowledge is always communicated. The world of traditionally inherited meanings reveals itself to the interpreter only to the extent to which his own world thereby becomes transparent to him at the same time. The man who understands the traditional meanings provides a link between the two worlds; he comprehends the factual content of what is handed down by applying the tradition to himself and his situation.

If, however, the procedural rules thus combine interpretation with application, then the following explanation suggests itself; in revealing reality, interpretational research is guided by a concern for the maintenance and extension of possible intersubjective understanding which is necessary for the orientation of any symbolic interaction. Meaning is understood according to its structure with a view to a possible consensus of interacting individuals within the frame of a traditional or culturally patterned self-understanding. This we shall call the practical, as distinct from the technical, interest of knowledge.

The systematic *sciences of action*, that is, economics, sociology and politics, just like the natural sciences, serve the purpose of producing nomological knowledge. A critical social science, however, is obviously not content with this; it tries in addition to discover which (if any) theoretical statements express unchangeable laws of social action and which, though they express relations of dependence, because they are ideologically fixed, are in principle subject to change. In so far as this is the case, the criticism of ideology, and, moreover, psycho-analysis, assumes that information about lawlike interrelations *(Gesetzeszusammenhänge)* produces a process of reflection in the consciousness of the individual concerned; the level of non-reflective awareness belonging to the initial conditions of such laws can in this way become changed. Although critically established knowledge of laws is unable, by reflection, to invalidate such a law itself, it can certainly eliminate necessary preconditions of its application.

The methodological frame which settles the meaning of the validity of this category of critical statements can be explained in terms of the notion of self-reflection. This frees the subject from dependence on hypostatised forces. Self-reflection is influenced by an emancipatory concern with

46

knowledge, and it is shared by the critically oriented sciences and philosophy.

Of course, as long as philosophy still remains attached to ontology, it is itself subject to an objectivism which conceals the relation of its knowledge to an interest in the autonomy *(Mündigkeit)* of self and society. Only when philosophy turns the criticism which it directs at the objectivism of the sciences towards its own illusion of pure theory as well, will it achieve any strength from the dependence it thus admits, and of which it, as a philosophy that is seemingly free from presuppositions, vainly attempts to prove itself innocent.[11]

VI

The two elements whose interrelationship we are attempting to clarify are already brought together in the notion of interest as a guide to knowledge: knowledge and interest. We know from our everyday experience that often ideas serve well enough to substitute for the true motives of our actions. What on this level we call rationalisation, on the level of collective actions we call ideology. In both cases the manifest content of statements is falsified through the unreflective attachment of an only seemingly autonomous consciousness to its interests. It is therefore right that the discipline of trained thought should aim at precluding all such interests. In all sciences procedures have been developed to guard against subjective opinion. And against the uncontrolled influence of deeper interests, characteristic not so much of individuals as of the objective situation of social groups, a new discipline has even come into existence, the sociology of knowledge. But this is just one side of the matter. Because science has to achieve objectivity for its statements nowithstanding the pressure and seduction of particular interests, it mistakenly disregards fundamental interests to which it owes not only its impulse, but also the very condition that makes objectivity possible.

The attitudes towards technical control, towards an understanding of life's activities and towards emancipation from the quasi-natural forces of history and society determine the specific points of view from which we are first able to conceive reality as such. By becoming aware of the fact that the transcendental limits of possible world conceptions cannot be surpassed, a piece of nature gains, in us, an autonomy in nature. If knowledge should ever be able to elude its innate interests, then it will be via this insight that the mediation of subject and object, which the philosophical consciousness claims exclusively as *its* synthesis, is from the very beginning produced by interests. The mind, by reflection, can become aware of this natural basis; its power, however, reaches even into the logic of scientific discovery.

Illustrations or descriptions are never independent of standards. And the choice of such standards rests on attitudes which, because they can be neither logically deduced nor empirically proved, are in need of critical evaluation through arguments. Procedural decisions about principles, about, for instance, such fundamental distinctions as those between categorical and non-categorical being, analytic and synthetic statements, descriptive and emotive content, all have the characteristic of being neither voluntary nor compulsory.[1 2] They prove to be either appropriate or inadequate, for they measure themselves against the meta-logical necessity of interests which we are able neither to determine nor to picture, but which we must grasp nevertheless. My *first thesis* runs therefore: the achievements of the transcendental subject have their basis in the natural history of mankind.

Taken by itself this thesis could lead to the misunderstanding that man's intellect, like the claws and teeth of animals, is an organ for adaptation. This is no doubt true. But the natural historical interests to which we trace these interests back in the achievements of knowledge, stem at once from nature and the cultural breach with nature. Together with the element of the pressure of natural needs they embody the element of freedom from natural compulsion. Even to the seemingly very natural interest in self-preservation there corresponds a social system which compensates for the deficiencies of man's organic equipment, and which secures his historical existence *against* a nature threatening from outside. However, society is not just a system of self-preservation. There is also a restless urge, present as a libido in the individual, which has unharnessed itself from the functions of self-preservation and presses

48

towards Utopian fulfilment. But even these individual claims which cannot be made congruent with the demands of collective self-preservation are embodied in the social system. Therefore the processes of cognition, which are inseparable from the creation of society, cannot function only as a means of maintenance and reproduction of life; they serve equally to establish the very definitions of this life. However basic survival may seem, in mankind it is always a historical event; for it measures itself in relation to what a society tends to regard as the good way of life. My *second thesis* runs therefore: knowledge is an instrument for self-preservation just to the same extent as it transcends mere self-preservation.

The specific points of view, from which we necessarily conceive reality in a transcendental way, determine three categories of possible knowledge: information, which increases the extent of our technical command; interpretation, which enables an orientation of action in the light of common traditions; and analysis, which sets the consciousness free from its dependence on hypostatised forces. These points of view have their origin in a system of interest of a kind which is in itself attached to certain media that function in the creation of society: work, language and authority *(Herrschaft)*. Mankind secures its existence in systems of social employment and forceful self-preservation; also through a common life handed down by tradition and transmitted through ordinary language; and finally, by means of I-identities *(Ich-Identitäten)*, which always and on each level of individualisation establish the awareness of the individuals in relation to the norms of the group. Thus the interests guiding cognition are attached to the functioning of an I which, through processes of learning, adjusts itself to its external conditions of life; and which, furthermore, through processes of education, becomes accustomed to the system of communication belonging to the life of a social world; and which, finally, establishes for itself an identity in the conflict between instinctual urges and social coercion. These achievements enter into the productive powers which become accumulated in a society, furthermore into the cultural values in terms of which society interprets itself, and, finally, also into the norms which a society adopts or criticises. My *third thesis* runs therefore: the interests guiding cognition

49

constitute themselves in the medium of work, language and authority.

The constellation of knowledge and interest is not, indeed, the same in all categories. Certainly the presuppositionless autonomy in which, theoretically, knowledge first of all conceives reality and is then put to the service of interests alien to knowledge, is always, on this level, simply illusion. The intellect can, however, refer itself back to the context in which subject and object had *a limine* come to be connected — and this is a matter solely for self-reflection. It can to some extent catch up with the interest, if not do away with it.

It is not fortuitous that the critical suspension of judgement appropriate for the standards of all other processes of knowledge does not apply in the case of the standards of self-reflection. In this case they are certain. The concern with emancipation from quasi-natural authority is not just a vague idea that hovers before one's eyes: it can be *a priori* comprehended. What raises us above nature is indeed the only fact of which, due to its very nature, we *can* have knowledge: namely, language. The idea of autonomy *(Mündigkeit)* is given to us with the structure of language. With the very first sentence the intention of a common and uncompelled consensus is unequivocally stated. Autonomy is thus the only idea of which we, that is, those in the philosophical tradition, are in command. That is perhaps the reason why the language of German Idealism, according to which reason embodies both elements, consciousness *and* will, is not yet quite obsolete. For idealism reason was at the same time the will towards reason. In self-reflection knowledge for the sake of knowledge *(um der Erkenntniswillen)* comes to us together with an interest in autonomy. The emancipatory concern with knowledge aims at the accomplishment of reflection as such. My *fourth thesis* runs therefore: in the power of self-reflection knowledge and interest are one.

And yet only in an emancipated society, which had realised the autonomy of its members, would communication have developed into that free dialogue of all with all which we always hold up as the very paradigm of a mutually formed self-identity, as well as the ideal condition of true consensus. To this extent the truth of statements is based on the

50

anticipation of a life without repression. The ontological guise of pure theory, behind which the interests guiding knowledge cannot be seen, consolidates the fiction, as though the Socratic dialogue were possible in general and at any time. Philosophy has from the very beginning assumed that the autonomy given with the structure of language was not just anticipated, but real at any time. It is precisely pure theory, with its claim to be self-contained, that surrenders itself to the interests it suppresses and becomes ideological. Not until philosophy, in the dialectical course of history, discovers the traces of the force which has distorted the repeatedly attempted dialogue and continuously driven it away from the course of uncompelled communication, will it once again set in motion that process whose stationary position it otherwise authorises: the advance of mankind towards autonomy. As the *fifth thesis* I should therefore like to put forward the proposition: the unity of knowledge and interest proves itself in a dialectic which restores what has been suppressed from the historical traces of a suppressed dialogue.

VII

The sciences have retained one thing from philosophy: the illusion of pure theory. This posture does not define the practice of their research but rather their way of understanding themselves. And in so far as their view of themselves influences practice, this does indeed make good sense.

The sciences earn the respect that is theirs by applying their methods imperturbably and without thought for their guiding interest. By being methodologically ignorant of what they are doing, the sciences are the more sure of their discipline, that is, of methodical advances within a non-problematic frame. This inadequate awareness of theirs has a safeguarding function, for at the self-reflective level the sciences lack the means of protection against the risks of a too clear view of the connection between knowledge and interest. Fascism was only able to hatch the changeling *(Wechselbalg)* of a national physics, and Stalinism, which is a more serious matter, only Soviet-Marxist genetics, because

51

the illusion of objectivism was missing — a factor which might have proved immunity against the more dangerous enchantments of a misguided reflection.

The good reputation of objectivism, however, has its limits; this was rightly the starting-point for Husserl's criticism, even though he went about it in the wrong way As soon as the attitude of objectivity is turned into an ideological affirmation, the difficulties of the methodologically unconscious individual distort themselves into the doubtful virtue of a scientistic creed. Objectivism by no means prevents the sciences, as Husserl believed, from entering into the practical affairs of life. In one way or another the sciences are integrated into them, but their growing practical efficacy does not *eo ipso* bestow upon action a growing rationality.

In the nomological sciences a positivistic self-understanding tends to further the substitution of technical control for enlightened action. It guides the application of empirical scientific information from the quite illusionary point of view, as if the practical grasp of history could be referred back to the technical control of objectified processes. The objectivistic way in which the hermeneutic sciences understand themselves is no less consequential. From reflectively understood, still living traditions it extracts a sterilised knowledge and ensures that everything that is in any way historical is consigned to the archives. Guided by the objectivistic attitude of fact-picturing theory, the nomological and the hermeneutic sciences supplement one another with respect to their practical consequences. While the latter remove from the system their commitment to tradition, the former, on the basis of a history swept bare and superseded, force the practice of life entirely into the confines of the functioning of instrumental action. The dimension in which the active subjects could come to a rational and mutual understanding of ends and purposes is thus handed over to the obscurity of mere decision between objectified value-systems and irrational powers of belief.[13] Moreover, even if this dimension, left untouched by all good spirits, could only be subject to a criticism which is itself just as much caught up in objectivism, the consequences of positivism were no less problematic. For a criticism which denies its connection with an emancipatory interest and adheres instead to the claims of pure theory, projects the undecided process of the development of mankind on the level of philosophy of history, which then dogmatically distributes directives for action. A delusive philosophy of history is the reverse side of blind decisionism; a bureaucratically ordained partiality goes only too well with a neutrality of value, contemplatively misunderstood.

A critique which dispels the illusion of objectivity can have some effect against these practical consequences of the limited scientistic consciousness of science. It is not, however, a renewed Theoria here exerting itself to dissolve objectivism, but only the pointing out of what objectivism conceals: namely, the relationship between knowledge and interest. In renouncing objectivism philosophy is being faithful to its great tradition; the insight that the truth of statements is ultimately tied up with the intention to live the true life can only be preserved today on the ruins of ontology. Philosophy, however, will remain a speciality apart from the sciences and outside public awareness so long as the heritage (of tradition), which it itself has critically released, continues to exist in the positivistic understanding that the sciences have of themselves.

NOTES

1. This paper was the basis for my inaugural lecture at the University of Frankfurt on 28 June 1965. References to literature are therefore limited to a few suggestions.

2. 'Schellings Werke', ed. Schröter (C. H. Beck, Munich, 1927) iii 299.

3. Georg Picht, 'Der Sinn der Unterscheidung von Theorie und Praxis in der griechischen Philosophie', in 'Evangelische Ethik', viii (1964) pp. 321 ff.

4. 'Die Krisis der europaischen Wissenschaften und transcendentale Phänomenologie', in 'Ges. Werke', vi (Martinus Nijhoff, The Hague, 1954).

5. 'Krisis', p. 4.

6. Cf. E. Topitsch, 'Logik der Sozialwissenschaften' (Kiepenhauer, Cologne, 1965); and my thesis, 'Logik der Sozialwissenschaften', Beiheft der 'Philosophischen Rundschau' (J. C. B. Mohr, Tübingen: forthcoming).

7. 'Krisis', p. 329.

8. K. O. Apel, 'Die Entfaltung der Sprachanalytischen Philosophie und der Problem der Geisteswissenschaften', in 'Philosophisches Jahrbuch', lxxii (Munich, 1965) 239 ff.

9. Cf. K. R. Popper 'The Logic of Scientific Discovery' (Routledge & Kegan Paul, London, 1959); and my thesis, 'Analytische Wissenschaftstheorie und Dialektik', in 'Zeugnisse' (Europäische Verlagsanstalt, Frankfurt am Main, 1963) pp. 473 ff.

10. Here I subscribe to the investigations of H. D. Gadamer, 'Wahrheit und Methode' (J. C. B. Mohr, Tübingen, 1960) part ii.

11. T. W. Adorno, 'Zur Metakritik der Erkenntnistheorie' (Kohlhammer, Stuttgart, 1956).

12. M. White, 'Toward Reunion in Philosophy' (Harvard University Press, Cambridge, Mass., 1956).

13. Cf. my thesis, 'Dogmatismus, Vernunft und Entscheidung', in 'Theorie und Praxis' (Luchterhand, Neuwied, 1963) pp. 231 ff.

4 Sociological Explanation*

Tom Burns

Having to give an inaugural lecture is a rather daunting affair
though, I am sure, a salutary one. Luckily, there is always
tradition to sustain one and to afford some guidance. There
are, one finds, models, or types, of inaugural lectures. I
cannot claim to be a connoisseur, but, judging from a small
and heavily biased sample, they seem to fall into three
groups. There are those, to begin with, which announce new
departures for a subject, new horizons, recent territorial
acquisitions in teaching or research, perhaps a reformed
constitution: they are, in short, manifestos — delivered, of
course, modestly, even diffidently sometimes, and with
proper deference to neighbours and previous tenants, but
manifestos nevertheless; muted manifestos. The second kind
defines itself more precisely. There is hardly a single field of
scholarship or science in which the contribution of Scotland,
of this university itself, has not been extensive and
weighty — even, at times, momentous; very few branches of
learning in which it is not possible to point to a noble and
inspiring tradition of intellectual endeavour. There is special
propriety on the occasion of an inaugural lecture, then, in
recalling — invoking — the achievements of predecessors, of
the giants on whose shoulders we presume to stand; there is a
special propriety in setting oneself the aim, not unduly
modest, either, of continuing or reviving the traditions they
formed. And for those who invest in this kind of inaugural,
there is the very large bonus to collect from the rich deposits
of portable quotations which lie embedded in so much of
Scottish intellectual history, with its unique and rewarding
blend of wit and sententiousness, of high thinking and low
living. Inaugurals of this kind are known to the trade as
Scotch, or Upper Library, jobs.

Third, and last, is the guided tour through the main

* 'British Journal of Sociology' xviii (1967).

55

thoroughfares of a new and unfamiliar subject. Less striking in its appeal than the first, less elegant in manner than the second, more pedestrian by definition of course than either, the guided tour runs the twin hazards of losing half one's audience by boring them with what is already distressingly familiar stuff, and the other half by hurrying them through the more complicated or remote precincts.

These risks I have to ask you to face with me, however, because this is the form and pattern I want to adopt for this lecture. I do so not because sociology is new or unfamiliar — for me to think so would be presumptuous — but because it has seemed to me a subject more than usually susceptible to misconception and misconstruction.

There is, I shall argue, a special reason for this. All branches of knowledge, scientific and other, are concerned with description as well as with explanation, have their substantive content as well as their methodology, are fact-finding, diagnostic or taxonomic activities as well as theoretical and model-building activities. It is indeed by their descriptive activities, their substantive area of study, that specialist studies are known to the non-specialist public. Sociology is no exception, and it is because of this, I believe, that the misconceptions have arisen. For the misconceptions, such as they are, relate to what is publicly known about the descriptive activities of sociology.

The title I have chosen for this lecture, therefore, while not deliberately misleading, is rather elliptical. I shall have to deal with sociology in its descriptive aspects, and, moreover, to try to show how both as description and as explanation sociology is always a critical activity. In considering sociological explanation, furthermore, I shall not seek either to present you with a review of the methods of research used in sociology or of customary procedures in analysing research data — which would be very tedious and exceedingly inappropriate. I shall also steer very clear of the gound which has been ploughed so heavily in recent years by British and American philosophers. My references will be to empirical sociology rather than to what is commonly designated by sociologists as social theory. My object is to try to point out by example and to explain as best I can what is distinctive about sociology in its approach to its subject-matter. And I shall do this cumulatively, adding items to the account as we go.

Let me begin by taking it as common and undisputed ground that we tend to live more and more in a world of organised, departmentalised, bodies of knowledge; and that this is not a matter merely of the exigencies of university curricula, or of the shortness of life and the accumulation of knowledge which forces increasing specialisation on us. Intellectual life, scholarship and science are subject increasingly to the principles which govern the division of labour in the rest of civilised existence. We have become acutely aware of the cultural divisions which can grow up as consequence, and, in time, as reinforcement, of specialisation, and there is an increasing number of enthusiastic or conscience-stricken attempts to bridge the gaps. But there are other consequences which we are perhaps less conscious of. Among them is the odd tendency for the world in which we live, the environment of physical matter, of natural circumstance, and of events, to shape itself and to become organised after the same pattern of specialisms, and in their terms. History is, of course, both the past and the study of the past — of course; more particularly it is the body of recorded and ascertainable facts about the past which is regarded by historians as relevant to historical studies. Law has the same familiar and entirely undeceptive ambiguity in common usage; it is both the body of law and the study of law. And it is difficult to think of a time or a possible circumstance in which it might have made sense in either case to regard the subject-matter in any different way from the study of it. But it also makes equal sense to talk of chemistry and physics in the same way; and there was certainly a time when even quite civilised people did not. For us there is a chemical world and a physical world: the chemistry of aircraft engines or their physics, the chemistry or the physics of the human body, are terms in general currency. More significantly, during the past few generations new disciplines have acted on the world and on circumstances in the same fashion. Instead of enumerating all the particulars of forms of livelihood, standard of living, division of labour, system of exchange, modes and rates of capital formation, range of products, and so on, it is meaningful, acceptable and common usage to speak of 'the economy'.

57

There is a specific reference here to those actions, events and objects which are the relevant objects of study to economists. And the reference is really quite specific. It is not uncommon, for instance, to find in accounts and explanations of movements in prices, or of fluctuations in consumption, allusions to 'non-economic' variables, so-called, which nevertheless do effect changes in 'the economy'. Psychology has acted as an organising principle in a similar fashion, so that the special attributes of individual attainment, emotional response, mental experience and development which have become appropriate for psychological study now make up a recognised and recognisable sector of the world as we experience it. One can speak meaningfully of the psychology of a person and mean something different from what we mean when we speak of 'a person'.

In all these instances, a science or a discipline has come to achieve so established a recognition as a map of a segment or a set of elements in the world of common experience that it serves as a handy way of discriminating the world of common experience itself. It is one of the ways in which the world becomes a manageable place to live in. Most of us, after all, do seem to think most easily of the world itself as a map. But the process by which economics maps into 'the economy' or by which chemistry maps into 'the chemistry' of our bodies tends for the most part to be taken for granted or completely elided.

Organising our experience of the world in this fashion, convenient, customary and unexceptionable as it is for the layman, is often unwelcome and embarrassing to the specialist himself. Every decade produces its fresh crop of new specialisms which transcend the boundaries of disciplines almost as soon as they are firmly established in the public mind. But the point of this excursion into the higher generalities is to underline what I am sure you have run ahead of me to perceive, namely, that there is no segment or set of elements in the world of common experience which is organised in this way by sociology. One cannot speak of the sociology of Scotland as one can of the Scottish economy, nor of the sociology of children as one can of child psychology. Interestingly enough, substantive fields of sociology, many of them at least, go by titles like the sociology of education, the sociology of law, the sociology of politics, the sociology of medicine. In all these cases, the substantive area of study is defined by another discipline. The mapping has been done by it, not by sociology.

It is for this reason that this guided tour is taking place under the advertised announcement of 'sociological explanation'. For the substantive areas of sociological studies are composed out of the way in which sociology operates upon previously organised bodies of knowledge, not, let me hasten to add, only and merely upon bodies of scientific and academic knowledge but also upon systems of belief, and codes of accepted practice. Sociology operates in and upon these fields in quite specific directions and in quite specific ways. It does so by questioning assumptions which seem to be made by people, and especially by people in authority in education, law, politics and so forth, about the behaviour of people. These assumptions are sometimes explicit in the form of expressed statements, more often implicit in the form of preference orderings or concealed value-judgements, but they are all formulated within what I can best call the territorial boundaries of each system of organised knowledge and practice; they are assumptions to the effect that the human behaviour visible to the educationist, the lawyer, the politician and so on, is ordered sufficiently for their purposes according to the principles and the vocabulary of ideas developed within the educational system, the law, political science, and so on. Let me try to make this rather opaque pronouncement clearer by instances of what I mean.

I can begin by what will be for many of you very familiar ground. The 1944 Education Act for England and Wales, like the later Scottish Act, was designed to provide for more education at the secondary level, for different kinds of secondary education, and altogether to ensure that opportunities for educational and thus occupational and social advancement would be equally accessible to all children. There is no reason at all to question the sincerity of those who framed and later administered the Act. Indeed, the strength of the point I wish to make lies in the very genuineness of the attempt to reduce to vanishing point the inequities which had been built into the educational system maintained by the state. Within the perfectly valid frame of

59

reference adopted by legislators, administrators and their advisers, the system of selection for secondary education was as psychologically sophisticated and as fair as one could possibly expect. Certainly, so far as I know, no fairer system of selection has since been devised. Yet a series of studies carried out during the 1950s by the London School of Economics demonstrated conclusively that equality of opportunity had certainly not been achieved. These studies were not, of course, concerned in the least with the techniques of selection themselves, the apparatus of tests, their administration, the impartiality of teachers and educationists — anything but. The inquiries were directed towards bringing to light considerations and factors affecting educational performance which, familiar as they are to all of us now, had simply not been taken into account in the design of the new educational system; it is not that the structure of families and their material and social circumstances were thought of as not affecting the school life and career of the child — of course they were. But those factors had not been treated as affecting attainment in the ways and to the extent they were now shown to do.

During the 1960s the considerations or assumptions treated as external to the frame of reference of education, or disregarded entirely, have been added to by educational sociologists. Educational performance is now being related to organisational features of the school system, to the institutional character of the class-room situation, to the particular difficulties and anomalies of the teacher's role, and the structure of the teaching profession. Those later researches, like the earlier, are directed towards eliciting considerations and determining factors which, previously lying outside the technical scope of the educational system, are nevertheless relevant to the educational process and should henceforward be taken into account. There is an important sense, therefore, in which educational sociology is tributary to the theory and practice of education.

I suggested that the clear definition of the boundary of a field of scholarship or science and the coherence and homogeneity of the kind of facts regarded as lying within it — the fact that we can talk about education as a body of knowledge, and as an administrative system, and as a developmental process of a special kind — that all this comes from the existence of a publicly accepted frame of reference and a particular coinage of ideas and beliefs which is in good currency. The frame of reference changes, of course, and so does the body of ideas, aspirations and values accepted as good currency. The main tradition of sociological writing in the field of education — a tradition which stretches through the work of Durkheim (himself, incidentally, a professor of Education), Weber, and Mannheim (who also, when he came to this country occupied a chair of Education) — this main tradition bears on the way in which ideas and beliefs about the purpose, the appropriate administration and the nature of education have changed in response to changing and emerging needs in society. The actual causes of change, as Mannheim said, are motivated acts, but the motives themselves are shaped by changes in social conditions. And these changes occur at an accelerating pace under industrialism, which throws new burdens on educational institutions — the progressive burdens of mass instruction, promotion of scientific and technological progress, occupational recruitment and now, it seems, social selection — for, in the case of the great majority of people in this country, the place they are going to occupy in the social system and the class structure is settled before they are twenty years old.

'Under conditions of advanced industrialism', as Mrs Floud and Dr Halsey have said, 'the economy becomes increasingly dominated by the institutions of research and technological innovation. ... So that the educational system comes to occupy a strategic place as a central determinant of the economic, political, social and cultural character of society.'[1] On this larger scale, as well as in the study of educational opportunity and educability, the role of educational sociology is to examine, to question, to raise doubts about, to criticise the assumptions on which current policy, current theory and current practice are based.

The essentially critical function of sociology at this level is just as clearly present in political sociology. I have to insist on this critical function in the case of this field of studies, because the rendering of the purpose of sociological explanation in this context that I want to put forward is not widely current. In particular, it is very different from that

61

advanced by Martin Lipset and Reinhard Bendix, who are individually two of the most distinguished contributors to this field of sociology, and who, in combination, carry a very formidable – a papal – weight of authority. They write: 'Like political science, political sociology is concerned with the distribution and exercise of power in society. Unlike political science, it is not concerned with the institutional provisions for that distribution and exercise, but takes these as given. Thus political science starts with the state and examines how it affects society, while political sociology starts with society and examines how it affects the state: i.e., the formal institutions for the distribution and exercise of power.'[2]

We all, as academic teachers and students, deal in over-simplifications and learn to live with those of other people. But this attempt to dichotomise the study of political science and political sociology by polarising them, so to speak, on different points of origin is more than a pardonable over-simplification. It seems to me false as to the facts, possibly with regard to political science, certainly with regard to political sociology, which began with the attempt to measure the extent to which political institutions of a particular kind – namely, political party machines – can and do influence the behaviour of people in society. It is categorically false; the two kinds of study do not occupy two halves of the same football pitch or defend two goals, one labelled 'state' and the other labelled 'society', and advance towards the other; they are different kinds of game, played on different pitches. And the statement is, I believe, false as to the relationship between the two studies. Political sociology is not just the study of the same substantive field as political science but from a different angle of approach. It is tributary to – or, if you like, parasitic upon – political science, in the same way as educational sociology is upon education – parasitic, in the sense in which criticism is parasitic.

There are several fairly distinct divisions of activity in political sociology. The best known is the study of voting behaviour which effectively begins, despite André Siegfried's notable work completed before the First World War, with Lazarsfeld, Berelson and Gaudet's panel study of the

62

American presidential election of 1940.[3] What Lazarsfeld and his research team did was to interview a sample of 3000 electors in a part of Ohio at the beginning of the election campaign, and to interview sections of the main sample at regular intervals up to the presidential election in November. The research design was concerned specifically with estimating the actual influence exerted on voting by the campaigns of the two parties throughout the whole six months preceding the election. From this, and subsequent studies in America, Britain and elsewhere, we have gained an increasingly vivid and detailed picture of how much voting is a matter of habit, how little rational choice seems to enter in, how far political allegiances are formed virtually in childhood, how few voters change that allegiance in normal election circumstances. We are getting to know more about the influence of demographic factors and about the curiously overlooked part played by religious affiliation in certain countries. None of this work, or of other work on party organisation or pressure groups, on the nature and social function of ideology contributes anything to the solution of the major issues of political principle or of political organisation. It is not an approach to the field of study of political science from another point of departure. But it does affect very much the terms in which these issues are to be debated, and the limits of the considerations which must henceforward be regarded as pertinent to political studies. W. G. Runciman has remarked that 'Lazarsfeld's work has placed an important limit on the scope of *a priori* theorising about democracy; and it has done so by producing sociological evidence directly relevant to the tenets of political theory. It is not evidence which necessarily supports a left-wing or a right-wing view; but it is important precisely because any theory of democracy, whether left or right, must take account of it.'[4] I would, while supporting this, also say that the importance of the sociological work in this field lies not in its limiting the scope of *a priori* theorising but in extending it – of pointing to considerations which political studies must take into account beyond those which were previously seen as 'politically relevant'.

There are two corollaries to which I think I can now point as proceeding from what I have said so far. The first I have already suggested – which is that the relationship of sociology to these and other fields of substantive study is tributary. Sociologists, more than most scientists perhaps, admit the force of the injunction to forget their past, since much of what of value there is in it has been incorporated and has taken root in other disciplines. Secondly, while the direction and purpose of sociological kinds of explanation has been to amend and supplement the kinds of evidence and consideration lying within substantive areas of organised knowledge mapped by other established disciplines, the outlines of what might turn out to be a substantive area peculiar to sociology are perhaps becoming perceptible. In the cases I have mentioned, sociology has not only pointed to uniformities and variations in performance and in choice which are inexplicable in terms of the existing rationale of education or of politics, but has identified the external factors in terms of unwitting regularities among groups and categories of individuals, of latent controls and limitations of action, of conventions and observances which hardly can be said to rise to the surface of articulate expression. We are, in fact, dealing with the institutional framework of social behaviour, the implicit, unthinking and unarticulated code of norms which govern or influence individual conduct. Vilhelm Aubert's study of the judiciary in Norway,[5] when it was first published, evoked violent reactions among the legal profession precisely because it pointed to the fact that, in giving sentence, judges appeared to be following a tacit code which contravened the explicit code of equality before the law. We are, in this country, aware of the embarrassing variations in the practices followed in different magistrates' courts in giving sentence — the large discrepancies in the penalties exacted for indentical infringements of the law in apparently very similar circumstances. These variations have been the subject of a good deal of discussion and criticism in recent years, and, indeed, investigations have been undertaken to establish just how far the inconsistencies range. But the presumption in this connection, so far as this country is concerned is, I believe, that the inconsistencies are just that — that the natural range of variation which must occur because of differences in temperament, idiosyncratic interpretation of the law, uncontrollable prejudice against persons, and so on, is perhaps wider than it should be. What

Aubert did was to scrutinise and compare the sentences and the utterances of judges (senior as well as junior) in giving sentence, relate those to the recorded circumstances of the cases on which sentence was pronounced, and demonstrate that the variation in sentencing behaviour correlated extremely closely with the social class of the accused person. Not an astonishing conclusion, perhaps, but interesting. Interesting, because the correlation bespeaks a rule, a normative principle influencing the sentences given, which is certainly external to the principles which overtly apply to the behaviour of judges, and even contravenes those principles. Other studies, notably the Chicago studies of the conduct of arbitration cases by lawyers, point to the existence of rather more complicated normative principles which seem, in the same latent, unwitting fashion, to distort or contravene the principles of action which prevail, and which are — I must emphasise — honestly maintained, within the system of law itself.

I have, so far, kept to what I have thought might be more familiar ground for this explanation of sociological explanation, largely because I hoped in doing so to make clear the way in which sociological explanation is shaped by its special purposes. I want now to discuss rather more closely the essentially critical, assumption-testing nature of sociological investigation. I can, I think, bring most light to bear by recounting some research experience of my own in industrial organisations.

Most empirical studies of organisations depend a good deal on interviews with managers. One begins these interviews conventionally with questions about the particular job one's respondent does, and how it fits in with other people's and with other departments. The next step is to examine the discrepancies between the picture one gets from different respondents of the organisation in which they all work. There always are discrepancies, of course. But the question presented by these inconsistencies is not 'Which version is right?' but 'How do these differences arise? How is it that these different versions of the same set of circumstances and actions have arisen in the minds of people who have to co-operate with each other in the very circumstances they view so differently?' The need to account for these differences marks the first stage beyond narrative description.

Some years ago, at the outset of one such inquiry, I encountered a major difficulty even before reaching this first stage when comparison becomes feasible. The firm was in a very rapidly expanding and technologically advanced industry. A whole series of interviews with managers followed a rather disconcerting pattern. After listening to my account of myself and of what I was interested in finding out, they would say, in answer to my first question, 'Well, to make all this clear, I'd better start from the beginning', and then proceed to give me an account of their careers in the firm. This account would be lucid, well-organised, and informative, but would stop short at some time beforehand — when, in fact, they had arrived at their present position. I would then ask again what they were in fact doing now, what the different functions were that they carried out, whom they saw in connection with them, and so on. After a pause, they would then go on to explain, equally lucidly, how they and their department would operate when the present crisis was past, or the very big job they were rushing through was completed or when the reorganisation I had doubtless heard about had been carried through, and they could all settle down to work to a plan. After a succession of such interviews I was fairly certain that I had encountered the sociologist's poor substitute for the natural scientist's 'discovery' — the feeling that what had looked like good, commonsense ground (and what could be more commonsense than that managers know what jobs they are supposed to be doing?) was turning into rather liquid assumptions.

Luckily, the managers who had provided me with this experience found my reaction, when I was sure enough of myself to tell them, as interesting as I did, and agreed, four of them in one department, to carry out an experiment. This consisted merely in each keeping a detailed record over a period of five weeks of how he spent his working time, whom he met, what problems he was concerned with, whether he issued instructions, whether he gave exchanged, or received information, and so on.

I should like to dwell on this account of the genesis of a particular piece of research a little. Like any other kind of inquiry which has a history and an establishment, sociology

66

seems at any one time to be pursuing not so much the right kind of knowledge as the right kind of questions, not definitive information but fresh hypotheses. Anyone who has done research in any field will testify to the truth of Agnes Arber's remark that the difficulty in most scientific work lies in framing the questions rather than in finding the answers. What is not so often insisted upon is that questions do not suggest themselves or rise at the bidding of the specialist student with a little time on his hands. They arise from doubt. Doubt, in turn, arises from the existence of an alternative where none was previously suggested; it arises from a discrepancy between facts, or between accepted interpretations, or between intended and achieved results. In this particular case, it arose from doubt as to whether what everybody regarded as an abnormal departure from the pattern of activities as they should be was not in fact the normal condition of things.

Let me go on to say a little more about the research project which followed. The four people who carried this through did so in quite exemplary manner, swamped me with thousands of record forms and launched a research project which kept me, and a hundred other managers in a number of different industrial concerns, fully occupied at intervals over the next two years. There is one aspect of the results of this first, pilot, study which I want to mention here. I extracted all the record forms on which the departmental manager and one or other of his subordinates had recorded meeting each other. There were 240 of these. In 165 of them, the departmental manager had noted that he was giving a subordinate instructions or decisions; when one turned to the records made by the subordinates of the same episodes, only 84 of them indicated that they were receiving instructions or decisions. In fact, then, half the time, what the manager thought he was giving as instructions or decisions was being treated as advice or simply information.

This result, which I talked over at some length with the people who had done the recording, is open to a number of interpretations, all of them throwing some light, I think, not only on what we may call the pathology of the systems of bureaucratic authority on which so much of organised life in society depends, but on the way in which people living in a world in which equality is their prescriptive right as citizens yet accommodate themselves to the working necessities of subordination and inferior status. But for my present purpose, what I want to underline is the way in which the rules of the game which was actually being played between these four people — all of them young, intelligent, hardworking, ambitious — were in fact unrecognised by them. There were many other ways in which the same suggestion made itself felt — that organisations are made to work very often by the unwitting observance by their members of rules of the game which are not only different from the formal articulated body of rules but are not realised in anything like explicit form by the players themselves. The management of this department, for example, when they were asked at the end of this five-week period — when they had been composing almost minute-by-minute records of their activities — how much of their time was spent on all matters directly related to production, gave roughly well over half of their combined time as the answer. And in this they were, they thought, being conservative; after all, they *were* running a production department. In fact, they spent less than a third. In other companies, estimates of how the whole management group's time was spent — given after each individual member had spent several weeks in unusually close attention to just this — were even more wildly out. These results, incidentally, have inclined me to attach rather less than full objective validity to the figures published in one of the appendices to the Robbins Report (which are based on an inquiry conducted by postal questionnaire) into the way in which university staff distribute their time among their various activities.

I have used a miniature, perhaps trivial, illustration to demonstrate the widespread and pervasive tendency for human action to proceed in a *context* of thought and belief and intention very largely at variance with the manifest import of the actions themselves. In his 1961 Trevelyan lectures, E. H. Carr argues that what the historian is called upon to do is to investigate what lies behind the act. It was, he went on to suggest, a serious error to assume, as Collingwood had, that this meant the investigation of the thought and purposes of the individual actor. These may, said

68

Carr, be quite irrelevant. 'The relations of individuals to one another in society and the social forces which act through them produce from the actions of individuals results often at variance with, and sometimes 'opposite to, the results they themselves intended.'[6]

Sociology also has been described — by Karl Popper among others — as concerned, in the way E. H. Carr suggests, with the unanticipated consequences of human action. There are innumerable examples of this in the field of administrative action and planning. I can take one from near home. In 1954, a group of professional people working in Pilton, a large Edinburgh ward which is almost wholly made up of municipal housing estates, asked the Department of Social Study to carry out a survey which would help clarify some of what they saw as the social problems of the area. Most of these, at the time, had to do with juvenile delinquency and with a whole series of related difficulties to do with the unruliness of children and adolescents and their hostility to ordinary controls. As part of the preliminaries to the survey, which was carried out by graduate students in the department, I looked at the make-up of the population of the ward — which, even at that time, numbered some 28,000 people — about the same size population as Stirling. There were three noteworthy features. First, there was a marked preponderance of young people. Virtually one in four of the population was between 10 and 20 years old; this compared with one in eight for Edinburgh as a whole, and one in eleven for the Central wards. In some parts of Pilton, this disproportionate number of children was even higher — in one section, over half the population was composed of school children and older teenagers. There was also a corresponding numerical deficiency of people between 25 and 35 years old — the most active section of the mature adult population, and there were very few old people.

Now it seemed to me then, and I still believe, that the implications of this state of affairs are quite obvious. The social control and social education of children is immeasurably more difficult in a population with mature adults so heavily outnumbered. The mere thickness on the ground of young children and adolescents will tend to make them a much more powerful force in any community than normally, will reinforce any resistance to adult control from inside or outside a community, and will tend to make adults look for their own entertainment and recreation away from the area. The incidence of unacceptable forms of individual and group activity among children and adolescents will appear to be much higher than in other districts of the city. The forms of activity at any given time, and the choice of companionships open to the individual child will be much more diverse than usual. Child and adolescent society will tend, therefore, to be more self-sufficient.

I think it is reasonable to conclude that the 'youth problem' of Pilton at the same time was largely demographic in character. And the population structure which produced a kind of dislocation in the normal system of relationships between adult and children, and in the behaviour of children, was the direct consequence of a housing policy which, in Edinburgh as everywhere else, filled large housing estates built in the 1930s with young families. From ten to fifteen years later, the population of course consisted largely of the middle-aged and the adolescent, and there appeared the sudden growth of delinquency rates in suburban areas which was a notable feature of so many English and Scottish cities. It is as though society played confidence tricks on itself.

On a larger scale, society seems to play not confidence tricks so much as self-confidence tricks on itself. These are a familiar element in social history. It took an immense amount of painstaking effort over many years to prove that a third of the working-class population of London was living in poverty; more years of work still, by Rowntree, to prove that the vast majority of families able to afford less food, clothing and warmth than on the most spartan of reckonings constituted bare subsistence level, had not been plunged into distress through some moral obliquity or defect of character, but through pressure of circumstances which they had no possible means of controlling. The astonishing feature of the *Our Towns* report on the condition of children evacuated from city slums in 1940 was not the squalor and unseemliness of the children but the blank ignorance of all other sections of society about them and the circumstances of urban life which had produced them. Within the last few weeks, Professor Townsend's survey of the millions of

70

families in Britian living at or below the subsistence level represented by national assistance has come, again as a shock. The results of Harrington's survey of the incidence of poverty in the United States three years ago came as a shock. Now, they are the stock-in-trade of the week-end political speaker.

The traditional role of descriptive sociology, in this country and elsewhere, has largely been to point out what is immediately obvious to everybody as soon as the task of collecting and presenting the facts has been done. In this sociology performs its familiar tributary function, this time in the formation and development of public opinion and common knowledge. In its other, more specialised, task of searching for explanations of behaviour, sociology often seems even more directly concerned with the obvious. A little while ago, I said that if one could point to a substantive area which constituted the field of study for sociology, it would be the institutional norms which seem to govern action in the sense of providing navigational rules for decision and action, or limits and constants which the behaviour of people seems to observe. But there exists already an enormous fund of knowledge — common knowledge based on common experience and commonsense — about the characteristic patterns of behaviour which can be observed among different groups of people and in different kinds of situation. Many years ago, Paul Lazarsfeld wrote a lengthy review of the first two volumes to be published on the studies conducted during the Second World War into the morale of American troops and the reactions of conscripted men to army life. He lists a number of conclusions, and suggests that most people would dismiss them as familiar, or as so obvious that there was no point at all in examining them. For example: better-educated men show more psycho-neurotic symptoms during training than those with less education — (the mental stability of the intellectual compared with the psychological resilience or impassivity of the ordinary man has often been commented upon). Second, men from rural backgrounds were usually in better spirits during their army life than men brought up in the city. Third, troops from the Southern states were better able to stand up to the climate in the hot Pacific Islands than Northerners. Fourth, white privates were more eager for promotion than Negroes. One can add a fifth, equally obvious: officers and men in units where promotion was most frequent and rapid were more satisfied with their present positions and prospects than were people in units where there were least chances of promotion.

'We have in these examples', Lazarsfeld remarks, 'a sample list of the simplest kind of interrelationships which provide the bricks from which an empirical social science can be built. But why, since they are so obvious, is so much money and energy given to establish such findings? Would it not be wiser to take them for granted and proceed directly to a more sophisticated type of analysis? This might be so except for one interesting point about the list. Every one of these statements is the direct opposite of what was actually found. Poorly educated soldiers were more neurotic than those with higher education; Southerners showed no greater ability than Northerners to adjust to a tropical climate; Negroes were more eager for promotion than whites; and so on.'[7]

In this last instance, as in all the others, sociology defines itself as a critical activity. The purpose of sociology is to achieve an understanding of social behaviour and social institutions which is different from that current among the people through whose conduct the institutions exist; an understanding which is not merely different but new and better. The practice of sociology is criticism. It exists to criticise claims about the value of achievement and to question assumptions about the meaning of conduct. It is the business of sociologists to conduct a critical debate with the public about its equipment of social institutions.

This purpose of critical understanding is more important now than it has ever been. Sociology, like other social sciences, is the creature of the new human situation which industrialism has brought about. It emerged, tentatively at first, as the need grew to understand, mitigate and possibly even control the transformations which individual lives and the social order continually undergo. As it has developed, it has become clothed with more and more of the objectivity and methodology of the natural sciences, and has become infused with more of their spirit of inquiry and discovery as ends in themselves; but like other social sciences, its character has nevertheless remained basically ideographic. All the social sciences are, I believe, governed by the need to understand

and to represent in adequate terms the nature of individual personality and mental experience, or the relationship of individuals to each other, or the varieties of economic and political institutions and relationships, or the social order itself.

The new impetus which has been given in our generation to the pace of scientific and technological development and to industrial and economic change all over the world gives a new urgency to these studies.

In many ways, the pressing need to know more about human behaviour in all its contexts — a need which has found increasingly popular expression during this century — is a manifestation of the disparity between man's understanding and control of nature and his insight into and command over his own conduct and his own affairs. Traditional wisdom, the oversight of the 'intelligent amateur', and the accumulation of experience over a lifetime, which served earlier generations, are now insufficient when we are so promptly confronted with the direct and the indirect, the projected and the unanticipated, consequences of discoveries and decisons. Earlier generations, however fast they saw their world changing, were at least persuaded that certain traditional institutions and values were immutable, and even that the passage of time alone might solve major difficulties and problems.

Time, indeed, was seen in the nineteenth century as on the side of man. Now, it seems, time is against us. More accurately, perhaps, if more prosaically, the difference lies in the sheer multiplicity and technical difficulty of the factors entering into the decision-making process. The point here is that we are in a fundamentally different situation from that obtaining when piecemeal changes could be made in social, economic or political systems as and when it seemed best, and when institutions could be discarded or replaced without much regard being paid to the social fabric of which they formed part. Decisons, planning and action in scientific, educational, economic and social affairs must now take cognisance of an ever-increasing span of considerations if they are both to be effective and not do more harm than good. Similar circumstances obtain for public and private corporations; and the concurrent growth of studies of decision-making in economics, sociology and psychology is again a manifestation of the way in which development in the social sciences reflects the emergent needs of society.

It is not fortuitous that all societies, whatever their political character or stage of economic development, have realised the need for some form of planning. 'Planning', in fact, is a word of dubious relevance to what is happening, if it is read in its traditional sense of producing a design which future actions, at set times, will convert into a finished construction in complete accordance with it. It is much more a matter of deciding the direction and the goals of activity, of setting the upper and lower constraints to the amounts and to the kinds of activity which are pertinent to the achievement of the goals. This new connotation places much more emphasis on selecting the sets of relevant variables and on understanding and controlling them and the factors which affect them. Planning, in short, has become a complicated process of social cybernetics, into which psychological, social, geographic, economic and educational factors enter, and a process which has to be implemented in terms of organisational and administrative expertise compared with which our existing procedures are but primitive craft skills.

The demands which present social needs are putting on the social sciences are already enormous. I am convinced that a far greater volume of demands and needs is present in latent form, or is building up. These demands are being expressed in a bewildering variety of forms. They are altogether out of proportion to the present capabilities and resources of the social sciences. If they are to come within measurable distance of an adequate response to the need which society has of them, positive and substantial efforts must be made to foster their development. These efforts are now, I believe, visible in a number of countries in Europe. They appear to be imminent in Britain.

I began this lecture by observing that sociology was not a new discipline. This is true, but it is, in one sense at least, new to this university. It has been born at a time when the demands on it, as on other social sciences, are growing, and at a time also when the character of the discipline itself is changing out of recognition. Sociology in Edinburgh looks forward to a strenuous but, I hope, an adventurous and lusty infancy.

74

NOTES

1. Jean Floud and A. H. Halsey, 'The Sociology of Education', 'Current Sociology', vii 3 (1958) 169.
2. Reinhard Bendix and Seymore M. Lipset, 'Political Sociology', 'Current Sociology', vii 3 (1958) p. 169.
3. Paul F. Lazarsfeld, B. Berelson and H. Gaudet, 'The People's Choice', 2nd ed. (Columbia University Press, 1948).
4. W. G. Runciman, 'Sociological Evidence and Political Theory' in Peter Laslett and W. G. Runciman (eds.), 'Philosophy, Politics and Society' (Blackwell, 1962) pp. 42-3.
5. Vilhelm Aubert, 'Sociology of Law', ch. 6, 'Law Courts and the Class Structure' (Institute for Social Research, Oslo, 1964, mimeographed).
6. E. H. Carr, 'What is History?' (Penguin Books, 1964) p. 52.
7. Paul F. Lazarsfeld, 'The American Soldier — an Expository Review', 'Public Opinion Quarterly' (1949) 380.

5 Methodological Individualism Reconsidered*

Steven Lukes

In what follows I discuss and (hopefully) render harmless a doctrine which has a very long ancestry, has constantly reappeared in the history of sociology and still appears to haunt the scene. It was, we might say, conceived by Hobbes, who held that 'it is necessary that we know the things that are to be compounded before we can know the whole compound' for 'everything is best understood by its constitutive causes', the causes of the social compound residing in 'men as if but even now sprung out of the earth, and suddenly, like mushrooms, come to full maturity, without all kinds of engagement to each other'.[1] It was begat by the thinkers of the Enlightenment, among whom, with a few important exceptions (such as Vico and Montesquieu) an individualist mode of explanation became pre-eminent, though with wide divergences as to what was included, in the characterisation of the explanatory elements. It was confronted by a wide range of thinkers in the early nineteenth century, who brought to the understanding of social life a new perspective, in which collective phenomena were accorded priority in explanation. As de Bonald wrote, it is 'society that constitutes man, that is, it forms him by social education . . .'[2] or, in Comte's words, a society was 'no more decomposable into individuals than a geometric surface is into lines, or a line into points'.[3] For others, however, such as Mill and the Utilitarians, 'the Laws of the phenomena of society are, and can be, nothing but the actions and passions of human beings'. namely 'the laws of individual human nature'.[4] This debate has recurred in many different guises — in the dispute between the 'historical' school in economics and the 'abstract' theory of classical economics, in endless debates among philosophers of history and between

* *The British Journal of Sociology*, xix (1968). The author thanks Martin Hollis of the University of East Anglia for his comments on this paper.

sociologists and psychologists,[5] and, above all, in the celebrated controversy between Durkheim and Gabriel Tarde.[6] Among others, Simmel[7] and Cooley[8] tried to resolve the issue, as did Gurvitch[9] and Ginsberg,[10] but it constantly reappears, for example in reactions to the extravagantly macroscopic theorising of Parsons and his followers[11] and in the extraordinarily muddled debate provoked by the wide-ranging methodological polemics of Hayek and Popper.[12]

What I shall try to do here is, first, to distinguish what I take to be the central tenet of methodological individualism from a number of different theses from which it has not normally been distinguished; and second, to show why, even in the most vacuous sense, methodological individualism is implausible.

Let us begin with a set of truisms. Society consists of people. Groups consist of people. Institutions consist of people plus rules and roles. Rules are followed (or alternatively not followed) by people and roles are filled by people. Also there are traditions, customs, ideologies, kinship systems, languages: these are ways people act, think and talk. At the risk of pomposity, these truisms may be said to constitute a theory (let us call it 'Truistic Social Atomism') made up of banal propositions about the world that are analytically true, i.e. in virtue of the meaning of words.

Some thinkers have held it to be equally truistic (indeed, sometimes, to amount to the same thing) to say that facts about society and social phenomena are to be explained solely in terms of facts about individuals. This is the doctrine of methodological individualism. For example, Hayek writes:

> There is no other way toward an understanding of social phenomena but through our understanding of individual actions directed toward other people and guided by their expected behaviour.[13]

Similarly, according to Popper,

> ... all social phenomena, and especially the functioning of all social institutions, should always be understood as resulting from the decisions, actions, attitudes, etc. of human individuals, and ... we should never be satisfied by an explanation in terms of so-called 'collectives' ...[14]

77

Finally we may quote Watkins's account of 'the principle of methodological individualism':

> According to this principle, the ultimate constituents of the social world are individual people who act more or less appropriately in the light of their dispositions and understanding of their situation. Every complex social situation or event is the result of a particular configuration of individuals, their dispositions, situations, beliefs, and physical resources and environment.

It is worth noticing, incidentally, that the first sentence here is simply a (refined) statement of Truistic Social Atomism. Watkins continues:

> There may be unfinished or half-way explanations of large-scale social phenomena (say, inflation) in terms of other large-scale phenomena (say, full employment); but we shall not have arrived at rock-bottom explanations of such large-scale phenomena until we have deduced an account of them from statements about the dispositions, beliefs, resources and inter-relations of individuals. (The individuals may remain anonymous and only typical dispositions etc., may be attributed to them.) And just as mechanism is contrasted with the organicist idea of physical fields, so methodological individualism is contrasted with sociological holism or organicism. On this latter view, social systems constitute 'wholes' at least in the sense that some of their large-scale behaviour is governed by macro-laws which are essentially sociological in the sense that they are *sui generis* and not to be explained as mere regularities or tendencies resulting from the behaviour of interacting individuals. On the contrary, the behaviour of individuals should (according to sociological holism) be explained at least partly in terms of such laws (perhaps in conjunction with an account, first of individuals' roles within institutions, and secondly of the functions of institutions with the whole social system). If methodological individualism means that human beings are supposed to be the only moving agents in history, and if sociological holism means that some superhuman agents or

78

factors are supposed to be at work in history, then these two alternatives are exhaustive.[15]

Methodological individualism, therefore, is a prescription for explanation, asserting that no purported explanations of social (or individual) phenomena are to count as explanations, or (in Watkins's version) as rock-bottom explanations, unless they are couched wholly in terms of facts about individuals.

It is now necessary to distinguish this theory from a number of others, from which it is usually not distinguished. It has been taken to be the same as any or all of the following:

1. Truistic Social Atomism. We have seen that Watkins, for example, seems to equate this with methodological individualism proper.

2. A theory of meaning to the effect that every statement about social phenomena is either a statement about individual human beings or else it is unintelligible and therefore not a statement at all. This theory entails that all predicates which range over social phenomena are definable in terms of predicates which range only individual phenomena and that all statements about social phenomena are translatable without loss of meaning into statements that are wholly about individuals. As Jarvie has put it, ' "Army" is merely a plural of soldier and *all* statements about the Army can be reduced to statements about the particular soldiers comprising the Army.'[16]

It is worth noticing that this theory is only plausible on a crude verificationist theory of meaning (to the effect that the meaning of p is what confirms the truth of p). Otherwise, although statements about armies are true only in virtue of the fact that other statements about individuals are true, the former are not equivalent in meaning to the latter, nor *a fortiori* are they 'about' the subject of the latter.

3. A theory of ontology to the effect that in the social world only individuals are real. This usually carries the correlative doctrine that social phenomena are constructions of the mind and 'do not exist in reality'. Thus Hayek writes, 'The social sciences . . . do not deal with "given" wholes but their task is to constitute these wholes by constructing

79

models from the familiar elements — models which reproduce the structure of relationships between some of the many phenomena which we always simultaneously observe in real life. This is no less true of the popular concepts of social wholes which are represented by the terms current in ordinary language; they too refer to mental models . . .'[17] Similarly, Popper holds that 'social entities such as institutions or associations' are 'abstract models constructed to interpret certain selected abstract relations between individuals'.[18]

If this theory means that in the social world only individuals are observable, it is evidently false. Some social phenomena simply can be observed (as both trees and forests can): and indeed, many features of social phenomena are observable (e.g. the procedure of a court) while many features of individuals are not (e.g. intentions). Both individual and social phenomena have observable and non-observable features. If it means that individual phenomena are easy to understand, while social phenomena are not (which is Hayek's view), this is highly implausible: compare the procedure of the court with the motives of the criminal. If the theory means that individuals exist independently of e.g. groups and institutions, this is also false, since, just as facts about social phenomena are contingent upon facts about individuals, the reverse is also true. Thus, as we have seen, we can only speak of soldiers because we can speak of armies: only if certain statements are true of armies are others true of soldiers. If the theory means that all social phenomena are fictional and all individual phenomena are factual, that would entail that all assertions about social phenomena are false or else neither true nor false, which is absurd. Finally, the theory may mean that only facts about individuals are explanatory, which alone would make this theory equivalent to methodological individualism.

4. A negative theory to the effect that sociological laws are impossible, or that lawlike statements about social phenomena are always false. Hayek and Popper sometimes seem to believe this, but Watkins clearly repudiates it, asserting merely that such statements form part of 'half-way' as opposed to 'rock-bottom' explanations.

This theory, like all dogmas of the form 'x is impossible' is open to refutation by a single counter-instance. Since such counter-instances are readily available[19] there is nothing left to say on this score.

5. A doctrine that may be called 'social individualism' which (ambiguously) asserts that society has as its end the good of individuals. When unpacked, this may be taken to mean any or all of the following: *(a)* social institutions are to be understood as founded and maintained by individuals to fulfil their ends (as in e.g. Social Contract theory); *(b)* social institutions in fact satisfy individual ends; *(c)* social institutions ought to satisfy individual ends. *(a)* is not widely held today, though it is not extinct; *(b)* is certainly held by Hayek with respect to the market, as though it followed from methodological individualism; and *(c)* which, interpreting 'social institutions' and 'individual ends' as a non-interventionist state and express preferences, becomes political liberalism, is clearly held by Popper to be uniquely consonant with methodological individualism.

However, neither *(b)* nor *(c)* is logically or conceptually related to methodological individualism, while *(a)* is a version of it.

II

What I hope so far to have shown is what the central tenet of methodological individualism is and what it is not. It remains to assess its plausibility.

It asserts (to repeat) that all attempts to explain social and individual phenomena are to be rejected (or, for Watkins, rejected as rock-bottom explanations) unless they refer exclusively to facts about individuals. There are thus two matters to investigate: (1) what is meant by 'facts about individuals'; and (2) what is meant by 'explanation'?

1. What is a fact about an individual? Or, more clearly, what predicates may be applied to individuals? Consider the following examples:

  (i) genetic make-up; brain-states,
  (ii) aggression; gratification; stimulus-response,

(iii) co-operation; power; esteem,
(iv) cashing cheques; saluting; voting.

What this exceedingly rudimentary list shows is that at least this: that there is a continuum of what I shall henceforth call individual predicates from what one might call the most non-social to the most social. Propositions incorporating only predicates of type (i) are about human beings *qua* material objects and make no reference to and presuppose nothing about consciousness or any feature of any social group or institution. Propositions incorporating only individual predicates of type (ii) presuppose consciousness but still make no reference to and presuppose nothing about any feature of any social group or institution. Propositions incorporating only predicates of type (iii) do have a minimal social reference: they presuppose a social context in which certain actions, social relations and/or mental states are picked out and given a particular significance (which makes social relations of certain sorts count as 'co-operative', which makes certain social positions count as positions of 'power' and a certain set of attitudes count as 'esteem'). They still do not presuppose or entail any particular propositions about any particular form of group or institution. Finally, propositions incorporating only individual predicates of type (iv) are maximally social, in that they presuppose and sometimes directly entail propositions about particular types of group and institution. ('Voting Labour' is at an even further point on the continuum.)

Methodological individualism has frequently been taken to confine its favoured explanations to any or all of these sorts of individual predicates. We may distinguish the following four possibilities:

(i) Attempts to explain in terms of type (i) predicates. A good example is H. J. Eysenck's *Psychology of Politics*. [20] According to Eysenck, 'Political actions are actions of human beings; the study of the direct cause of these actions is the field of the study of psychology. All other social sciences deal with variables which affect political action indirectly.'[21] (Compare this with Durkheim's famous statement that 'every time that a social phenomenon is directly explained by a

82

psychological phenomenon, we may be sure that the explanation is false'.)[22] Eysenck sets out to classify attitudes along two dimensions — the Radical—Conservative and the Tough-minded—Tender-minded — on the basis of evidence elicited by carefully constructed questionnaires. Then, having classified the attitudes, his aim is to *explain* them by reference to antecedent conditions and his interest here is centred upon the modifications of the central nervous system.

(ii) Attempts to explain in terms of type (ii) predicates. Examples are Hobbes's appeal to appetites and aversions, Pareto's residues and those Freudian theories in which sexual activity is seen as a type of undifferentiated activity that is (subsequently) channelled in particular social directions.

(iii) Attempts to explain in terms of type (iii) predicates. Examples are those sociologists and social psychologists (from Tarde to Homans[23]) who favour explanations in terms of general and 'elementary' forms of social behaviour, which do invoke some minimal social reference but are unspecific as to any particular form of group or institution.

(iv) Attempts to explain in terms of type (iv) predicates. Examples of these are extremely widespread, comprising all those who appeal to facts about concrete and specifically located individuals in order to explain. Here the relevant features of the social context are, so to speak, built into the individual. Open almost any empirical (though not theoretical) work of sociology, or history, and explanations of this sort leap to the eye.

Merely to state these four alternative possibilities is to suggest that their differences are more important than their similarities. What do they show about the plausibility of methodological individualism? To answer this it is necessary to turn to the meaning of 'explanation'.

2. To explain something is (at least) to overcome an obstacle — to make what was unintelligible intelligible. There is more than one way of doing this.

It is important to see, and it is often forgotten, that to *identify* a piece of behaviour, a set of beliefs, etc., is sometimes to explain it. This may involve seeing it in a new way, picking out hidden structural features. Consider an anthropologist's interpretation of ritual or a sociological study of

83

(say) bureaucracy. Often explanation resides precisely in a successful and sufficiently wide-ranging identification of behaviour or types of behaviour (often in terms of a set of beliefs). Again, to take an example from Mandelbaum,[24] a Martian visiting earth sees one man mark a piece of paper that another has handed to him through some iron bars: on his being told that the bank-teller is certifying the withdrawal slip he has had the action explained, through its being identified. If the methodological individualist is saying that no explanations are possible (or rock-bottom) except those framed exclusively in terms of individual predicates of types (i), (ii) and (iii), i.e. those not presupposing or entailing propositions about particular institutions and organisations, then he is arbitrarily ruling out (or denying finality to) most ordinarily acceptable explanations, as used in everyday life, but also by most sociologists and anthropologists for most of the time. If he is prepared to include individual predicates of type (iv), he seems to be proposing nothing more than a futile linguistic purism. Why should we be compelled to talk about the tribesman but not the tribe, the bank-teller but not the bank? And let no one underestimate the difficulty or the importance of explanation by identification. Indeed, a whole methodological tradition (from Dilthey through Weber to Winch) holds this to be the characteristic mode of explanation in social science.

Another way of explaining is to deduce the specific and particular from the general and universal. If I have a body of coherent, economical, well-confirmed and unfalsified general laws from which, given the specifications of boundary and initial conditions, I predict (or retrodict) x and x occurs, then, in one very respectable sense, I have certainly explained x.[25] This is the form of explanation which methodological individualists characteristically seem to advocate, though they vary as to whether the individual predicates which are uniquely to constitute the general laws and specifications of particular circumstances are to be of types (i), (ii), (iii) or (iv).

If they are to be of type (i), either of two equally unacceptable consequences follow. Eysenck writes, 'It is fully realised that most of the problems discussed must ultimately be seen in their historical, economic, sociological, and

84

perhaps even anthropological context, but little is to be gained at the present time by complicating the picture too much.'[26] But the picture is already so complicated at the very beginning (and the attitudes Eysenck is studying are only identifiable in social terms); the problem is how to simplify it. This could logically be achieved either by developing a theory which will explain the 'historical, economic, sociological . . . anthropological context' exclusively in terms of (e.g.) the central nervous system or by demonstrating that this 'context' is simply a backdrop against which quasi-mechanical psychological forces are the sole causal influences at work. Since, apart from quaint efforts that are of interest only to the intellectual historian, no one has given the slightest clue as to how either alternative might plausibly be achieved, there seems to be little point in taking it seriously, except as a problem in philosophy. Neurophysiology may be the Queen of the Social Sciences, but her claim remains entirely speculative.

If the individual predicates are to be of type (ii), there is again no positive reason to find the methodological individualist's claim plausible. Parallel arguments to those for type (i) predicates apply: no one has yet provided any plausible reason for supposing that e.g. (logically) pre-social drives uniquely determine the social context or that this context is causally irrelevant to their operation. As Freud himself saw, and many neo-Freudians have insisted, the process of social channelling is a crucial part of the explanation of behaviour, involving reference to features of both small groups and the wider social structure.

If the individual predicates are to be of type (iii), there is still no positive reason to find the methodological individualist's claim plausbile. There may indeed be valid and useful explanations of this type, but the claim we are considering asserts that all proper, or rock-bottom, explanations must be. Why rule out as possible candidates for inclusion in an *explicans* (statement of general laws + statement of boundary and initial conditions) statements that are about, or that presuppose or entail other statements that are about, social phenomena? One reason for doing so might be a belief that, in Hume's words, 'mankind are . . . much the same in all times in all places'.[27] As Homans puts it, the characteristics

85

of 'elementary social behaviour, far more than those of institutionalised behaviour, are shared by all mankind':

> Institutions, whether they are things like the physician's role or things like the bureaucracy, have a long history behind them of development within a particular society; and institutions, societies differ greatly. But within institutions, in the face-to-face relations between individuals . . . characteristics of behaviour appear in which mankind gives away its lost unity.[28]

This may be so, but then there are still the differences between institutions and societies to explain.

Finally, if the claim is that the individual predicates must be of type (iv), then it appears harmless, but also pointless. Explanations, both in the sense we are considering now and in the sense of identifications, may be wholly couched in such predicates but what uniquely special status do they possess? For, as we have already seen, propositions incorporating them presuppose and/or entail other propositions about social phenomena. Thus the latter have not really been eliminated; they have merely been swept under the carpet.

It is worth adding that since Popper and Watkins allow 'situations' and 'interrelations between individuals' to enter into explanations, it is difficult to see why they insist on calling their doctrine 'methodological individualism'. In fact the burden of their concerns and their arguments is to oppose certain sorts of explanations in terms of social phenomena. They are against 'holism' and 'historicism', but opposition to these doctrines does not entail acceptance of methodological individualism. For, in the first place, 'situations' and 'interrelations between individuals' can be described in terms which do not refer to individuals without holist or historicist implications. And secondly, it may be impossible to describe them in terms which do refer to individuals,[29] and yet they may be indispensable to an explanation, either as part of an identifying explanation in the statement of a general law, or of initial and boundary conditions.

NOTES

1. 'The English Works of Thomas Hobbes' ed. Sir William Molesworth (London, 1839) i 67; ii xiv; ii 109.

2. L. de Bonald, 'Theorie du Pouvoir' (Paris, 1854) i 103.

3. A. Comte, 'Système de Politique Positive' (Paris, 1851) ii 181.

4. J. S. Mill, 'A System of Logic', 9th ed. (London, 1875) ii 469. 'Men are not', Mill continues, 'when brought together, converted into another kind of substance, with different properties'.

5. See D. Essertier, 'Psychologie et Sociologie' (Paris, 1927).

6. Cf. E. Durkheim, 'Les Règles de la Méthode Sociologique' (Paris, 1895; 2nd ed. 1901), and G. Tarde, 'Les Lois Sociales' (Paris, 1898).

7. See 'The Sociology of Georg Simmel', trans. and ed. with introd. by K. H. Wolff (Glencoe, Ill., 1950) esp. chs i, ii and iv. (e.g. 'Let us grant for the moment that only individuals "really" exist. Even then, only a false conception of science could infer from this "fact" that any knowledge which somehow aims at synthesizing these individuals deals with merely speculative abstractions and unrealities': pp. 4-5).

8. See C. H. Cooley, 'Human Nature and the Social Order' (New York, 1902). For Cooley, society and the individual are merely 'the collective and distributive aspects of the same thing' (pp. 1-2).

9. See G. Gurvitch, 'Les Faux Problèmes de la Sociologie au XIXe Siècle', in 'La Vocation Actuelle de la Sociologie' (Paris, 1950) esp. pp 25-37.

10. See M. Ginsberg, 'The Individual and Society', in 'On the Diversity of Morals' (London, 1956).

11. See G. C. Homans, 'Bringing Men Back In', 'American Sociological Review' (1964) and D. H. Wrong, 'The Oversocialised Conception of Man in Modern Sociology', 'American Sociological Review' (1961).

12. See the following discussions: F. A. Hayek, 'The Counter-Revolution of Science' (Glencoe, Ill., 1952) chs 4, 6 and 8; K. R. Popper, 'The Open Society and its Enemies' (London, 1945) ch. 14 and 'The Poverty of Historicism' (London, 1957) chs. 7, 23, 24 and 31; J. W. N. Watkins, 'Ideal Types and Historical Explanation', 'British Journal for the Philosophy of Science' (1952) (reprinted in H. Feigl and M. Brodbeck, 'Readings in the Philosophy of Science' (New York, 1953)), 'Methodological Individualism' (note), ibid., 'Historical Explanation in the Social Sciences', ibid. (1957); M. Mandelbaum, 'Societal Laws', ibid. (1957). L. J. Goldstein, 'The Two Theses of Methodological Individualism' (note), ibid. (1958); Watkins, 'The Two Theses of Methodological Individualism' (note) ibid. (1959); Goldstein, 'Mr Watkins on the Two Theses' (note) ibid. (1959), Watkins 'Third Reply to Mr Goldstein' (note), ibid. (1959); R. J. Scott, 'Methodological and Epistemological Individualism' (note), ibid. (1961); Mandelbaum, 'Societal Facts', 'British Journal of Sociology (1955); E. Gellner, 'Explanations in History', 'Proceedings of the Aristotelian Society' (1956) (these last two articles together with Watkins's 1957 article above are reprinted in P. Gardiner (ed.), 'Theories of History'

(Glencoe, Ill and London, 1959) together with a reply to Watkins by Gellner. Gellner's paper is here retitled 'Holism and Individualism in History and Sociology'); M. Brodbeck, 'Philosophy of Social Science', 'Philosophy of Science' (1954); Watkins, 'Methodological Individualism: A Reply' (note), ibid. (1955); Brodbeck, 'Methodological Individualisms: Definition and Reduction', ibid. (1958); Goldstein, 'The Inadequacy of the Principle of Methodological Individualism', 'Journal of Philosophy' (1956); Watkins 'The Alleged Inadequacy of Methodological Individualism' (note), ibid. (1958); C. Taylor, 'The Poverty of the Poverty of Historicism', 'Universities and Left Review' (Summer 1958) followed by replies from I. Jarvie and Watkins, ibid. (Spring 1959); J. Agassi, 'Methodological Individualism', 'British Journal of Sociology (1960); E. Nagel, 'The Structure of Science' (London, 1961) pp. 535-46; A. C. Danto, 'Analytical Philosophy of History' (Cambridge, 1965) ch. xii; and W. H. Dray, 'Holism and Individualism in History and Social Science' in P. Edwards (ed.), 'The Encyclopedia of Philosophy' (New York, 1967).

13. 'Individualism and Economic Order' (London, 1949) p. 6.

14. 'The Open Society' 4th ed. ii 98.

15. 'Historical Explanation in the Social Sciences' in Gardiner (ed.) 'Theories of History', p. 505. Cf. '. . . large-scale *social* phenomena must be accounted for by the situations, dispositions and beliefs of *individuals*. This I call methodological individualism': Watkins, 'Methodological Individualism: A Reply', 'Philosophy of Science' (1955) 58 (see n. 12 above).

16. 'Universities and Left Review' (spring 1959) 57.

17. 'The Counter-Revolution of Science', p. 56.

18. 'The Poverty of Historicism', p. 140.

19. Popper himself provides some: see 'The Poverty of Historicism', pp. 62-3.

20. London, 1960.

21. 'Psychology of Politics', p. 10.

22. 'Les Règles de la Méthode Sociologique', p. 103.

23. See 'Social Behaviour' (London, 1961).

24. 'British Journal of Sociology' (1955).

25. E.g. Hempel calls this 'deductive-nomological explanation'. For a recent defence of this type of explanation in social science, see R. Rudner, 'Philosophy of Social Science' (Englewood Cliffs, N.J., 1965). I have not discussed 'probabilistic explanation', in which the general laws are not universal and the *explicans* only makes the *explicandum* highly probable, in the text; such explanations pose no special problems for any argument.

26. 'Psychology of Politics', p. 5.

27. D. Hume, 'Essays Moral and Political', ed. T. H. Green and T. H. Grose (London, 1875) ii 68.

28. 'Social Behaviour', p. 6.

29. E.g. in the cases of rules and terminologies of kinship or of language generally.

6 The Problem of Rationality in the Social World*

Alfred Schutz

The problem suggested by the terms 'rationality' or 'rational action' as used in current literature is most certainly central to the methodology and epistemology of the scientific study of the social world. The terms themselves, however, are not only used with many different meanings — and this sometimes in the writings of the same author as, for instance, Max Weber — but they represent only very inadequately the underlying conceptual scheme. In order to bring out the concealed equivocations and connotations, and to isolate the question of rationality from all the other problems surrounding it, we must go further into the structure of the social world and make more extensive inquiries into the different attitudes toward the social world adopted, on the one hand, by the actor within his world, and, on the other hand, by the scientific observer of it.

What is commonly understood by the term 'rational action' is best shown by the definition of 'rationality' or 'reasonableness' given by Professor Talcott Parsons in his remarkable study on *The Structure of Social Action* (McGraw-Hill, New York, 1937) p. 58.

'Action is rational in so far as it pursues ends possible within the conditions of the situation, and by the means which, among those available to the actor, are intrinsically best adapted to the end for reasons understandable and verifiable by positive empirical science.' Indicating in his usual careful manner the methodological point of view from which he contemplates his problem, Professor Parsons comments upon this definition as follows: 'Since science is the rational achievement par excellence, the mode of approach here outlined is in terms of the analogy between the scientific investigator and the actor in ordinary practical

* 'Economica', x (1943) 130-49. 'Collected Papers', ii 64-88, ed. Arvid Brodersen (Martinus Nijhoff, The Hague, 1964).

activities. The starting point is that of conceiving the actor as coming to know the facts of the situation in which he acts and thus the conditions necessary and means available for the realisation of his ends. As applied to the means—end relationship this is essentially a matter of the accurate prediction of the probable effects of various possible ways of altering the situation (employment of alternative means) and the resultant choice among them. Apart from questions relating to the choice of ends and from those relating to 'effort' . . . there is, where the standard is applicable at all, little difficulty in conceiving the actor as thus analogous to the scientist whose knowledge is the principal determinant of his action so far as his actual course conforms with the expectations of an observer who has, as Pareto says, "a more extended knowledge of the circumstances".'

This definition gives an excellent résumé of the widely used concept of rational action in so far as it refers to the level of social theory. It seems important, however, to make more precise the peculiarity of this theoretical level by contrasting it with the other levels of our experience of the social world. We must, therefore, start by examining what we really mean when we speak of different levels in observing the social world. Following this a short description of the social world as it appears to the actor within this world in his everyday life will give us an opportunity of examining whether or not the category of rationality becomes determinative for his actions. Only after these preliminaries shall we examine the social world as it is given to the scientific observer; and together with it we shall have to examine the question whether the categories of interpretation used by the scientist coincide with those used by the observed actor. Anticipating our results we may say at once that with the shift from one level to another all the conceptual schemes and all the terms of interpretation must be modified.

II

The fact that the same object has a different appearance to various observers has been illustrated by some philosophers by the example of a city which, though always the same, appears different to different persons according to their individual standpoints. I do not wish to overwork this metaphor, but it helps to make clear the difference between our view of the social world in which we naïvely live and the social world which is the object of scientific observation. The man brought up in a town will find his way in its streets by following the habits he has acquired in his daily occupations. He may not have a consistent conception of the organisation of the city, and, if he uses the underground railway to go to his office, a large part of the city may remain unknown to him. Nevertheless, he will have a proper sense of the distances between different places and of the directions in which the different points are situated relatively to whatever he regards as the centre. This centre will usually be his home, and it may be sufficient for him to know that he will find nearby an underground line or a bus leading to certain other points to bring them all within his reach. He can, therefore, say that he knows his town, and, though this knowledge is of a very incoherent kind, it is sufficient for all his practical needs.

When a stranger comes to the town, he has to learn to orientate himself in it and to know it. Nothing is self-explanatory for him and he has to ask an expert, in this case a native, to learn how to get from one point to another. He may, of course, refer to a map of the town, but even successfully to use the map he must know the meaning of the signs on the map, the exact point within the town where he stands and its correlative on the map, and at least one more point in order correctly to relate the signs on the map to the real objects in the city.

Entirely different means of orientation must be used by the cartographer who has to draw a map of the city. There are several ways open to him. He can start with a photograph taken from an aeroplane; he can place a theodolite at a known point, measure a certain distance and calculate trigonometrical functions, etc. The science of cartography has developed a standard for such operations, elements the cartographer must know before he begins to draw his map, and rules he must observe if he is to draw his map correctly.

The town is the same for all the three persons we have mentioned — the native, the foreigner and the cartographer — but for the native it has a special meaning: 'my home town'; for the foreigner it is a place within which he has to live and work for some time: for the cartographer it is an object of his science, he is interested in it only for the purposes of drawing a map. We may say that the same object is considered from different levels.

We should certainly be surprised if we found a cartographer in mapping a town restricting himself to collecting information from natives. Nevertheless, social scientists frequently choose this strange method. They forget that their scientific work is done on a level of interpretation and understanding different from the naïve attitudes of orientation and interpretation peculiar to people in daily life. When these social scientists speak of different levels, they frequently consider the difference between the two levels as entirely and simply one of the degree of concreteness or generality. These two terms, however, are no more than chapter headings for much more complicated problems than those which they directly suggest.

In our daily life, as in our scientific world, we, as human beings, all have the tendency to presume, more or less naïvely, that what we have once verified as valid will remain valid throughout the future, and that what appeared to us beyond question yesterday will still be beyond all question tomorrow. This naïve presumption may be made without danger if we deal with propositions of a purely logical character, or with empirical statements of a very high generality, though it can be shown that these kinds of propositions, too, have only a limited realm of applicability. On the other hand, at a so-called concrete level, we are forced to admit very many suppositions and implications as beyond question. We can even consider the level of our actual research as defined by the total of unquestioned presuppositions which we make by placing ourselves at the specific standpoint from which we envisage the interrelation of problems and aspects under scrutiny. Accordingly, passing from one level to another would involve that certain presuppositions of our research formerly regarded as beyond all question would now be called in question; and what was formerly a datum of our problem would now become problematic itself. But the simple fact that new problems and aspects of facts emerge with the shift in the point of view, while others that were formerly in the centre of our question disappear, is sufficient to initiate a thorough modification of the meaning of all the terms correctly used at the former level. Careful control of such modifications of the meaning is, therefore, indispensable if we are to avoid the risk of naïvely taking over from one level to another terms and propositions whose validity is essentially limited to a certain level, that is, to its implied suppositions.

Philosophical and in particular phenomenological theory has made very important contributions toward the better understanding of this phenomenon. However, we need not concern ourselves here with this very complicated problem from the phenomenological viewpoint. It will be sufficient to refer to an outstanding thinker of the English-speaking world; to William James and his theory of conception. It was he who taught us that each of our concepts has its fringes surrounding a nucleus of its unmodified meaning. 'In all our voluntary thinking,' he says, 'there is some topic or subject about which all the members of the thought revolve. Relation to our topic or interest is constantly felt in the fringe of our concepts. Each word in a sentence is felt, not only as a word, but as having a meaning. The meaning of a word taken thus dynamically in a sentence may be quite different from its meaning if taken statically or without context.'

It is not for us to discuss here James's theory of the nature of such fringes and their genesis in the stream of thought. For our purpose it will be sufficient to say that already the connection in which a concept or a term is used, and its relation to the topic of interest (and this topic of interest is in our case the *problem*), create specific modifications of the fringes surrounding the nucleus, or even of the nucleus itself. It was also William James who explained that we do not apperceive isolated phenomena, but rather a field of several interrelated and interwoven things as it emerges in the stream of our thought. This theory explains sufficiently for our purposes the phenomenon of the meaning of a term being modified as we pass to another level. I think that these superficial references will be sufficient to indicate the nature of the problem we are dealing with.

The term 'rationality', or at least the concept it envisages,

93

has, within the framework of social science, the specific role of a 'key concept'. It is peculiar to key concepts that, once introduced into an apparently uniform system, they constitute the differentiations between the points of view which we call levels. The meaning of such key concepts, therefore, does not depend on the level of the actual research, but, on the contrary, the level on which the research may be done depends upon the meaning attributed to the key concept, the introduction of which has for the first time divided what formerly appeared as a homogeneous field of research into several different levels. Anticipating what we shall have to prove later, we shall say that the level made accessible by the introduction of the term 'rational action' as a chief principle of the method of social sciences is nothing else than the level of theoretical observation and interpretation of the social world.

III

As scientific observers of the social world, we are not practically but only cognitively interested in it. That means we are not acting in it with full responsibility for the consequences, but rather contemplating it with the same detached equanimity as physicists contemplate their experiments. But let us remember that notwithstanding our scientific activity we all remain human beings in our daily life — men among fellow-men with whom we are interrelated in very many ways. To be precise, even our scientific activity itself is based on the co-operation between us, the scientists, and our teachers and the teachers of our teachers, a co-operation by mutual influence and mutual criticism; but in so far as scientific activity is socially founded, it is one among other emanations of our human nature and certainly pertains to our daily life, governed by the categories of vocation and avocation, of work and leisure, of planning and accomplishing. Scientific activity as a social phenomenon is one thing, the specific attitude the scientist has to adopt toward his problem is another. Considered purely as a human activity, scientific work is distinguished from other human activities merely by the fact that it constitutes the archetype for rational interpretation and rational action.

In our daily life it is only very rarely that we act in a rational way if we understand this term in the meaning envisaged in Professor Parsons's previously quoted statement. We do not even interpret the social world surrounding us in a rational way, except under special circumstances which compel us to leave our basic attitude of just living our lives. Each of us, so it seems, has naïvely organised his social world and his daily life in such a way that he finds himself the centre of the social cosmos surrounding him. Or, better, he was already born into an organised social cosmos. For him it is a cosmos and it is organised in so far as it contains all the comfortable equipment to render his daily living and that of his fellow-men a routine matter. There are, on the one hand, institutions of various kinds, tools, machines, etc.; on the other hand, habits, traditions, rules and experiences, both actual and vicarious. Furthermore, there is a scale of systematised relations which everyone has with his fellows, starting from the relations with members of his immediate family, relations with kinsmen, with personal friends, with people he knows personally, with people he met once in his life, through relations with those anonymous men who work somewhere and in a way he cannot imagine, but with the result that the letter he puts into the pillar box reaches the addressee in time, and that his lamp is lit by the turn of a switch.

Thus the social world with the 'alter ego's in it is arranged around the self as a centre in various degrees of intimacy and anonymity. Here am I and next to me are 'alter ego's of whom, as Kipling says, I know 'their naked souls'. Then come those with whom I share time and space and whom I know more or less intimately. Next in order are the manifold relations I have with people in whose personality I am interested, though I have only an indirect knowledge of them such, for instance, as may be obtained from their works or writings or from reports from others. For example, my social relation with the author of the book I am reading is of this kind. On the other hand, I have social relations (in the technical meaning of this term), though superficial and inconsistent ones, with others in whose personalities I am not interested, but who merely happen to perform functions in

95

which I am interested. Perhaps the salesgirl in the store where I buy my shaving cream, or the man who polishes my shoes, are much more interesting personalities than many of my friends. I do not inquire. I am not interested in social contact with those people. I just want to get my shaving cream and to have my shoes polished by whatever means. In this sense it makes very little difference to me whether, when I want to make a telephone call, an operator or a dial intervenes. Incidentally — and here we enter the remotest sphere of social relations — the dial, too, has its social function because it derives, as do all products of human activity, from the man who invented, designed and produced it. But if I am not guided by a special motive, I do not ask for the history, genesis, and construction of all the tools and institutions created by other people's activity. Likewise I do not ask about the personality and destiny of fellow-men whose activity I consider as a purely *typical* function. In any case, and this is important for our problem, I can use the telephone with success without knowing how it functions; I am interested only in the fact that it does function. I do not care whether the result achieved, which alone interests me, is due to the intervention of a human being whose motives remain undisclosed to me or to a mechanism whose operation I do not understand. What counts is the typical character of the occurrence within a typified situation.

Thus, in this organisation of the social world by the human being living naïvely in it, we already find the germ of the system of types and typical relations which we shall recognise later in its fullest ramification as the essential feature of scientific method. This typification is progressive in the same proportion as the personality of the fellow-man disappears beyond the undisclosed anonymity of his function. If we want to do so, we may interpret this process of progressive typification also as one of rationalisation. At least it is envisaged by one of the several meanings Max Weber attributes to the term 'rationalisation' when he speaks of the 'disenchantment of the world' *(Entzauberung der Welt)*. This term means the transformation of an uncontrollable and unintelligible world into an organisation which we can understand and therefore master, and in the framework of which prediction becomes possible.

In my opinion, the fundamental problem of the different aspects under which our fellow-men and their behaviour and actions seem given to us has not yet received from sociologists the attention it merits. But if social science, with few exceptions, has failed to consider this kind of rationalisation of its conceptual framework, each of us human beings, in 'just living along', has already performed this task, and this without planning to do so and without any effort in the performance of his job. In doing so, we are guided neither by methodological considerations nor by any conceptual scheme of means—end relations, nor by any idea of values we have to realise. Our practical interest alone, as it arises in a certain situation of our life, and as it will be modified by the change in the situation which is just on the point of occurring, is the only relevant principle in the building up of the perspective structure in which our social world appears to us in daily life. For, just as all our visual apperceptions are in conformity with the principles of perspective and convey the impressions of depths and distance, so all our apperceptions of the social world necessarily have the basic character of perspective views. Of course the social world of a sixty-year-old Chinese Buddhist in the time of the Ming dynasty will be organised in quite a different way from the social world of a twenty-year-old American Christian of our own day, but the fact remains that both worlds would be organised, and this within the framework of the categories of familiarity and strangeness, of personality and type, of intimacy and anonymity. Furthermore, each of these worlds would be centred in the self of the person who lives and acts in it.

IV

But let us proceed in our analysis of the knowledge that a man living naïvely has about the world, the social world as well as the natural. In his daily life the healthy, adult and wide-awake human being (we are not speaking of others) has this knowledge, so to speak, automatically at hand. From heritage and education, from the manifold influences of tradition, habits and his own previous reflection, his store of experiences is built up. It embraces the most heterogeneous kinds of knowledge in a very incoherent and confused state. Clear and distinct experiences are intermingled with vague conjectures; suppositions and prejudices cross well-proven evidences; motives, means and ends, as well as causes and effects, are strung together without clear understanding of their real connections. There are everywhere gaps, inter-missions, discontinuities. Apparently there is a kind of organisation by habits, rules and principles which we regularly apply with success. But the origin of our habits is almost beyond our control; the rules we apply are rules of thumb and their validity has never been verified. The principles we start from are partly taken over uncritically from parents and teachers, partly distilled at random from specific situations in our lives or in the lives of others without having made any further inquiry into their consistency. Nowhere have we a guarantee of the reliability of all of these assumptions by which we are governed. On the other hand, these experiences and rules are sufficient to us for mastering life. As we normally have to act and not to reflect in order to satisfy the demands of the moment, which it is our task to master, we are not interested in the 'quest for certainty'. We are satisfied if we have a fair chance of realising our purposes, and this chance, so we like to think, we have if we set in motion the same mechanism of habits, rules and principles which formerly stood the test and which still stand the test. Our knowledge in daily life is not without hypotheses, inductions and predictions, but they all have the character of the approximate and the typical. The ideal of everyday knowledge is not certainty, nor even probability in a mathematical sense, but just likelihood. Anticipations of future states of affairs are conjectures about what is to be hoped or feared, or at best, about what can be reasonably expected. When afterwards the anticipated state of affairs takes some form in actuality, we do not say that our pre-diction has come true or proved false, or that our hypothesis has stood the test, but that our hopes or fears were or were not well founded. The consistency of this system of know-ledge is not that of natural *laws*, but that of *typical* sequences and relations.

This kind of knowledge and its organisation I should like to call 'cookery-book knowledge'. The cookery-book has recipes, lists of ingredients formulae for mixing them, and directions for finishing off. This is all we need to make an apple pie, and also all we need to deal with the routine matters of daily life. If we enjoy the apple pie so prepared, we do not ask whether the manner of preparing it as indicated by the recipe is the most appropriate from the hygienic or alimentary point of view, or whether it is the shortest, the most economical, or the most efficient. We just eat and enjoy it. Most of our daily activities from rising to going to bed are of this kind. They are performed by following recipes reduced to automatic habits or unquestioned platitudes. This kind of knowledge is concerned only with the regularity as such of events in the external world irrespective of its origin. Because of this regularity it can be reasonably expected that the sun will rise tomorrow morning. It is equally regular, and it can, therefore, with as good reason be anticipated too that the bus will bring me to my office if I choose the right one and pay my fare.

V

The foregoing remarks characterise in a very superficial manner the conceptual scheme of our everyday behaviour in so far as the term 'conceptual scheme' can be applied at all. Are we to classify a behaviour of the type just described as rational or irrational? In order to answer this question we must analyse the various equivocal implications which are hidden in the term 'rationality' as it is applied to the level of everyday experience.

1. 'Rational' is frequently used as synonymous with 'reasonable'. Now we certainly act in our daily life in a reasonable way if we use the recipes we find in the store of our experience as already tested in an analogous situation. But acting rationally often means avoiding mechanical applications of precedents, dropping the use of analogies, and searching for a new way to master the situation.

2. Sometimes rational action is put on a par with acting deliberately, but the term 'deliberately' itself implies many equivocal elements.

(a) Routine action of daily life is deliberated in so far as it always relates back to the original act of deliberation which once preceded the building up of the formula now taken by the actor as a standard for his actual behaviour.

(b) Conveniently defined, the term 'deliberation' may cover the insight into the applicability to a present situation of a recipe which has proved successful in the past.

(c) We can give the term 'deliberation' a meaning covering the pure anticipation of the end — and this anticipation is always the motive for the actor to set the action going.

(d) On the other hand, the term 'deliberation' as used, for instance, by Professor Dewey in his *Human Nature and Conduct*, means 'a dramatic rehearsal in imagination of various competing possible lines of action'. In this sense, which is of the greatest importance for the theory of rationality, we cannot classify as rational the type of everday actions which we have examined up to now as deliberated actions. On the contrary, it is characteristic of these routine actions that the problem of choice between different possibilities does not enter into the consciousness of the actor. We shall have to come back to the problem of choice immediately.

3. Rational action is frequently defined as 'planned' or 'projected' action without a precise indication of the meaning of the terms 'planned' or 'projected'. We cannot simply say that the non-rational routine acts of daily life are not consciously planned. On the contrary, they rest within the framework of our plans and projects. They are even instruments for realising them. All planning presupposes an end to be realised by stages, and each of these stages may be called, from one point of view or another, either means or intermediate ends. Now the function of all routine work is a a standardisation and mechanisation of the means—end relations as such by referring standardised means to standardised classes of ends. The effect of this standardisation is that the intermediate ends disappear from the consciously envisaged chain of means which have to be brought about for performing the planned end. But here arises the problem of subjective meaning which we have mentioned before. We cannot speak of the unit-act as if this unit were constituted or demarcated by the observer. We

must seriously ask: when does one act start and when is it accomplished? We shall see that only the actor is in a position to answer this question.

Let us take the following example: Assume the professional life of a business man to be organised and planned to the extent that he intends to continue with his business for the next ten years, after which he hopes to retire. To continue his work involves going to his office every morning. For this purpose he has to leave his home at a certain hour, buy a ticket, take the train, etc. He did so yesterday and he will do so tomorrow if nothing extraordinary intervenes. Let us assume that one day he is late and that he thinks: 'I shall miss my train – I shall be late at my office. Mr "X" will be there already, waiting for me. He will be in a bad humour, and perhaps he will not sign the contract on which so much of my future depends.' Let us further assume that an observer watches this man rushing for the train 'as usual' (as he thinks). Is his behaviour planned, and if so, what is the plan? Only the actor can give the answer because he alone knows the span of his plans and projects. Probably all routine work is a tool for bringing about ends which are beyond routine work and which determine it.

4. 'Rational' is frequently identified with 'predictable'. It is not necessary to return to this question. We have already analysed the specific form of prediction in everyday knowledge as simply an estimate of likelihood.

5. According to the interpretation of some authors, 'rational' refers to 'logical'. Professor Parsons's definition is one example and Pareto's theory of non-logical action to which he refers is another. In so far as the scientific concept of the rational act is in question, the system of logic may be fully applied. On the other hand, on the level of everyday experience, logic in its traditional form cannot render the services we need and expect. Traditional logic is a logic of concepts based on certain idealisations. In enforcing the postulate of clearness and distinctness of the concepts, for instance, traditional logic disregards all the fringes surrounding the nucleus within the stream of thought. On the other hand, thought in daily life has its chief interest precisely in the relation of the fringes which attach the nucleus to the actual situation of the thinker. This is clearly a very

101

important point. It explains why Husserl classifies the greater part of our propositions in daily thought as 'occasional propositions', that means, as valid and understandable only relative to the speaker's situation and to their place in his stream of thought. It explains, too, why our everyday thoughts are less interested in the antithesis 'true—false' than in the sliding transition 'likely—unlikely'. We do not make everyday propositions with the purpose of achieving a formal validity within a certain realm which could be recognised by someone else, as the logician does, but in order to gain knowledge valid only for ourselves and to further our practical aims. To this extent, but only to this extent, the principle of pragmatism is incontestably well founded. It is a description of the style of everyday thought, but not a theory of cognition.

6. A rational act presupposes, according to the interpretation of other authors, a choice between two or more means toward the same end, or even between two different ends, and a selection of the most appropriate. This interpretation will be analysed in the following section.

VI

As Professor John Dewey has pointed out, in our daily life we are largely preoccupied with the next step. Men stop and think only when the sequence of doing is interrupted, and the disjunction in the form of a problem forces them to stop and rehearse alternative ways — over, around or through — which their past experience in collision with this problem suggest. The image of a dramatic rehearsal of future action used by Professor Dewey is a very fortunate one. Indeed, we cannot find out which of the alternatives will lead to the desired end without imagining this act as already accomplished. So we have to place ourselves mentally in a future state of affairs which we consider as already realised, though to realise it would be the end of our contemplated action. Only by considering the act as accomplished can we judge whether the contemplated means of bringing it about are appropriate or not, or whether the end to be realised accommodates itself to the general plan of our life. I like to call this technique of deliberation 'thinking in the future perfect tense'. But there is a great difference between action actually performed and action only imagined as performed. The really accomplished act is irrevocable and the consequences must be borne whether it has been successful or not. Imagination is always revocable and can be revised again and again. Therefore, in simply rehearsing several projects, I can ascribe to each a different probability of success, but I can never be disappointed by its failure. Like all other anticipations, the rehearsed future action also has gaps which only the performance of the act will fill in. Therefore the actor will only retrospectively see whether his project has stood the test or proved a failure.

The technique of the choice is this: The mind of the actor runs through one alternative and then through the other till the decision falls from his mind — to use the words of Bergson — as a ripe fruit falls from the tree. But it is a prerequisite of all choice that the actor have clearly in mind that alternative ways of applying different means or even alternative ends do actually exist. It is erroneous to assume that consciousness of such alternatives and therefore choice is necessarily given before every human action, and that in consequence all acting involves deliberation and preference. This interpretation uncritically confuses selection in the sense of just singling out without comparison of alternatives, and choice in the sense of electing the preferred. Selection is, as has already been pointed out by James, a cardinal function of human consciousness. Interest is nothing else than selection, but it does not necessarily involve conscious choice between alternatives which presupposes reflection, volition and preference. When I walk through a garden discussing a problem with a friend and I turn left or right, I do not choose to do so. I have no alternative in mind. It is a question for psychology to determine the motives for such behaviour, but I cannot say that I prefer one direction to another.

Undoubtedly there are situations in which each of us sits down and thinks over his problems. In general he will do so at critical points in his life when his chief interest is to master a situation. But even then he will accept his emotions as guides in finding the most suitable solution as well as rational deliberation, and he is right in doing so, because these

103

This short analysis shows that we cannot speak of an *isolated* rational act, if we mean by this an act resulting from deliberated choice, but only of a *system* of rational acts.[1]

But where is this *system* of rational action to be found? We have already noted that the concept of rationality has its native place not at the level of the everyday conception of the social world, but at the theoretical level of the scientific observation of it, and it is here that it finds its field of methodological application. Therefore, we have to proceed to the problem of the social sciences and to the scientific methods of its interpretation.

VII

Our analysis of the social world in which we live has shown that each of us considers himself as the centre of this world, which he groups around himself according to his own interests. The observer's attitude towards the social world is quite different. This world is not the theatre of his activities, but the object of his contemplation on which he looks with detached equanimity. As a scientist (not as a human being dealing with science) the observer is essentially solitary. He has no companion and we can say that he has placed himself outside the social world with its manifold relations and its system of interests. Everyone, to become a social scientist, must make up his mind to put somebody else instead of himself as the centre of this world, namely, the observed person. But with the shift in the central point, the whole system has been transformed, and, if I may use this metaphor, all the equations proved as valid in the former system now have to be expressed in terms of the new one. If the social system in question had reached an ideal perfection, it would be possible to establish a universal transformation formula such as Einstein has succeeded in establishing for translating propositions in terms of the Newtonian System of Mechanics into those of the Theory of Relativity.

The first and fundamental consequence of this shift in the point of view is that the scientist replaces the human beings he observes as actors on the social stage by puppets created by himself and manipulated by himself. What I call 'puppets' corresponds to the technical term 'ideal types' which Weber has introduced into Social Science.

Our analysis of our common social world has shown us the origin of typification. We typify, in daily life, human activities which interest us only as appropriate means of bringing about intended effects, but not as emanations of the personality of our fellow-men. The procedure of the scientific observer is on the whole the same. He observes certain events as caused by human activity and he begins to establish a type of such proceedings. Afterwards he co-ordinates with these typical acts typical actors as their performers. He thus ends up by constructing personal ideal types which he imagines as having consciousness. This fictitious consciousness is constructed in such a way that the fictitious actor, if he were not a dummy but a human being of flesh-and-blood, would have the same stream of thought as a living man acting in the same manner, but with the important modification that the artificial consciousness is not subjected to the ontological conditions of human existence. The puppet is not born, he does not grow up, and he will not die. He has no hopes and no fears; he does not know anxiety as a chief motive of all his deeds. He is not free in the sense that his acting could transgress the limits his creator, the social scientist, has fixed. He cannot, therefore, have other conflicts of interest and motives than those the social scientist has implanted in him. The personal ideal type cannot err if to err is not its typical destiny. It cannot perform an act which is outside the typical motives, the typical means—ends relations, and outside the typical situation provided for by the scientist. In short, the ideal type is but a model of a conscious mind without the faculty of spontaneity and without a will of its own. In typical situations of our daily life we all, too, assume certain typical roles. By isolating one of our activities from its interrelations with all the other manifestations of our personality, we disguise ourselves as consumers or tax-payers, citizens, members of a church or of a club, clients, smokers, bystanders, etc. The traveller, for instance, has to behave in the specific way he believes the type 'railway agent' to expect from a typical passenger. For us in our daily lives these attitudes are but roles which we voluntarily assume as expedients and which we may drop whenever we want to do so. But assuming this role does not change our general attitude towards the social world or towards our own life. Our knowledge remains incoherent, our propositions occasional, our future uncertain, our general situation unstable. The next moment may bring the great cataclysm which will affect our choice, modify all our plans, perhaps destroy the value of all our experience. And we keep,— even in the role — the liberty of choice, as far as such liberty exists at all within the scope of our human and social conditions. This liberty embraces the possibility of taking off our disguise, of dropping the role, of recommencing our orientation in the social world. We continue to be subjects, centres of spontaneous activities, actors.

The puppet called 'personal ideal type' is, on the contrary, never a subject or a centre of spontaneous activity. He does not have the task of mastering the world, and, strictly speaking, he has no world at all. His destiny is regulated and determined beforehand by his creator, the social scientist, and in such a perfect pre-established harmony as Leibniz imagined the world created by God. By the grace of its constructor, he is endowed with just that kind of knowledge he needs to perform the job for the sake of which he was brought into the scientific world. The scientist distributes his own store of experience, and that means of scientific experience in clear and distinct terms, among the puppets with which he peoples the social world. But this social world, too, is organised in quite another way; it is not centred in the ideal type; it lacks the categories of intimacy and anonymity, of familiarity and strangeness: in short, it lacks the basic character of perspective appearance. What counts is the point of view from which the *scientist* envisages the social world. This point of view defines the general perspective framework in which the chosen sector of the social world presents itself to the scientific observer as well as to the fictitious consciousness of the puppet type. This central point of view of the scientist is called his 'scientific problem under examination'.

In a scientific system the problem has exactly the same significance for the scientific activity as the practical interests have for activities in everyday work. The scientific problem as formulated has a twofold function:

(a) It determines the limits within which possible propositions become relevant to the inquiry. It thus creates the realm of the scientific subject-matter within which all concepts must be compatible.

(b) The simple fact that a problem is raised creates a scheme of reference for the construction of all ideal types which may be utilised as relevant.

For the better understanding of the last remark we have to consider that the concept 'type' is not an independent one but always needs a supplement. We cannot speak simply of an 'ideal type' as such; we must indicate the reference scheme with which this ideal type may be utilised, that is, the problem for the sake of which the type has been constructed. To borrow a mathematical term we may say that the ideal type always needs a subscript referring to the problem which determines the formation of all the types to be used. In this sense, the problem under scrutiny is the locus of all possible types which may pertain to the system investigated.

I cannot go further here into the logical foundations of this thesis which I call the *principle of relevance*. But we can interpret it as an application of James's theory concerning the fringes of concepts. The ideal type, too, like all other concepts, has fringes referring to the main topic about which all the members of the thought revolve. It is easy to understand that a shift in the main topic — that is, in the problem — automatically involves a modification in the fringes of each concept revolving about it. And, as a shift in the problem means a modification in the scope of relevance too, we can explain, for the same reason, why new facts emerge with the shift in the point of view, whereas others that were formerly in the centre of our question disappear. But this statement is nothing else than the original definition we have given of the passing from one level to another. To be sure, it must be admitted that the term 'level' applies strictly only to whole systems of problems; nevertheless, the consequences are, in principle, the same. It seems important to me that the scientist keep in mind that each shift in the problem involves a thorough modification of all the concepts and of all the types with which he is dealing. A great many misunderstandings and controversies in the social sciences have their root in the unmodified application of concepts and types at a level other than that where they have their natural place.

But why form personal ideal types at all? Why not simply collect empirical facts? Or, if the technique of typological interpretation may be applied successfully, why not restrict oneself to forming types of impersonal events, or types of the behaviour of groups? Do we not have modern economics as an example of a social science which does not deal with personal ideal types, but with curves, with mathematical functions, with the movement of prices, or with such institutions as bank systems or currency? Statistics has performed the great work of collecting information about the behaviour of groups. Why go back to the scheme of social action and to the individual actor?

The answer is this: It is true that a very great part of social science can be performed and has been performed at a level which legitimately abstracts from all that happens in the individual actor. But this operating with generalisations and idealisations on a high level of abstraction is in any case nothing but a kind of intellectual shorthand. Whenever the problem under inquiry makes it necessary, the social scientist must have the possibility of shifting the level of his research to that of individual human activity, and where real scientific work is done this shift will always become possible.

The real reason for this is that we cannot deal with phenomena in the social world as we do with phenomena belonging to the natural sphere. In the latter, we collect facts and regularities which are not understandable to us, but which we can refer only to certain fundamental assumptions about the world. We shall never understand why the mercury in the thermometer rises if the sun shines on it. We can only interpret this phenomenon as compatible with the laws we have deduced from some basic assumption about the physical world. Social phenomena, on the contrary, we want to understand and we cannot understand them otherwise than within the scheme of human motives, human means and ends, human planning – in short – within the categories of human action.

The social scientist must therefore ask, or he must, at least, always be in a position to ask, what happens in the mind of an individual actor whose act has led to the phenomenon in question. We can formulate this *postulate of the subjective interpretation* more correctly as follows: The scientist has to ask what type of individual mind can be constructed and what typical thoughts must be attributed to it to explain the fact in question as the result of its activity within an understandable relation.

This postulate finds its complement in another which I propose to call, borrowing a term of Max Weber, the *postulate of adequacy*. It may be formulated as follows: 'Each term used in a scientific system referring to human action must be so constructed that a human act performed within the life world by an individual actor in the way indicated by the typical construction would be reasonable and understandable for the actor himself, as well as for his fellow-men.' This postulate is of extreme importance for the methodology of social science. What makes it possible for a social science to refer at all to events in the life world is the fact that the interpretation of any human act by the social scientist might be the same as that by the actor or by his partner.

The principle of relevance, the postulate of the subjective interpretation, and that of adequacy, are applicable at each level of social study. For instance, all the historical sciences are governed by them. The next step would be to circumscribe within the social sciences the category of those we call the theoretical ones. The outstanding feature of these theoretical sciences is the interpretation of the social world in terms of a system of determinate logical structure (Parsons, *Structure of Social Action*, p. 7). This system of means—ends relations is also an ideal typical one, but as Professor Parsons has pointed out, it is an analytical one and not a system dealing with concrete actions as he calls it. I once formulated the same idea in the statement that the personal ideal-types of action constructed by the so-called theoretical sciences are of a maximum anonymity, that means, what is typified is the behaviour of 'people as such' or of 'everyman'. Whatever formula we may use to describe the peculiarity of the theoretical realm, it is clear that a logically interrelated system presupposes that the means—end relations together with the system of constant motives and the system of life plans must be constructed in such a way that:

(*a*) it remains in full compatibility with the principles of formal logic;

(*b*) all its elements are conceived in full clearness and distinctness;

(*c*) It contains only scientifically verifiable assumptions which have to be in full compatibility with the whole of our scientific knowledge.

All these three requirements may be condensed into another *postulate* for the building up of the ideal types, that of *rationality*. It may be formulated as follows: The ideal type of social action must be constructed in such a way that the actor in the living world would perform the typified act if he had a clear and distinct scientific knowledge of all the elements relevant to his choice and the constant tendency to choose the most appropriate means for the realisation of the most appropriate end. Indeed, as we had anticipated in the beginning, only by the introduction of the key concept of rationality can all the elements be provided for the constitution of the level called 'pure theory'. The postulate of rationality implies, furthermore, that all other behaviour has to be interpreted as derivative from the basic scheme of rational acting. The reason for this is that only action within the framework of rational categories can be scientifically discussed. Science does not have at its disposal other methods than rational ones and it cannot, therefore, verify or falsify purely occasional propositions.

As we stated before, each type formed by the scientist has its subscript referring to the main problem. In a theoretical system, therefore, only pure rational types are admitted. But where can the scientist find the guarantee that he is establishing a real unified system? Where are the scientific tools to perform that difficult task? The answer is that in every branch of the social sciences which has arrived at the theoretical stage of its development there is a fundamental hypothesis which both defines the fields of research and gives the regulative principle for building up the system of ideal types. Such a fundamental hypothesis, for instance, is in classical economics the utilitarian principle, and in modern economics the marginal princple. The sense of this postulate is the following: 'Build your ideal types as if all actors had

112

oriented their life plan and, therefore, all their activities to the chief end of realising the greatest utility with the minimum of costs; human activity which is oriented in such a way (and only this kind of human activity) is the subject-matter of your science.'

But at the back of all these statements arises a very disturbing question. If the social world as object of our scientific research is but a typical construction, why bother with this intellectual game? Our scientific activity and, particularly, that which deals with the social world, is also performed within a certain means—ends relation, namely, in order to acquire knowledge for mastering the world, the real world, not the one created by the grace of the scientist. We want to find out what happens in the real world and not in the fantasies of a few sophisticated eccentrics.

There are a few arguments for quieting such an interlocutor. First of all, the construction of the scientific world is not an arbitrary act of the scientist which he can perform at his own discretion:

1. There are the historical boundaries of the realm of his science which each scientist has inherited from his ancestors as a stock of approved propositions.

2. The postulate of adequacy requires that the typical construction be compatible with the totality of both our daily life and our scientific experience.

But to one who is not satisfied with such guarantees and asks for greater reality, I want to say that I am afraid I do not exactly know what reality is, and my only comfort in this unpleasant situation is that I share my ignorance with the greatest philosophers of all time, Again, I want to quote William James and his profound theory of the different realities in which we live at the same time. It is a misunderstanding of the essential character of science to think that it deals with reality if we consider as the pattern of reality the world of daily life. The world of both the natural and the social scientist is neither more nor less real than the world of thought in general can be. It is not the world within which we act and within which we are born and die. But it is the real home of those important events and achievements which humanity at all times calls culture.

The social scientist, therefore, may continue his work in

113

full confidence. His clarified methods, governed by the postulates mentioned, give him the assurance that he will never lose contact with the world of daily life. And as long as he uses with success methods which have stood this test and still do so, he is quite right in continuing without worrying about methodological problems. Methodology is not the preceptor or the tutor of the scientist. It is always his pupil, and there is no great master in his scientific field who could not teach the methodologists how to proceed. But the really great teacher always has to learn from his pupils. Arnold Schoenberg, the famous composer, starts the preface to his masterly book on the theory of harmony with the sentence: 'This book I have learned from my pupils.' In this role, the methodologist has to ask intelligent questions about the technique of his teacher. And if those questions help others to think over what they really do, and perhaps to eliminate certain intrinsic difficulties hidden in the foundation of the scientific edifice where the scientists never set foot, methodology has performed its task.

NOTES

1. See the excellent study which Professor Parsons has devoted to this problem under the heading 'Systems of Action and their Unit', at the end of his 'Structure of Social Action'.

7 Concepts and Society*

Ernest Gellner

1. This paper is concerned with the application of Functionalism to the interpretation of concepts and beliefs.

Concepts and beliefs are themselves, in a sense, institutions amongst others; for they provide a kind of fairly permanent frame, as do other institutions, independent of any one individual, within which individual conduct takes place. In another sense, they are correlates of *all* the institutions of a society; and to understand the *working* of the concepts of a society is to understand its institutions.[1] Hence, a discussion of the application of Functionalism to interpretation (of concepts and beliefs), rather than Functionalism as such, is not really much of a restriction of the subject-matter.

Concepts and beliefs are, of course, of particular concern to social anthropology. Sociology can sometimes be a matter of ascertaining facts within an institutional framework which is taken for granted. The anthropologist can virtually never take anything for granted in this way. For anthropology is also the discipline most associated with Functionalism. The connection is not fortuitous.

2. Nevertheless the problem of the *interpretation* of concepts is almost as important within sociology – in the narrower sense in which it excludes Social Anthropology. For instance, the problem which is one of the mainsprings of sociological theory and which remains at the very centre of sociology – the question concerning the impact of theological doctrines on the emergence of economic rationality – hinges in large part on how one *interprets* the relevant theological concepts and arguments. Is one merely to take what the recorded theological text says and explicitly recommends? In that case, the connection seems very tenuous. Or is one to take what the text says *and* interpret its

* 'Transactions of the Fifth World Congress of Sociology', i (International Sociological Association).

meaning, for the people influenced by it, in the light of what they actually *did*? In that case, the explanation of behaviour in terms of doctrine risks becoming vacuous and circular. There must, one hopes, be some middle way, which allows interpretation, which allows some but not all of the context to be incorporated into the meaning of the concept, thus avoiding both an unrealistic literal-minded scholasticism, and yet also escaping circularity of explanation. The problem concerns the rules and limits of invocation of social *context* in interpreting the participants' concepts.

Consider as an example one of the most recent contributions to this debate, Professor Kurt Samuelsson's *Religion and Economic Action* (London, 1961; Swedish edition, *Ekonomi och Religion*, Stockholm, 1957). This work is an onslaught on the Weberian thesis. '. . . our scrutiny of Puritan doctrine and capitalist ideology . . . has rendered untenable the hypothesis of a connection between Puritanism and capitalism . . .' (p. 153). Samuelsson employs a battery of arguments to support his conclusion, and some of these are highly relevant to the present theme. For one, he refers (p. 153) to '. . . the impossibility, in the last resort, of correlating concepts as broad and vague as those in question'. Here he seems to mean primarily the sociologist's own concepts (Puritanism, capitalism), but indirectly the alleged breadth and vagueness of these reflects the vagueness of Puritan or capitalist notions themselves. But it would be an absurd requirement to restrict sociological interpretation to clear and distinct concepts: these are historically a rarity, and there is nothing to make one suppose that vague and broad notions, whose logical implications for conduct are ill-determined, do not in fact have a powerful and specific impact on actual behaviour. We are faced here with the unfortunate need to *interpret* just what the concepts in question meant to the participants – and the problems connected with such interpretation are the theme of the present paper.

Samuelsson is not content with a declaration of the impossibility 'in the last resort' of establishing such correlations at all, but also specifically tries to refute the correlation by adducing contrary evidence. This counter-evidence largely consists, reasonably enough, of examining

116

just what the Puritans actually said, and the kind of conduct they actually commended. Considering this, Samuelsson concludes (p. 41) that 'unquestionably, this ought to have impeded rather than promoted a capitalist trend'. He then considers counter-objections to this, such as Tawney's: these consist of arguing that the 'Christian casuistry of economic conduct', which *logically* should have impeded capitalism (i.e. if one considers what the statements in the text actually entail), in fact, in virtue of what they *meant* to the people concerned, 'braced the energies' and 'fortified the temper' of the capitalist spirit. In other words, he convicts Tawney of claiming to know better than the texts what Puritanism really meant to its devotees. Samuelsson appears to have a great contempt for such implicit claims to access to hidden meanings: it is (p. 41) 'a somersault in the best Weberian style'. With irony he comments (p. 42, italics mine) that on the view he opposes, the capitalist spirit '*was the true and genuine* Puritan spirit' (as opposed to the spirit actually found in the texts), and that thus 'Puritanism *in some other and more capitalist sense* . . . becomes the capitalistic spirit's principal source of power . . .'.

I am not concerned, nor competent, to argue whether Samuelsson's employment, in this particular case, of his tacit principle that one must not reinterpret the assertions one actually finds, is valid. What is relevant here is that if such a principle is made explicit and generalised, it would make nonsense of most sociological studies of the relationship of belief and conduct. We shall find anthropologists driven to employ the very opposite principle, the insistence rather than refusal of contextual reinterpretation.

3. This is where Functionalism is relevant. The essence of Functionalism is perhaps the stress on context (rather than origin or overt motive) in the explanation of social behaviour. Formulated as an extreme doctrine, it asserts that each social institution is ideally suited to its context. The paradigm of explanation then becomes an account of just how a given institution does ideally fit its context, which means presumably just how it serves the survival and stability of the whole better than would any available alternative.

One of the charges made against this doctrine is that it is 'teleological', that it explains the present behaviour in terms of its consequences in the future, i.e. in terms of the manner in which those consequences *will* be desirable from the given society's viewpoint.

It seems to me that it is not difficult to answer this particular charge. All that is required is that each 'functional' explanation be as it were *read backwards*. The 'explanation' of institution X is not really the proper, causal explanation of *it*, but of the manner in which it contributes to the society as a whole. The 'real' explanation of X is provided when the functional accounts of the *other* institutions is given — of all of them, or of a relevant subset of those of them which contribute towards the maintenance of X — which jointly make up a 'real', causal explanation of X itself (just as the 'functional' account of X figures in *their* causal explanation). This of course implies that good, proper explanations can only be had when a whole society is seen as a unity, and that partial studies of institutions in isolation are incomplete, and only a step towards proper understanding. But such a stress on societies seen as unities is indeed a part of the 'Functionalist' syndrome of ideas.

But there cannot be many people today who hold Functionalism in its extreme form.[2] What needs to be said about that has been most brilliantly and succinctly said by Professor Lévi-Strauss:

> Dire qu'une société fonctionne est un truisme; mais dire que tout, dans une société, fonctionne est absurdité.
> (*Anthropologie Structurale* (Paris, 1958) p. 17.)

The thesis of social adjustment is not really a theory: it is a promise of a theory, a promise that somewhere along the spectrum between an absurdity and truism there is a point where truth without triviality is to be found. Until the precise point along that spectrum is located, it will not be a theory, and as far as I know no one has attempted to locate it, and it is difficult to see how one could. The corollary of the doctrine in its *extreme form*, the claim of perfect stability and self-maintenance of societies, is plainly false. The requirement that societies be seen as unities is unsatisfiable for most societies in the modern world, and in view of their size, complexity and in view of the difficulties

118

of delimiting 'societies'.

But whilst, for these reasons, 'strong' Functionalism is dead or moribund, moderate Functionalism, or Functionalism as a method rather than a theory, is happily very much alive. Lévi-Strauss is perhaps right when he speaks of

> . . . cette forme primaire du structuralisme qu'on appelle fonctionnalisme.
>
> (*Anthropologie Structurale*, p. 357.)

The exploration of social structure is one of the main preoccupations of sociology. It must require of the investigator of any one institution an awareness of its context, of the 'structure' within which that institution finds itself.

But if moderate Functionalism is justifiably alive, its application to the interpretation of concepts and doctrines is particularly relevant. It consists of the insistence on the fact that concepts and beliefs do not exist in isolation, in texts or in individual minds, but in the life of men and societies. The activities and institutions, in the context of which a word or phrase or set of phrases is used, must be known before that word or those phrases can be understood, before we can really speak of a *concept* or a *belief*.

4. The particular application of the functional, context-stressing method to concepts is nothing new. it can be found above all in the work of Emile Durkheim which is one of the fountain-heads of Functionalism in general, in *Les Formes Élémentaires de la Vie Religieuse*. I think that less than justice is done to Durkheim when he is remembered as the author of a doctrine to the effect that primitive societies or societies in general really 'worship themselves'. The real essence of his doctrine in that remarkable work seems to me to lie elsewhere, in the view that concepts, as opposed to sensations, are only possible in a social context[3] (and *a fortiori* that they can only be understood when the social context is known), and that important, categorical concepts, on which all others depend, require ritual if they are to be sustained. It tends to be forgotten that Durkheim's main problem, as he saw it, was not to explain religion but to explain conceptual thought and above all the *necessity*, the compulsive nature of certain of our general concepts. This is

119

a Kantian problem, and Durkheim claimed to have solved it in a way which resembled Kant's, but differed from it in various important ways.

Above all, it differed from it in two ways: the machinery, so to speak, which was responsible for a compulsive nature of our categorial concepts was collective and observable, rather than hidden in the backstage recesses of the individual mind; and secondly, it did not, like a Balliol man, function effortlessly, but needed for its effective working to keep in training, to be forever flexing its muscles and keeping them in trim — and just this was Durkheim's theory of ritual, which for him was the method by which the intelligibility and compulsiveness of crucial categories was maintained in the minds of members of a given society. Ritual and religion did publicly what the Kantian transcendental ego did only behind the impassable iron curtain of the noumenal. It was thus that Durkheim paved the way for modern anthropological field-work: it was his view that in observing (say) the rituals associated with a clan totem, we were privileged to observe the machinery which explains the conceptual, logical and moral compulsions of the members of *that* society, compulsions similar, for instance to our inability to think of the world outside time. Much later, a linguistic philosopher, commenting somewhere on transcendental beliefs, hinted that their source lay in language by saying that men needed a god of time as little as they needed a god of tenses. Durkheim's much more plausible point was precisely this in reverse: in order to have and understand tenses, we need first of all to have or to have had (something like) a god and a ritual of time.

Our contemporary invocations of the functional, social-context approach to the study and interpretation of concepts is in various ways very different from Durkheim's. Durkheim was not so much concerned to defend the concepts of primitive societies: in their setting, they did not need a defence, and in the setting of modern and changing societies he was not anxious to defend what was archaic, nor loath to suggest that some intellectual luggage might well be archaic. He was really concerned to explain the compulsiveness of what in practice did not seem to need any defence (and in so doing, he claimed he was solving the problem of knowledge

120

whose solution had in his view evaded Kant and others, and to be solving it without falling into either empiricism or apriorism). Whether he was successful I do not propose to discuss: for a variety of reasons it seems to me that he was not.[4]

By contrast, the modern user of the Functionalist approach to concepts is concerned to defend, rather than to explain a compulsion. In anthropology, he may be concerned to defend the objects of his particular study from the charge of absurdity or pre-logical thought; in philosophy he may be concerned with applying the crypto-Functionalist theory of language which is the basis of so much contemporary philosophy. And behind either of these motives, there is, more potent than either, the consideration springing from our general intellectual climate — the desire to assist or reinforce the tacit *concordat* which seems to have been reached between intellectual criticism and established concepts in the middle of the twentieth century.

5. The situation facing a social anthropologist who wishes to interpret a concept, assertion or doctrine in an alien culture is basically simple. He is, say, faced with an assertion S in the local language. He has at his disposal the large or infinite set of possible sentences in his own language. His task is to locate the nearest equivalent or equivalents of S in his own language.

He may not be wholly happy about this situation, but he cannot avoid it. There is no third language which could mediate between the native language and his own, in which equivalences could be stated and which would avoid the pitfalls arising from the fact that his own language has its own way of handling the world, which may not be those of the native language studied, and which consequently are liable to distort that which is being translated.

Naïvely, people sometimes think that *reality* itself could be this kind of mediator and 'third language': that equivalences between expressions in different languages could be established by locating just which objects in the world they referred to. (If the objects were identical, then so were the expressions. . . .) For a variety of powerful reasons, this is of course no good. Language functions in a variety of ways other than 'referring to objects'. Many objects are simply not there, in any obvious physical sense, to be located: how could one, by this method, establish the equivalences, if they exist, between abstract or negative or hypothetical or religious expressions? Again, many 'objects' are in a sense created by the language, by the manner in which its terms carve up the world or experience. Thus the mediating third party is simply not to be found: either it turns out to be an elusive ghost ('reality'), or it is just one further language, with idiosyncrasies of its own which are as liable to distort in the translation as did the original language of the investigator. Using it only multiplies the probability of distortion by adding to the number of conceptual middle men, and in any case the procedure involves a vicious regress.

This situation is described, for instance, in a recent important study of primitive religion: '[The] unity and multiplicity of Divinity causes no difficulty in the context of Dinka language and life, but it is impossible entirely to avoid the logical and semantic problems which arise when Dinka statements bearing upon it are translated, together, into English.' (Godfrey Lienhardt, *Divinity and Experience*: *The Religion of the Dinka* (Oxford, 1961) p. 56.)

Or, as the same author puts it in the context of a general discussion of anthropology, in *The Institutions of Primitive Society*, by various authors (Oxford, 1954) ch. VIII: 'The problem of describing to others how members of a remote tribe think then begins to appear *largely as one of translation*, of making the coherence primitive thought has ... as clear as possible in our own' (p. 97, italics mine).

The situation facing the historical sociologist is not very different Samuelsson says (*Religion and Economic Action* p. 36): 'neither in St Paul nor in Baxter do the texts ... form coherent chains of reasoning .... The source material, in both cases, consists of a few sentences, statements made on isolated occasions ... often clearly contradictory and not infrequently framed with such oracular sophistry that it is impossible for the reader of a later age to determine with certainty the "intrinsic meaning". ...'.

The problem is analogous, though there are differences. One is that if the historical sociologist's material is disjointed and fragmentary, there is less he can do about it than the anthropologist confronting a still continuing culture. Another
122

difference is that this particular sociologist is not over-charitable in attributing coherence to the authors of his texts, whilst the anthropologist cited appears to make it a condition of a good translation that it conveys the coherence which he assumes is there to be found in primitive thought. Such charity, or lack of it, is a matter of fashion in various disciplines. Most anthropologists at present are, I think, charitable: in sociology the situation is not so clear and there is no reason to think that Samuelsson is similarly typical.[5]

One main stream of contemporary philosophy is inclined towards similar charity towards the concepts of the philosopher's own society. Mr R. Wollheim, for instance, in *F. H. Bradley* (Penguin Books, 1959) p. 67, observes '. . . there are those [philosophers] who think that . . . what we think is far truer, far profounder than we ordinarily take it to be . . .' and goes on, correctly, to cite as the contemporary origin of this charitable view the later Wittgenstein. But Wittgenstein is also the author of the insistence on seeing the meaning of utterances as their use, and on seeing language as a 'form of life': in anthropological terms, on interpreting them in the light of their function in the culture of which they are a part. This influential movement is of course liable to confirm anthropologists in their attitude, and at least one of them, in a brilliant essay,[6] has drawn attention to the parallelism. Time was when neither philosophers nor anthropologists were so charitable.

6. Thus the basic situation is simple. I am schematising it below. Indigenous or textual sentence S faces a long or

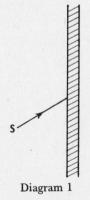

Diagram 1

infinite column of all possible (say) English sentences. The investigator, with some misgivings, locates the nearest equivalent of S in the column.

7. Having done this, the anthropologist simply cannot, whether he likes it or not, and however much he may strive to be *wertfrei*, prevent himself from noticing whether the equivalents found in his own language for S are sensible or silly, as assertions. One's first reaction to assertions in one's own language, inseparable from appreciating their meaning, is to classify them in some way as Good or Bad. (I do not say 'true' or 'false', for this only arises with regard to some types of assertion. With regard to others, other dichotomies, such as 'meaningful' and 'absurd' or 'sensible' and 'silly' might apply. I deliberately use the 'Good' and 'Bad' so as to cover all such possible polar alternatives whichever might best apply to the equivalent of S.)

So in terms of our diagram, we have two boxes, G(ood) and B(ad); and having located the equivalents of S in his own language, the anthropologist willy-nilly goes on to note whether these equivalents go into G or B. (He may of course think that he is doing this purely in his own private capacity, and not professionally as an anthropologist. No matter, he does do it.) So the schema becomes slightly more complex. Let us assume in this case that the anthropologist judges the equivalents of S to be silly, B(ad). The schema now is:

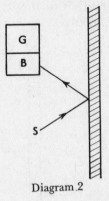

Diagram 2

8. But what diagram 2 describes is, as an account of

124

contemporary interpretations, unrealistic. On the contrary, it describes a state of affairs much more characteristic of an earlier period, of what may almost be called the pre-history of anthropology. To come out with an interpretation of the indigenous sentence which classifies it as B(ad), as false or irrational or absurd, or at any rate to do it often, is a sign of *ethnocentricity*. Ethnocentricity is a grave defect from the viewpoint of the standards of the anthropological community.

Like members of other tribes, anthropologists are socialised by means of legends. These legends of course need not be false: indeed the one I am about to describe has much truth in it. Nevertheless, it is their socialising, indoctrinating function rather than their historical accuracy which is relevant. The legend by means of which a new anthropologist is moulded runs something as follows: Once upon a time, the anthropological world was inhabited by a proto-population who were *ethnocentric*. They collected information about primitives mainly in order to poke fun at them, to illustrate the primitive's inferiority to themselves. The information collected, even if accurate (which it often wasn't) was worthless because it was torn out of context.

The pre-enlightenment anthropologist, struck by the frequency with which the interpretations resulted in assertions which were B(ad), and crediting this to the backwardness of the societies whose beliefs were being described, tended to explain this in terms of one of two theories: *(a)* Primitive Mentality theories, or *(b)* Jacob's Ladder (Evolutionist) theories of moral and intellectual growth. The former theory amounts to saying that savages get things wrong and confused so systematically, rather than being just occasionally in error, that one can characterise their thought as 'pre-logical'. The latter theory is somewhat more charitable and supposes that the savages are on the same ladder as we are, but so far behind that most of what they believe, whilst resulting from the application of the same logical principles as our own, is also an example of so unskilled an application of them that it is all too frequently' wrong. Neither of these theories is much favoured at present.

For one day the Age of Darkness came to an end. Modern anthropology begins with good, genuine, real modern field-

125

work. The essence of such field-work is that it does see institutions, practices, beliefs etc. *in context*. At the same time, ethnocentrism is overcome. It is no longer the aim of studies to titillate a feeling of superiority by retailing piquant oddities. The two things, the seeing of institutions etc. in context, and the overcoming of ethnocentrism, are of course intimately connected. The schema which now applies is somewhat different:

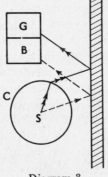

Diagram 3

The circle C around the original indigenous assertion S stands for its social context. The context so to speak refracts the line of interpretation: with the aid of context, one arrives at a different equivalent in English of the original sentence S. And, lo and behold, if one *then* asks oneself about the merit of the newly interpreted S, one finds oneself giving it a high mark for sensibleness, truth or whatnot. One ends at G(ood) rather than B(ad). The earlier, bad old practice is indicated on this diagram by a dotted line.

9. There are various motives and/or justifications for the new, contextual approach. One of them is simply that it contains a good deal of validity: one does indeed get incomparably better appreciation of a doctrine by seeing its setting and use. But there are other motives. One of them is the laudable desire to be tolerant, understanding and liberal, to refrain from an uncomprehending and presumptuous superiority in one's attitude to other (notably 'primitive') societies.

In the modern world, this can be an urgent concern and

126

connected with the need to combat racialism. A notable example of this use of anthropological sophistication is Professor Lévi-Strauss's *Race and History* (UNESCO, Paris, 1952). In a chapter entitled 'The Ethnocentric Attitude' he describes the widespread tendency to discount and despise members of other cultures as savages or barbarians, and speaks of it (p. 11) as 'this naïve attitude . . . deeply rooted in most men' and adds that 'this [i.e. his] booklet . . . in fact refutes it'. The main method he employs here to dissuade us from ethnocentricity is to point out that ethnocentrism characterises above all just those whom one would describe as savages. 'This attitude of mind, which excludes as 'savages' (or any people one may choose to regard as savages) from human kind, is precisely the attitude most strikingly characteristic of those same savages.' One may be worried by the fact that the second occurrence of the word *savages* in the preceding sentence does not occur in inverted commas: in other words, that Lévi-Strauss is attempting to dissuade us from speaking of 'savages' by warning us that *savages* do so. Does he not here presuppose their existence and a condemnation of them? The liberal is in great danger of falling into paradox: either he condemns the ethnocentrism of savages and thus his tolerance has an important limit, or he does not, and then he at least condones *their* intolerance.

The paradox emerges even more clearly in an aphoristic definition he offers a little later (p. 12) of the 'barbarian'. 'The barbarian is, first and foremost, the man who believes in barbarism.' What makes one a savage, in other words, is the belief that some others *are* such.

Let us follow out this definition, taking it literally. A barbarian is he who believes that some others are barbarians. Notoriously, there are such people. They, therefore, are barbarians. *We* know they believe it. Hence, we believe they are barbarians. Ergo, we too are barbarians (by reapplication of the initial definition). And so is anyone who has noticed this fact and knows that *we* are, and so on. Lévi-Strauss's definition has the curious property that, by a kind of regression or contagion, it spreads barbarism like wildfire through the mere awareness of it.

This paradox follows logically from Lévi-Strauss's innocuous-seeming definition. But this is not merely a logical oddity, arising from some quirk or careless formulation. It reflects something far more fundamental. It springs from a dilemma deep in the very foundations of the tolerant, understanding liberalism, of which sophisticated anthropology is a part, and it goes back at least to the thought of the Enlightenment which is the ancestor of such liberalism. The (unresolved) dilemma, which the thought of the Enlightenment faced, was between a relativistic-functionalist view of thought, and the absolutist claims of enlightened Reason. Viewing man as part of nature, as enlightened Reason requires, it wished to see his cognitive and evaluative activities as parts of nature too, and hence as varying, legitimately, from organism to organism and context to context. (This is the relativist-functional view.) But at the same time in recommending life according to Reason and Nature, it wished at the very least to exempt this view itself (and, in practice, some others) from such a relativism.

This dilemma was never really resolved in as far as a naturalistic or third-person view of beliefs (individual or collective) leads us to relativism, whilst our thought at the same time makes an exception in its own favour. We are here only concerned with the working out of this dilemma in anthropology. What characteristically happened in anthropology is rather like that pattern of alliances in which one's neighbours are one's enemies, but one's neighbours-but-one are one's allies. Anthropologists were relativistic, tolerant, contextually-comprehending vis-à-vis the savages who are after all some distance away, but absolutistic, intolerant vis-à-vis their immediate neighbours or predecessors, the members of our own society who do not share their comprehending outlook and are themselves 'ethnocentric'.

The anthropologists were roughly liberals in their own society and tories on behalf of the society they were investigating: they 'understood' the tribesman but condemned the District Officer or the Missionary. A bitter and misinformed attack on this attitude occurs in A. J. Hanna's *European Rule in Africa* (London, 1961) p. 22: 'The rise of social anthropology did much to foster [the] attitude [of trying to perpetuate tribalism] ... exploring with fascinated interest the subtle and complex ramifications of tribal structure, and disdaining to mention ... murder, mutilation,

128

torture, witch-hunting [*sic*], cattle-raiding, wife-raiding. . . .
A . . . psychological tendency led the anthropologist to
become the champion not only of the tribe whose customs
he studied, but of its customs themselves.'

It is interesting to note, however, that the pattern of
alliances, as it were, has changed since the days of the liberals
who were, in relativist spirit, tolerantly understanding of the
intolerant absolutism of the distant tribesman, but less so of
the absolutist beliefs in their own society. Nowadays, more
sociological students of religion are themselves believers: in
other words, contextual charity ends at home.

10. My main point about the tolerance-engendering
contextual interpretation is that it calls for caution: that as a
method it can be rather more wobbly than at first appears.
Let us return to the diagram. What the last diagram
expressed — the diagram schematising context-respecting,
enlightened investigation — can involve some self-deception.
What really happens, at any rate sometimes, is this:

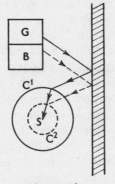

Diagram 4

This diagram differs from the preceding one partly in the
direction of the arrows. What I mean is this: it is the *prior*
determination that S, the indigenous affirmation, be interpreted favourably, which determines just how much context
will be taken into consideration. The diagram shows how
different ranges of context — C_1 or C_2 — are brought in
according to whether the starting point is charitable or not.
The context 'refracts' the line of interpretation' take

a little more, or a little less, (as in the dotted lines), and a different interpretation of S in English will result. Or rather, the prior disposition concerning what kind of interpretation one wishes to find, determines the range of context brought in. (Apart from varying the range, there will also be different views of what the context is, either empirically, or in the way it is described and seen. A believing and an agnostic anthropologist may have differing views about what contexts there are to be seen.) The dotted circle represents a different — in this case, smaller — range of context taken into consideration.

It may be that the sympathetic, positive interpretations of indigenous assertions are not the result of a sophisticated appreciation of context, but *the other way round*: that the manner in which the context is invoked, the amount and kind of context and the way the context itself is interpreted, depends on prior tacit determination concerning the kind of interpretation one wishes to find. After all, there is nothing in the nature of things or societies to dictate visibly just how much context is relevant to any given utterance, or how that context should be described.

Professor Raymond Firth has remarked in 'Problem and Assumption in an Anthropological Study of Religion' (Huxley Memorial Lecture, 1959) p. 139: 'From my own experience, I am impressed by the ease with which it is possible to add one's own personal dimension to the interpretation of an alien religious ideology, to raise the generalisations to a higher power than the empirical content of the material warrants.' My point is, really that it is more than a matter of *ease* — it is a matter of necessity: for interpretation cannot be determinate without assumptions concerning the success or failure of the interpreted communication, and the criteria of such success are not manifest in the 'content of the material' itself. One has to work them out as best one can, and it will *not* do to take the short cut of reading them off the material by assuming that the material is always successful, i.e. that the statements investigated do satisfy and exemplify criteria of coherence, and hence that interpretation is not successful until this coherence has been made manifest in the translation. The logical *assessment* of an assertion, and the identification of its

130

nearest equivalent in our language, are intimately linked and inseparable.

11. But this formal argument may carry more conviction if illustrated by concrete examples. The first I shall take is Professor Evans-Pritchard's treatment of 'Nuer religion notably in chapter V, 'The Problem of Symbols', of *Nuer Religion* (Oxford, 1956). Evans-Pritchard's main theoretical concern in this book is to refute Lévy-Bruhl's thesis concerning 'pre-logical mentality'. Evans-Pritchard's method in the pursuit of this aim is to take Nuer assertions and doctrines which, on the face of it, would indeed provide excellent evidence for a doctrine of the 'pre-logical mentality' of primitives, and then to proceed with the help of contextual interpretation to show that in fact they do not.

Evans-Pritchard begins his discussion as follows (p. 123): 'Our problem . . . can be simply stated by the question: What meaning are we to attach to Nuer statements that such-and-such a thing is *kwoth*, spirit? The answer is not so simple.' For the point is that the Nuer do make assertions which, prima facie, support a Lévy-Bruhl-type theory of 'primitive mentality', as Evans-Pritchard himself admits and stresses: 'It seems odd, if not absurd, to a European when he is told that a twin is a bird as though it were an obvious fact, for Nuer are not saying that a twin is like a bird but that he is a bird. There seems to be a complete contradiction in the statement: and it was precisely on statements of this kind recorded by observers of primitive peoples that Lévy-Bruhl based his theory of the pre-logical mentality of these peoples, its chief characteristic being, in his view, that it permits such evident contradictions — that a thing can be what it is and at the same time something altogether different' (p. 131). Or again, 'When a cucumber is used as a sacrificial victim Nuer speak of it as an ox. In doing so they are asserting something rather more than that it takes the place of an ox' (p. 128).

But this is not the only kind of apparently odd assertion in which the Nuer indulge. This kind of statement appears to be in conflict with the principle of identity or non-contradiction, or with common sense, or with manifest observable fact: human twins are *not* birds, and vice versa. But they *also* make assertions which are in conflict with good theology, or at any rate with the theology which, according

131

to Evans-Pritchard, they really hold: '... Nuer religious thought ... is pre-eminently dualistic.' '... there is ...a duality between *kwoth*, Spirit, which is immaterial ... and *cak*, creation, the material world known to the senses. Rain and lightning and pestilences and murrains belong to this created world ...' (p. 124).

Nevertheless, Nuer do make assertions which appear to be in conflict with this theology as well: '... certain things are said, or may be said, "to be" God — rain, lightning, and various other natural ... things ...' (p. 123). 'They may say of rain or lightning or pestilence "*e kwoth*", "it is God" ...' (p. 124).

What is the solution? How are the Nuer saved for both common sense *and* for dualistic theology, when their assertions appear to convict them of self-contradiction *and* of a doctrine of the immanence of the Deity in the world?

I shall present the solution in Professor Evans-Pritchard's own words. Concerning the apparent contradiction in Nuer thought, arising from the identification of twins and birds, it appears (p. 131) that 'no contradiction is involved in the statement, which, on the contrary, appears quite sensible and even true, to one who presents the idea to himself in the Nuer language and within their system of religious thought. ... *They are not saying that a twin has a beak, feathers, and so forth. Nor in their everyday relations as twins do Nuer speak of them as birds or act towards them as though they were birds.*' (Italics mine.)

One may ask here — but what, then, *would* count as pre-logical thought? Only, presumably, the behaviour of a totally demented person, suffering from permanent hallucinations, who *would* treat something which is perceptibly a human being as though it had all the physical attributes of a bird. But could Lévy-Bruhl conceivably have meant this when he was putting forward the doctrine of pre-logical mentality? He knew, and could hardly have helped knowing, that savages like everyone else are capable of distinguishing objects which are so unlike physically as a human being who happens to be a twin, and a bird. (In as far as there is nothing about the physical appearance of a human being who happens to be a twin — unless perhaps some socially significant markings, but Evans-Pritchard does not say that Nuer twins have something

132

of this kind — to distinguish him from other human beings, the Nuer capacity to distinguish him from a bird follows from their very capacity to distinguish humans in general from birds, a capacity which can hardly be in doubt.) This being so, Lévy-Bruhl's thesis can hardly with fairness be interpreted as entailing that errors such as the confusion of human and bird bodies is genuinely committed by primitives. He could not have meant this: or rather, we may not attribute this doctrine to him if we extend to *him* too the courtesy or charity of contextual interpretation, which requires that we do not credit people with beliefs — whatever they *say* — which are plainly in conflict with what they can be assumed to know in the light of what they actually do. (e.g. Nuer cannot believe twins to be birds as their conduct distinguishes between the two).

If it be adopted as a principle that people cannot mean what at some level (e.g. implicitly, through their conduct) they also know to be false or absurd, then this principle must be applicable to Lévy-Bruhl too. The trouble with the principle is, of course, that it is *too* charitable: it absolves too many people of the charge of systematically illogical or false or self-deceptive thought.

It is worth considering just why the principle is so indiscriminately charitable. It insists, as Evans-Pritchard does when applying it, on interpreting assertions in the light of actual *conduct*. But no ongoing viable system of conduct — and any society, and also any sane surviving man, exemplifies such a system — *can* be self-contradictory. Assertions, doctrines, can easily be illogical: conduct, and in particular the conduct of a *society* which is, by definition, a human group persisting over time, cannot easily be illogical. The object of anthropological inquiries are precisely human groups persisting over time. Their very persistence entails that they are reasonably viable: and this viability in turn ensures that a 'context' is available for the sympathetic interpretation which will make sense of the local doctrines and assertions, however odd they may seem on the surface. This principle, tacitly employed by Evans-Pritchard, is too strong, for it ensures that no reasonably viable society can be said to be based on or to uphold absurd or 'pre-logical' doctrines. The trouble with such all-embracing logical charity is, for one

133

thing, that it is unwittingly quite *a priori*: it may delude anthropologists into thinking that they have *found* that no society upholds absurd or self-contradictory beliefs, whilst in fact the principle employed has ensured in advance of any inquiry that nothing may count as pre-logical, inconsistent or categorially absurd though it may be. And this, apart from anything else, would blind one to at least one socially significant phenomenon: the social role of absurdity.

12. But before proceeding with this general consideration, one should also look at Evans-Pritchard's second reinterpretation of Nuer assertions. The first one was to save them for common sense or consistency from the charge of self-contradiction. The second was to save them for a dualist theology and from an immanentist one. Again, it is best to present the case in Evans-Pritchard's own words. Referring to the fact that Nuer appear to speak of certain things — rain, lightning etc. — as being God (as quoted above), in contradiction of the dualist theology with which he credits them, Evans-Pritchard comments (p. 123 and 124): 'There is here an ambiguity, or an obscurity, to be elucidated, for Nuer are not now saying that God or Spirit is like this or that, but that this or that "is" God or Spirit.'

In interpreting this crucial sentence, a good deal depends on just what Evans-Pritchard meant by putting the final occurrence of the word *is* in inverted commas. He might simply have wished to accentuate it, by contrast to the expression *is like* in the preceding clause. But there are two good objections to this interpretation: had this been his intention, he might simply have italicised it, as is more customary, and secondly, he should have given the same treatment, whether inverted commas or italicisation, to the contrasted expression *is like*. In fact, I interpret him as saying that the Nuer do not really say that these things are God, but merely that they 'are' God. They mean something other than what they say.

And indeed, we are told (p. 125), 'When Nuer say of rain or lightning that it is God they are making an elliptical statement. What is understood is not that the thing in itself is Spirit but that it is what we could call a medium or manifestation or sign of divine activity in relation to men and of significance for them.' And, no doubt, elliptical statements

134

are common in all languages. What is at issue are the procedures for filling in the gaps left by ellipsis.

It is important of course that the Nuer themselves, being illiterate, do not put any kind of inverted commas around their word for *is*, nor do they adopt any kind of phonetic equivalent of such a device. (Evans-Pritchard at no point suggests that they do.) Hence the attribution of the inverted commas, of the non-literal meaning, is a matter of interpretation, not of direct observation of the utterance itself.

And what is the logic of this interpretation? How are the gaps filled? In part, the argument is based on the assumption that the Nuer *cannot* mean the assertion literally because (their notion of) Deity is such that this would make no sense. 'Indeed it is because Spirit is conceived of in itself, as the creator and the one, and quite apart from any of its material manifestations, that phenomena can be said to be sent by it or to be its instruments' (p. 125). But to argue thus is of course to assume precisely that they do have such a self-sufficient, substantial-Creator notion of Spirit as they are credited with, *and* that they follow out the implications consistently. Indeed one may doubt whether and in what sense the Nuer can be said to possess a notion of the One, self-sufficient substance and Creator, independent of his material manifestations, etc., difficult notions which, explicitly formulated in this way, seem to presuppose the context of scholastic philosophy. It is something like this that Schoolmen have done for God: can the same be meaningfully said of the Nuer God, the Nuer having no Schoolmen?

But the position is supported not only by this argument, but also by some good independent evidence. One argument is that '. . . Nuer readily expand such statements by adding that thunder, rain, and pestilence are all instruments . . . of God or that they are sent by . . . God . . .' (p. 125). This is indeed a good and independent piece of evidence. Another argument is from the irreversibility of the judgements which claim that those certain mundane manifestations 'are' God: God or Spirit cannot in Nuer be said to 'be' them. This does not seem to me to be so valid a point. It is of course difficult for one who speaks no Nuer to judge, but in English it is possible, in some contexts, to say that A is B without the statement being reversible, but at the same time implying that A is a part of B and in that sense identical with it (or rather with a part of it). To someone who inquires about my suburb, I may in some contexts say that Putney is London (it is not Surrey): and I cannot say that London is Putney. It could be that for Nuer, rain etc. is in this sense (part of) the deity, and this would then indicate that the Nuer view of God is at least in part an immanent one, and not as severely transcendent as Evans-Pritchard seems to be arguing. ('. . . God not being an observable object, [the situation could scarcely arise] in which Nuer would require or desire to say about him that he is anything', p. 125.) Again one may also wonder whether Nuer can be credited with so firm a theological position on a question which they can hardly have explicitly posed in such terms.

I do not wish to be misunderstood: I am *not* arguing that Evans-Pritchard's account of Nuer concepts is a bad one. (Nor am I anxious to revive a doctrine of pre-logical mentality à *la* Lévy-Bruhl.) On the contrary, I have the greatest admiration for it. What I am anxious to argue is that contextual interpretation, which offers an account of what assertions 'really mean' in opposition to what they seem to mean in isolation, does not by itself clinch matters. It cannot arrive at determinate answers (concerning 'what they mean') without doing a number of things which may in fact prejudge the question: without delimiting just which context is to be taken into consideration, without crediting the people concerned with consistency (which is precisely what is *sub judice* when we discuss, as Evans-Pritchard does, Lévy-Bruhl's thesis), or without assumptions concerning what they can mean (which, again, is precisely what we do not know but are trying to find out). In fairness, one should add that Evans-Pritchard is aware of this, as just before he severely rebukes Lévy-Bruhl and others for their errors, he also remarks (p. 140): 'I can take the analysis no further: but if it is inconclusive it at least shows, if it is correct, how wide of the mark have been . . . [Lévy-Bruhl and some others].'

13. To say all this is not to argue for a scepticism or agnosticism concerning what members of alien cultures and speakers of alien languages mean, still less to argue for an abstention from the contextual method of interpretation.

(On the contrary, I shall argue for a fuller use of it, fuller in the sense of allowing for the possibility that what people mean is sometimes absurd.)

In a sense, Evans-Pritchard's saving of the Nuer for a dualistic theology is a more difficult exercise than is his saving of them from a charge of pre-logical mentality. We know anyway, without field-work, that they could in conduct distinguish birds from men and bulls from cucumbers, and to argue from these premisses to the absence of pre-logical thought does not perhaps really advance the question of whether pre-logical thought occurs. On the other hand nothing prior to field-work evidence could give us any reasons for having views about whether Nuer theology was or was not dualistic.

14. It is interesting at this stage to contrast Evans-Pritchard's use of the method with that of another distinguished practitioner of it, Mr Edmund Leach.

We have seen how Evans-Pritchard takes Nuer statements which, on the face of it, violate common sense and also others which go counter to a dualistic theology which separates a transcendent deity from the immanent world, and how, by holding these statements to be metaphorical or elliptical, he squares them with common sense and an acceptable theology. Mr Leach, in *Political Systems of Highland Burma* (London 1954), copes with other odd statements, made by Burmese Kachins.

Again, these statements are odd. It appears (p. 14) that a Kachin found killing a pig and asked what he is doing may reply that he is 'giving to the *nats*'. The oddity arises simply from the non-existence of *nats*. On the face of it, we might accuse the Kachins, if not of 'pre-logical mentality', at any rate of populating the world with imaginary creatures in their own image. Indeed, this seems to be so, for Leach tells us (p. 173) that *nats* are 'magnified non-natural men', and that 'in the *nat* world, as in the human world, there are chiefs, aristocrats, commoners and slaves'.

Nevertheless, Leach does not, like Evans-Pritchard, intend to give us a picture of what that supernatural world is like. (Evans-Pritchard gave us a picture of the Nuer vision of the supernatural which was sufficiently determinate to exclude some superficially plausible interpretations of some Nuer assertions.) On the contrary, he tells us (p. 172) 'it is nonsensical to discuss the actions or qualities of supernatural beings except in terms of human action'. 'Myth . . . is not so much a justification for ritual as a description of it.' Or (p. 13), 'Myth [and] .,. . ritual . . . are one and the same.' '. . . myth regarded as a statement in words "says" the same thing as ritual regarded as a statement in action. To ask questions about the content of belief which are not contained in the content of ritual is nonsense.'[7] '. . . a very large part of anthropological literature on religion [is] a discussion of the content of belief and of the rationality or otherwise of that content. Most such arguments seem to me scholastic nonsense.'

Or again (p. 14), when a Kachin is killing a pig and says he is giving it to the *nats*, 'it is nonsense to ask such questions as: "Do nats have legs? Do they eat flesh? Do they live in the sky?"' (Given the fact that they are 'magnified non-natural men' and that they are 'chiefs, aristocrats, commoners and slaves', it seems odd that it should be nonsense to credit them with legs, a diet, and a habitat.)

Concerning his own procedure, Leach tells us (p. 14): 'I make frequent reference to Kachin mythology but I . . . make no attempt to find any logical coherence in the myths to which I refer. Myths for me are simply one way of describing certain types of human behaviour. . . .' And, later, not only are myth and ritual one so that it makes no sense to ask non-contextual questions about the former, but also (p. 182) 'it becomes clear that the various *nats* of Kachin religious ideology are, in the last analysis, nothing more than ways of describing the formal relationships that exist between real persons and real groups in ordinary Kachin society'.

It is possible to discern what has happened. Leach's exegetic procedures have also saved the Kachins from being credited with meaning what they *appear* to be saying. Their assertions are reinterpreted in the light of the author's disregard for the supernatural, in the light of the doctrine that myths simply mean the ritual which they accompany and nothing else, and that the ritual in turn 'means', symbolises, the society in which it occurs. The 'Social' theory of religion appears to have, in our society, the following

138

function (amongst others possible): to enable us to attribute meaning to assertions which might otherwise be found to lack it.

Again, I am not concerned, nor indeed inclined, to challenge Leach's specific interpretations of the Kachins; though one wishes that some enterprising teacher of anthropology would set his students the task of writing an essay on *kwoth* as it would be written by Leach, and another on *nats* as it would be written by Evans-Pritchard. The point with which I am concerned is to show how the range of context, and the manner in which the context is seen, necessarily affect the interpretation. Both Evans-Pritchard and Leach are charitable to their subjects, and neither allows them to be credited with nonsense: but in the case of Leach, the 'sense' with which they are credited is identified by means of an essentially *social* doctrine of religion, a doctrine which is also precisely that which Evans-Pritchard strives to refute with the help of *his* interpretations.

15. The crux of the matter is that when, in a sense rightly, the interpretation of people's assertions must be made in the light of what they do and the social setting they do it in, this requirement is profoundly ambiguous. Two quite different things may be intended (though those who postulate the requirement may have failed to be clear in their own minds about this). The distinction between these two things can best be brought out, at any rate to begin with, by means of a simplified imaginary social situation.

Assume that in the language of a given society, there is a word *boble* which is applied to characterise people. Research reveals that *bobleness* or *bobility* is attributed to people under *either* of the following conditions: *(a)* a person who antecedently displays certain characteristics in his conduct, say uprightness, courage and generosity, is called *boble*. *(b)* any person holding a certain office, or a certain social position, is also *ipso facto* described as *boble*. One is tempted to say that bobility *(a)* is a descriptive term whose operational definition consists of tests for the possession of certain attributes (and might consist of seeing how large a portion of his income he distributed as largesse, how he behaved in danger, etc.), whereas *(b)* is simply an ascription, depending on the will or whim of those in authority, or on the social situation, but not in any reasonable direct or identifiable way dependent on the characteristics of the person in question. But the point is: the society in question does not distinguish *two concepts*, boble *(a)* and boble *(b)*. It only uses one word, boble *tout court*; and again its theories about bobility, expressed in proverbs, legends or even disquisitions of wise elders, only know bobility, one and indivisible. As a first and simplified approximation, the logic of bobility is not an unrecognisable model, perhaps, of some familiar concepts in our own languages.

But what is the observer to say about bobility, like, so to speak, semi-operational concepts? Bobility is a conceptual device by which the privileged class of the society in question acquires some of the prestige of certain virtues respected in that society, without the inconvenience of needing to practise them, thanks to the fact that the same word is applied either to practitioners of those virtues or to occupiers of favoured positions. It is, at the same time, a manner of reinforcing the appeal of those virtues, by associating them, through the use of the same appellation, with prestige and power. But all this needs to be said, and to say it is to bring out the internal logical incoherence of the concept — an incoherence which, indeed, is socially functional.

What this shows, however, is that the over-charitable interpreter, determined to defend the concepts he is investigating from the charge of logical incoherence, is bound to misdescribe the social situation. To make sense of the concept is to make nonsense of the society. Thus the *uncharitable* may be 'contextualist' in the second, deeper and better sense.

It seems to me that anthropologists are curiously charitable to concepts. They are not unduly charitable to individuals. On the contrary, they are all too willing to describe how individuals 'manipulate' each other and the rules of the local game: indeed the word 'manipulation' has a certain vogue and is encountered with very great frequency. But why should concepts not be similarly open to manipulation? Why should it not be a part of their use that the ambiguity of words, the logically illicit transformation of one concept into another (like a spirit appearing in diverse forms) is exploited to the full by the users of what seems to

140

be 'one' concept?

Excessive indulgence in contextual charity blinds us to what is best and what is worst in the life of societies. It blinds us to the possibility that social change may occur through the replacement of an inconsistent doctrine or ethic by a better one, or through a more consistent application of either. It equally blinds us to the possibility of, for instance, social control through the employment of absurd, ambiguous, inconsistent or unintelligible doctrines. I should not accept for one moment the contention that neither of these things ever occurs: but even if they never occurred it would be wrong to employ a method which excludes their possibility *a priori*.

16. It may be worth illustrating the point further with a real rather than schematised example, amongst central Moroccan Berbers, and I shall draw on my own field-work for this. Two concepts are relevant: *baraka* and *agurram* (pl. *igurramen*). *Baraka* is a word which can mean simply 'enough', but it also means plenitude, and above all blessedness, manifested amongst other things in prosperity and the power to cause prosperity in others by supernatural means. An *agurram* is a possessor of *baraka*.[8] The concept *baraka* has been explored before, notably by Westermarck's *Ritual and Belief in Morocco* (London, 1926) chs II and III. The concept of *agurram* has not to my knowledge previously been properly explored.

Igurramen are a minority in the wider tribal society of which they are a part. They are a fairly privileged and influential one, and they perform essential and important functions as mediators, arbitrators etc. amongst the feuding tribal population around them. They are selected from a range of potential *igurramen*, who are defined by descent — roughly speaking, to be one it is necessary that one's ancestors or at least some of them should have been *igurramen* too. The crucial question is — *how* are they selected?

The local belief is that they are selected by God. Moreover, God makes his choice manifest by endowing those whom he has selected with certain characteristics, including magical powers, and great generosity, prosperity, a consider-the-lilies attitude, pacifism and so forth.

The reality of the situation is, however, that the *igurramen* are in fact selected by the surrounding ordinary tribesmen who use their services, by being called to perform those services and being preferred to the rival candidates for their performance. What appears to be *vox Dei* is in reality *vox populi*. Moreover, the matter of the blessed characteristics, the stigmata of *agurram*-hood, is more complicated. It is essential that successful candidates to *agurram* status be *credited* with these characteristics, but it is equally essential, at any rate with regard to some of them, that they should not really possess them. For instance, an *agurram* who was extremely generous in a consider-the-lilies spirit would soon be impoverished and, as such, fail by another crucial test, that of prosperity.

There is here a crucial divergence between concept and reality, a divergence which moreover is quite essential for the working of the social system. It is no use saying, as has been suggested to me by an advocate of the hermeneutic method which I am criticising, that the notion of divine selection of *igurramen* is simply the local way of conceptualising a popular election. This interpretation is excluded for a number of reasons. For one thing, the Berbers of central Morocco are perfectly familiar with *real* elections. In their traditional system, they also have, apart from the *igurramen*, lay tribal chiefs, (*amghar*, pl. *imgharen*) who are elected, annually, by tribal assembly. In these real elections the tribesmen do indeed hope for and request divine guidance, but they are quite clear that it is they themselves who do the electing. They distinguish clearly between this kind of genuine annual election, and the very long-drawn-out process (stretching over generations) by which *igurramen* are selected, in fact by the tribesmen, but ideally by God. But it would be presumptuous and blasphemous for tribesmen to claim to appoint an *agurram*. Secondly, it is of the essence of the function of an *agurram* that he is given from the outside: he has to be a neutral who arbitrates and mediates between tribes. If he were chosen, like a chief or an ally, by the tribesmen, or rather if he were seen to be chosen by tribesmen (as in fact he is), for a litigant to submit to his verdict would be in effect to submit to those other tribesmen who had chosen the *agurram*. This, of course, would involve a

142

loss of face and constitute a confession of weakness. Tribesmen sometimes do choose lay arbitrators: but they then know that they are doing so and the point of invoking *igurramen* is the invoking ʲof *independent* authority. Submission to a divinely chosen *agurram* is a sign not of weakness but of piety. Not to submit to him is, and is explicitly claimed to be, *shameful*. (This illustrates a point which seems to me enormously important, namely that concepts generally contain *justifications* of practices, and hence that one misinterprets them grossly if one treats them simply as these practices, and their context, in another dress. The justifications are independent of the thing justified.)

It might be objected that my unwillingness to accept the indigenous account at its face value merely reflects my theological prejudices, i.e. my unwillingness to believe that the deity interferes in the political life of the central High Atlas. But this kind of objection does not have even a prima facie plausibility with regard to the other social mechanism mentioned. There is nothing in my conceptual spectacles to make me unwilling to conceive that some people might be generous and uncalculating, nor should I be unwilling to describe them in these terms if I found them to be so. It is just that field-work observation of *igurramen* and the social context in which they operate has convinced me that, whilst indeed *igurramen* must entertain lavishly and with an air of insouciance, they *must* also at least balance their income from donations from pilgrims with the outgoings from entertaining them, for a poor *agurram* is a no-good *agurram*. Here again, we are faced with a socially essential discrepancy between concept and reality. What is required is not disregard for social context, but, on the contrary, a fuller appreciation of it which is not wedded *a priori* to finding good sense in the concepts.

One might sum up all this by saying that nothing is more false than the claim that, for a given assertion, *its use is its meaning*. On the contrary, its use may depend on its lack of meaning, its ambiguity, its possession of wholly different and incompatible meanings in different contexts, *and* on the fact that, at the same time, it as it were emits the impression of possessing a consistent meaning throughout — on retaining, for instance, the aura of a justification valid only in one

143

context when used in quite another.

17. It is worth exploring this in connection with the other concept mentioned, *baraka*. I shall not say much about it, as the literature concerning it is already extensive (Westermarck's *Ritual and Belief in Morocco*, chs II and III). Suffice it to say that the concept is a source of great joy to me, for it violates, simultaneously, no fewer than three of the major and most advertised categorial distinctions favoured by recent philosophers. It is an evaluative term, but it is used as though it were a descriptive one: possessors of *baraka* are treated as though they were possessors of an objective characteristic rather than recipients of high moral grades from their fellow-men. And in as far as it is claimed to be an objective characteristic of people, manifest in their conduct, it could only be a dispositional one — but it is treated as though it were the name of some *stuff*: apart from being transmitted genetically, it can also be transmitted by its possessor to another person by means of spitting into the mouth, etc. Thirdly, its attribution is really a case of the performative use of language, for people in fact become possessors of *baraka* by being treated as possessors of it — but nevertheless, it is treated as though its possession were a matter wholly independent of the volition of those who attribute it. (This has already been explained in connection with the account of *agurram*, the possessor of *baraka*, and it has also been explained how this deception is essential for the working of the social system in question.)

In other words, the actual life of this concept goes dead against the celebrated work of recent philosophers. One may well speculate that the society in question could be undermined by acquainting its members with the works of Ryle, Ayer, Stevenson and J. L. Austin. The question is somewhat academic, for in its traditional form the society is virtually illiterate (that is, illiterate but for a small number of Muslim scribes whose range is severely circumscribed) and not amenable to the persuasion of external teachers, and by the time it has ceased to be illiterate and unreceptive, it will have been disrupted anyway.

But this does illustrate a number of important points. I have already stressed that it is no use supposing that one can deal with this by claiming that the indigenous societies always live, as it were, in a conceptual dimension of their own, in which our categorial boundaries do not apply. On the contrary, we can sometimes only make sense of the society in question by seeing how the manipulation of concepts and the violation of categorial boundaries helps it to work. It is precisely the logical *in*consistency of *baraka* which enables it to be applied according to social need and to endow what is a social need with the appearance of external, given and indeed authoritative reality.

18. There are, both in philosophy and the wider intellectual climate of our time, considerable forces giving support to the kind of Functionalism which makes good sense of everything. In philosophy, it springs from the doctrine which identifies *meaning* with *use*, and there is already in existence at least one work by a philosopher about the social sciences in general — Mr P. Winch's, cited above — which elaborates (and commends) the consequences of this doctrine. A proper discussion of the philosophic questions involved would of course take longer.

In the world at large, there is much incentive to paper over the incoherence, and inconveniences, of current ideologies by emulating this anthropological technique. How many ideologists treat their *own* beliefs with a technique similar to that employed by anthropologists for tribesmen! I for one do not feel that, in the realm of concepts and doctrines, we may say that *tout comprendre c'est tout pardonner*. On the contrary, in the social sciences at any rate, if we forgive too much we understand nothing. The attitude of *credo quia absurdum* is *also* a social phenomenon, and we miss its point and its social role if we water it down by interpretation to make it just one further form of non-absurdity, sensible simply in virtue of being viable.

19. One major charge against Functionalism in the past has been the allegation that it cannot deal with social change. With regard to Functionalism in general this charge has now little relevance, as it only applies to strong or extreme formulations of it, and these are held by few. But with regard to the Functionalist approach to interpretation of concepts, it applies very strongly. For it precludes us from making sense of those social changes which arise at least in part from the fact that people sometimes notice the incoherences of

145

doctrines and concepts and proceed to reform the institutions justified by them. This may never happen *just like that*: it may be that it invariably is a discontented segment of society, a new rising class for instance, which exploits those incoherences. But even if this were so, and the discovery of incoherences were never more than a contributory rather than a sufficient cause, it still would not be legitimate for us to employ a method which inherently prevents any possible appreciation of this fact. When anthropologists were concerned primarily with stable societies (or societies held to be such), the mistake was perhaps excusable: but nowadays it is not.

In the end, it is illuminating to return to one of the sources of the Functionalist approach, Durkheim. Durkheim is sometimes accused of overrating the cohesion-engendering function of belief. In the *Elementary Forms of Religious Life*, which is the object of these charges, he did also put forward, albeit briefly, a theory of social change.[9] This theory he sums up in one brief passage, and it is a theory plainly parallel to his theory of social cohesion.

Car une société [est] constituée ... avant tout, par l'idée qu'elle se fait d'elle-meme. Et sans doute, il arrive qu'elle hésite sur la manière dont elle doit se concevoir: elle se sent tiraillée en des sens divergents ... ces conflicts, quand ils éclatent, ont lieu non entre l'idéal et la realité, mais entre idéaux différents. ...

Les Formes Élémentaires de la Vie Réligieuse, 125, ed., p. 604.

This theory, the germ of which is contained in Durkheim, has been elaborated by Mr E. R. Leach's *Political Systems of Highland Burma*, esp. pp. 8-9. My main point here is that there was no need for Durkheim to look even that far for a theory of social change. He apparently thought that if one set of ritually reinforced and inculcated concepts explained social stability, then it took the presence of *two sets* to account for social change. But ironically, such a refinement is not necessary. Some social change may be accounted for precisely because *one* set of ideas has been inculcated too well, or has come to have too great a hold over the loyalties and imaginations of the members of the society in question, or because one of its subgroups has chosen to exploit the imperfect application of those ideas, and to iron out the inconsistencies and incoherences. Over-charitable exegesis would blind us to this.

Contextual interpretation is in some respects like the invocation of *ad hoc* additional hypotheses in science: it is inevitable, proper, often very valuable, and at the same time dangerous and liable to disastrous abuse. It is probably impossible in either case to draw up general rules for delimiting the legitimate and illegitimate uses of it. In science, the best safeguard may be a vivid sense of the possibility that the initial theory which is being saved may have been false after all; in sociological interpretation, an equally vivid sense of the possibility that the interpreted statement may contain absurdity.

20. There remains the issue in the wider society outside the social sciences, the question of the justifiability of 'Functionalist' white-washing of concepts and doctrines. Professor Evans-Pritchard sternly rebukes Durkheim at the end of his book *Nuer Religion*, p. 313: 'It was Durkheim and not the savage who made society into a god.' Perhaps, but it is ironic that if the savage did not, modern man *does* seem to worship his own society through his religion.[10]

My plea against charity did not have as its aim the revival of a 'pre-logical primitive mentality' theory. On the contrary: I hope rather we shall be less charitable to ourselves. I agree entirely with Mr Leach's point in his contribution to *Man and Culture*, that when it comes to the general way in which concepts are embedded in use and context, there is no difference between 'primitives' and us. There is no need to be too charitable to *either*.

My own view of Durkheim is that at the core of his thought there lies not the doctrine of worshipping one's own society, but the doctrines that concepts are essentially social and that religion is the way in which society endows us with them and imposes their hold over us. But, consistently or not, he did not combine this with a static view of society and intellectual life. It would be ironic if neo-Functionalist interpretation now became the means by which our own concepts were ossified amongst us.

147

1. It is, however, very important not to misunderstand this point. For it is *not* true to say that to understand the concepts of a society (in the way its members do) is to understand the society. Concepts are as liable to mask reality as to reveal it, and masking some of it may be a part of their function. The profoundly mistaken doctrine that to understand a society is to understand its concepts has a certain vogue and has recently been revived and argued, for instance, in Mr P. Winch's 'The Idea of a Social Science' (London, 1958). Some of the reasons why this view is false are discussed below.

2. But they do still exist. Consider Professor Ralph Piddington's essay, 'Malinowski's Theory of Needs', in 'Man and Culture', ed. Professor Raymond Firth (London, 1957) esp. p. 47.

3. *Much* later. L. Wittgenstein was credited with just this discovery.

4. Somewhat to my surprise, Mr D. G. MacRae appears to think that he was: '. . . Durkheim *showed* . . . how time, space, causality and other fundamental categories . . . are in great measure social products . . .': 'Ideology and Society' (London, 1961) p. 83. (Italics mine.) Much depends of course on how great a measure 'great measure' is. Durkheim was concerned to explain the compulsiveness of categories. He succeeded in showing, I think, how our power of *apprehending* them depended on society. He did not explain why, once they are in our possession, we cannot escape them.

The distinction is important. Precisely the same is also true of Durkheim's (quite unwitting) follower and successor, Wittgenstein, who also supposed categories were validated by being parts of a 'form of life' and who, incidentally, like Durkheim also vacillated between supposing all concepts could be validated in this manner, and restricting this confirmation to categories.

I am quite prepared to believe that at the root of our ability to count, to relate things along a time series or spatially, is a social order which exemplifies and 'ritually' brings home to us the concepts involved. But I do not think this accounts either for their compulsiveness or for occasional lapses from it. There is something comic about this idea. Are we to say that Riemann and Lobachevsky were inadequately exposed to those rituals of Western society which make the Euclidean picture of space compulsive to its members?

5. For instance, Dr W. Stark, in 'The Sociology of Knowledge' (London, 1958), recommends almost universal charity in this respect, with the help of arguments which differ both from Durkheim's and from those of Functionalists. See also 'Sociology of Faith', 'Inquiry' (1958, no. 4).

6. E. R. Leach, in 'The Epistemological Background to Malinowski's Empiricism', in 'Man and Culture', ed. Firth, p. 119.

7. If Mr Leach meant this quite literally, he should of course give us only the Kachin expression itself plus a description of the ritual and of the society — and *not*, as in fact he does, *translation* of the ritual statements.

148

8. The term *baraka* is in use throughout North Africa by Arabs and Berbers, and also elsewhere. The term *agurram* is only known among Berbers, and not among all of these. It is used in central and southern Morocco, but not among the northern Berbers of the Rif mountains. It is also used by Algerian Berbers, but I do not know how extensively.

9. The work also contains some other suggestions on this subject, not so relevant to my argument here.

10. Cf. Will Herberg, 'Catholic-Protestant-Jew' (1955).

8 Symbols in Ndembu Ritual*

Victor Turner

Some Preliminary Definitions

Among the Ndembu of Northern Rhodesia, the importance
of ritual in the lives of villagers is striking. Hardly a week
passes, in a small neighbourhood, without a ritual drum being
heard in one or other of its villages.

By 'ritual' I mean prescribed formal behaviour for
occasions not given over to technological routine, having
reference to beliefs in mystical beings or powers. The symbol
is the smallest unit of ritual which still retains the specific
properties of ritual behaviour; it is the ultimate unit of
specific structure in a ritual context. Since this essay is in the
main a description and analysis of the structure and
properties of symbols, it will be enough to state here,
following the *Concise Oxford Dictionary,* that a 'symbol' is a
thing regarded by general consent as naturally typifying or
representing or recalling something by possession of
analogous qualities or by association in fact or thought. The
symbols I observed in the field were, empirically, objects,
activities, relationships, events, gestures, and spatial units in a
ritual situation.

Following the advice and example of Professor Monica
Wilson, I asked Ndembu specialists as well as laymen to
interpret the symbols of their ritual. As a result, I obtained
much exegetic material. I felt that it was methodologically
important to keep observational and interpretative material
distinct from one another. The reason for this will soon
become apparent.

I found that I could not analyse ritual symbols without

* Reprinted from Max Gluckman, ed., 'Closed Systems and Open
Minds' (Aldine, Chicago, 1964); copyright © 1964 by Max Gluckman,
Ely Devons, V. W. Turner, F. G. Bailey, A. L. Epstein, Tom Lupton,
Sheila Cunnison, William Watson.

studying them in a time-series in relation to other 'events'. For symbols are essentially involved in social process. I came to see performances of ritual as distinct phases in the social processes whereby groups became adjusted to internal changes and adapted to their external environment. From this standpoint the ritual symbol becomes a factor in social action, a positive force in an activity-field. The symbol becomes associated with human interests, purposes, ends and means, whether these are explicitly formulated or have to be inferred from the observed behaviour. The structure and properties of a symbol become those of a dynamic entity, at least within its appropriate context of action.

Structure and Properties of Ritual Symbols

The structure and properties of ritual symbols may be inferred from three classes of data:

- (a) External form and observable characteristics.
- (b) Interpretations offered
  - (1) by specialists
  - (2) by laymen.
- (c) Significant contexts largely worked out by the anthropologist.

Here is an example. At Nkang'a, the girl's puberty ritual, a novice is wrapped in a blanket and laid at the foot of a *mudyi* sapling. The *mudyi* tree *(Diplorrhyncus mossambicensis)* is conspicuous for its white latex, which exudes in milky beads if the thin bark is scratched. For Ndembu this is its most important observable characteristic. I therefore propose to call it 'the milk-tree' henceforward. Most Ndembu women can attribute several meanings to this tree. In the first place, they say that the milk-tree is the 'senior' *(mukulumpi)* tree of the ritual. Each kind of ritual has this 'senior' or, as I will call it, 'dominant' symbol. Such symbols fall into a special class which I will discuss more fully later. Here it is enough to state that dominant symbols are regarded not merely as means to the fulfilment of the avowed purposes of a given ritual but also and more importantly refer to values which are

151

regarded as ends in themselves, i.e., to axiomatic values. Secondly, the women say with reference to its observable characteristics that the milk-tree stands for human breastmilk and also for the breasts which supply it. They relate this meaning to the fact that Nkang'a is performed when a girl's breasts begin to ripen, not after her first menstruation, which is the subject of another and less elaborate ritual. The main theme of Nkang'a is indeed the tie of nurturance between mother and child, not the bond of birth. This theme of nurturance is expressed at Nkang'a in a number of supplementary symbols indicative of the act of feeding and of foodstuffs. In the third place, the women describe the milk-tree as 'the tree of a mother and her child'. Here the reference has shifted from description of a biological act, breast-feeding, to a social tie of profound significance both in domestic relations and in the structure of the widest Ndembu community. This latter meaning is brought out most clearly in a text I recorded from a male ritual specialist. I translate literally.

The milk-tree is the place of all mothers of the lineage (*ivumu*, literally 'womb' or 'stomach'). It represents the ancestress of women and men. The milk-tree is where our ancestress slept when she was initiated. 'To initiate' here means the dancing of women round and round the milk-tree where the novice sleeps. One ancestress after another slept there down to our grandmother and our mother and ourselves the children. That is the place of our tribal custom (*muchidi*),[1] where we began, even men just the same, for men are circumcised under a milk-tree.

This text brings our clearly those meanings of the milk-tree which refer to principles and values of social organisation. At one level of abstraction the milk-tree stands for matriliny, the principle on which the continuity of Ndembu society depends. Matriliny governs succession to office and inheritance of property, and it vests dominant rights of residence in local units. More than any other principle of social organisation it confers order and structure on Ndembu social life. But beyond this, *mudyi* means more than matriliny, both according to this text and according to many

152

other statements I have collected. It stands for tribal custom *(muchidi wetu)* itself. The principle of matriliny, vertebral in Ndembu social organisation, as an element in the semantic structure of the milk-tree, itself symbolises the total system of interrelations between groups and persons which makes up Ndembu society. Some of the meanings of important symbols may themselves be symbols, each with its own system of meanings. At its highest level of abstraction, therefore, the milk-tree stands for the unity and continuity of Ndembu society. Both men and women are components of that spatio-temporal continuum. Perhaps that is why one educated Ndembu, trying to cross the gap between our cultures, explained to me that the milk-tree was like the British flag above the administrative headquarters: *'Mudyi* is our flag', he said.

When discussing the milk-tree symbolism in the context of the girl's puberty ritual, informants tend to stress the harmonising, cohesive aspects of the milk-tree symbolism. They also stress the aspect of dependence. The child depends on its mother for nutriment: similarly, say the Ndembu, the tribesman drinks from the breasts of tribal custom. Thus nourishment and learning are equated in the meaning content of the milk-tree. I have often heard the milk-tree compared to 'going to school', the child is said to swallow instruction as a baby swallows milk and *kapudyi*, the thin cassava gruel which Ndembu liken to milk. And do we not ourselves speak of 'a thirst for knowledge'? Here the milk-tree is a shorthand for the process of instruction in tribal matters which follows the critical episode in both boys' and girls' initiation — circumcision in the case of the boys and the long trial of lying motionless in that of the girls. The mother's role is the archetype of protector, nourisher and teacher. For example, a chief is often referred to as the 'mother of his people', while the hunter-doctor who initiates a novice into a hunting cult is called 'the mother of huntsmanship' *(mama dawuyang'a)*. An apprentice circumciser is referred to as 'child of the circumcision medicine' and his instructor as 'mother of the circumcision medicine'. In all the senses hitherto described the milk-tree represents harmonious, benevolent aspects of domestic and tribal life.

But when the third mode of interpretation, contextual

153

analysis, is applied, the interpretations of informants are contradicted by the way people actually behave with reference to the milk-tree. It becomes clear that the milk-tree represents aspects of social differentiation, and even opposition between the components of a society which ideally it is supposed to symbolise as a harmonious whole. The first relevant context we shall examine is the role of the milk-tree in a series of action situations within the framework of the girl's puberty ritual. Symbols, as I have said, produce action, and dominant symbols tend to become focuses of interaction. Groups mobilise around them, worship before them, perform other symbolic activities near them, and add other symbolic objects to them, often to make composite shrines. Usually these groups of participants themselves stand for important components of the secular social system, whether these components consist of corporate groups, such as families and lineages, or of mere categories of persons possessing similar characteristics such as old men, women, children, hunters or widows. In each kind of Ndembu ritual a different group or category becomes the focal social element. In Nkang'a this focal element is the unity of Ndembu women. It is the women who dance around the milk-tree and initiate the recumbent novice by making her the hub of their whirling circle. Not only is the milk-tree the 'flag of the Ndembu'; more specifically, in the early phases of Nkang'a, it is the 'flag' of Ndembu women. In this situation it does more than focus the exclusiveness of women; it mobilises them in opposition to the men. For the women sing songs taunting the men, and for a time will not let men dance in their circle. Therefore, if we are to take account of the operational aspect of the milk-tree symbol, including not only what Ndembu say about it but also what they do with it in its 'meaning', we must allow that it distinguishes women as a social category and indicates their solidarity.

But the milk-tree makes further discriminations. For example, in certain action contexts it stands for the novice herself. One such context is the initial sacralisation of a specific milk-tree sapling. Here the natural property of the tree's immaturity is significant. Informants say that a young tree is chosen because the novice is young. The girl's particular tree symbolises her new social personality as a

154

mature woman. In the past, and occasionally today, the girl's puberty ritual was part of her marriage ritual, and marriage marked her transition from girlhood to womanhood. Much of the training and most of the symbolism of Nkang'a are concerned with making the girl a sexually-accomplished spouse, a fruitful woman and a mother able to produce a generous supply of milk For each girl this is a unique process. She is initiated alone and is the centre of public attention and care. From her point of view it is *her* Nkang'a, the most thrilling and self-gratifying phase of her life. Society recognises and encourages these sentiments, even though it also prescribes certain trials and hardships for the novice, who must suffer before she is glorified on the last day of the ritual. The milk-tree then, celebrates the coming-of-age of the new social personality, and distinguishes her from all other women at this one moment in her life. But, in terms of its action context, the milk-tree here also expresses the conflict between the girl and the moral community of adult women she is entering. Not without reason is the milk-tree site known as 'the place of death' or 'the place of suffering', terms also applied to the site where boys are circumcised, for the girl novice must not move a muscle throughout a whole hot and clamant day.

In other contexts the milk-tree site is the scene of opposition between the novice's own mother and the group of adult women. The mother is debarred from attending the ring of dancers. She is losing her child, although later she recovers her as an adult co-member of her lineage. Here we see the conflict between the matricentric family and the wider society which, as I have said, is dominantly articulated by the principle of matriliny. The relationship between mother and daughter persists throughout the ritual, but its content is changed. It is worth pointing out that, at one phase in Nkang'a, mother and daughter interchange portions of clothing. This may perhaps be related to the Ndembu custom whereby mourners wear small portions of a dead relative's clothing. Whatever the interchange of clothing may mean to a psycho-analyst — and here we arrive at one of the limits of our present anthropological competence — it seems not unlikely that Ndembu intend to symbolise the termination for both mother and daughter of an important

155

aspect of their relationship. This is one of the symbolic actions — one of very few — about which I found it impossible to elicit any interpretation in the puberty ritual. Hence it is legitimate to infer, in my opinion, that powerful unconscious wishes, of a kind considered illicit by Ndembu, are expressed in it. Opposition between the tribeswomen and the novice's mother is mimetically represented at the milk-tree towards the end of the first day of the puberty ritual. The girl's mother cooks a huge meal of cassava and beans — both kinds of food are symbols in Nkang'a with many meanings — for the women visitors, who eat in village groups and not at random. Before eating, the women return to the milk-tree from their eating-place a few yards away and circle the tree in procession. The mother brings up the rear holding up a large spoon full of cassava and beans. Suddenly she shouts: 'Who wants the cassava of *chipwampwilu*?' All the women rush to be first to seize the spoon and eat from it. *Chipwampwilu* appears to be an archaic word and no one knows its meaning. Informants say that the spoon represents the novice herself in her role of married woman, while the food stands both for her reproductive power *(lusemu)* and her role as cultivator and cook. One woman told my wife: 'It is lucky if the person snatching the spoon comes from the novice's own village. Otherwise the mother believes that her child will go far away from her to a distant village and die there. The mother wants her child to stay near her.' Implicit in this statement is a deeper conflict than that between the matricentric family and mature female society. It refers to another dominant articulating principle of Ndembu society, namely virilocal marriage according to which women live at their husbands' villages after marriage. Its effect is sometimes to separate mothers from daughters by considerable distances. In the episode described the women symbolise the matrilineal cores of villages. Each village wishes to gain control through marriage over the novice's capacity to work. Its members also hope that her children will be raised in it, thus adding to its size and prestige. Later in Nkang'a there is a symbolic struggle between the novice's matrilineal kin and those of her bridegroom, which makes explicit the conflict between virilocality and matriliny.

Lastly, in the context of action situations the milk-tree is

156

sometimes described by informants as representing the novice's own matrilineage. Indeed, it has this significance in the competition for the spoon just discussed. For women of her own village try to snatch the spoon before members of other villages. Even if such women do not belong to her matrilineage but are married to its male members they are thought to be acting on its behalf. Thus, the milk-tree in one of its action-aspects represents the unity and exclusiveness of a single matrilineage with a local focus in a village against other such corporate groups. The conflict between yet another subsystem and the total system is given dramatic and symbolic form.

By this time it will have become clear that considerable discrepancy exists between the interpretations of the milk-tree offered by informants and the behaviour exhibited by Ndembu in situations dominated by the milk-tree symbolism. Thus we are told that the milk-tree represents the close tie between mother and daughter. Yet the milk-tree separates a daughter from her mother. We are also told that the milk-tree stands for the unity of Ndembu society. Yet we find that in practice it separates women from men, and some categories and groups of women from others. How are these contradictions between principle and practice to be explained?

Some Problems of Interpretation

I am convinced that my informants genuinely believed that the milk-tree represented only the linking and unifying aspects of Ndembu social organisation. I am equally convinced that the role of the milk-tree in action situations, where it represents a focus of specified groups in opposition to other groups, forms an equally important component of its total meaning. Here the important question must be asked, 'meaning for whom?' For if Ndembu do not recognise the discrepancy between their interpretation of the milk-tree symbolism and their behaviour in connection with it, does this mean that the discrepancy has no relevance for the social anthropologist? Indeed, some anthropologists claim, with Nadel, that 'uncomprehended symbols have no part in social

157

enquiry; their social effectiveness lies in their capacity to indicate, and if they indicate nothing to the actors, they are, from our point of view, irrelevant, and indeed no longer symbols (whatever their significance for the psychologist or psycho-analyst)'.[2] Professor Monica Wilson holds a similar point of view. She writes that she stresses 'Nyakysa interpretations of their own rituals, for anthropological literature is bespattered with symbolic guessing, the ethnographer's interpretations of the rituals of other people'.[3] Indeed, she goes so far as to base her whole analysis of Nyakysa ritual on 'the Nyakyusa translation or interpretation of the symbolism'. In my view, these investigators go beyond the limits of salutary caution and impose serious, and even arbitrary, limitations on themselves. To some extent their difficulties derive from their failure to distinguish the concept of *symbol* from that of a mere *sign*. Although I am in complete disagreement with his fundamental postulate that the collective unconscious is the main formative principle in ritual symbolism, I consider that Carl Jung has cleared the way for further investigation by making just this distinction. 'A sign' he says, 'is an analogous or abbreviated expression of a *known* thing. But a symbol is always the best possible expression of a relatively *unknown* fact, a fact, however, which is none the less recognised or postulated as existing.'[4] Nadel and Wilson, in treating most ritual symbols as signs, must ignore or regard as irrelevant some of the crucial properties of such symbols.

Field Setting and Structural Perspective

How, then, can a social anthropologist justify his claim to be able to interpret a society's ritual symbols more deeply and comprehensively than the actors themselves? In the first place the anthropologist, by the use of his special techniques and concepts, is able to view the performance of a given kind of ritual as 'occurring in, and being interpenetrated by, a totality of coexisting social entities such as various kinds of groups, subgroups, categories, or personalities, and also barriers between them, and modes of interconnexion'.[5] In other words, he can place this ritual in its significant field setting, and describe the structure and properties of that field. On the other hand, each participant in the ritual views it from his own particular corner of observation. He has what Lupton has called his own 'structural perspective'. His vision is circumscribed by his occupancy of a particular position, or even of a set of situationally conflicting positions, both in the persisting structure of his society, and also in the role structure of the given ritual. Moreover, the participant is likely to be governed in his actions by a number of interests, purposes, and sentiments, dependent upon his specific position, which impair his understanding of the total situation. An even more serious obstacle against his achieving objectivity is the fact that he tends to regard as axiomatic and primary the ideals, values and norms which are overtly expressed or symbolised in the ritual. Thus, in the Nkang'a ritual, each person or group in successive contexts of action, sees the milk-tree only as representing her or their own specific interests and values at those times. But the anthropologist who has previously made a structural analysis of Ndembu society, isolating its organisational principles, and distinguishing its groups and relationships, has no particular bias, and can observe the real interconnexions and conflicts between groups and persons, in so far as these receive ritual representation. What is meaningless for an actor playing a specific role may well be highly significant for an observer and analyst of the total system.

On these grounds, therefore, I consider it legitimate to include within the total meaning of a dominant ritual symbol aspects of behaviour associated with it which the actors themselves are unable to interpret, and indeed of which they may be unaware, if they are asked to interpret the symbol outside its activity-context. But there still remains for us the problem of the contradiction between the expressed meanings of the milk-tree symbol and the meaning of the stereotyped forms of behaviour closely associated with it. Indigenous interpretations of the milk-tree symbolism in the abstract appear to indicate that there is no incompatibility or conflict between the persons and groups to which it refers. Yet, as we have seen, it is between just such groups that conflict is mimed at the milk-tree site.

159

But before we can interpret, we must further classify our descriptive data, collected by the methods described above. Such a classification will enable us to state some of the properties of ritual symbols. The simplest property is that of *condensation*. Many things and actions, etc., are represented in a single formation. Secondly, a dominant symbol is a *unification of disparate significata*. The disparate *significata* are interconnected by virtue of their common possession of analogous qualities or by association in fact or thought. Such qualities or links of association may in themselves be quite trivial, or random, or widely distributed over a range of phenomena. Their very generality enables them to bracket together the most diverse ideas and phenomena. Thus, as we have seen, the milk-tree stands for, *inter alia*, women's breasts, motherhood, a novice at Nkang'a, the principle of matriliny, a specific matrilineage, learning, and the unity and persistence of Ndembu society. The themes of nourishment and dependence run through all these diverse *significata*.

The third important property of dominant ritual symbols is *polarisation of meaning*. Not only the milk-tree, but all other dominant Ndembu symbols possess two clearly distinguishable poles of meaning. At one pole is found a cluster of *significata* which refer to components of the moral and social orders of Ndembu society, to principles of social organisation, to kinds of corporate grouping, and to the norms and values inherent in structural relationships. At the other pole, the *significata* are usually natural and physiological phenomena and processes. Let us call the first of these the 'ideological pole', and the second the 'sensory pole'. At the sensory pole, the meaning content is closely related to the outward form of the symbol. Thus one meaning of the milk-tree — breast-milk — is closely related to the exudation of milky latex from the tree. One sensory meaning of another dominant symbol, the *mukula* tree is blood; and this tree secretes a dusky red gum.

At the sensory pole are concentrated those *significata* that may be expected to arouse desires and feelings; at the ideological pole one finds an arrangement of norms and values which guide and control persons as members of social groups

160

and categories. The sensory, emotional *significata* tend to be 'gross' in a double sense. In the first place they are gross in a general way, taking no account of detail, or the precise qualities of emotion. For it cannot be sufficiently stressed that such symbols are social facts, 'collective representations', even though their appeal is to the lowest common denominator of human feeling. The second sense of 'gross' is 'frankly, even flagrantly, physiological'. Thus the milk-tree has the gross meanings of breast-milk, breasts and the process of breast-feeding. These are also gross in the sense that they represent items of universal Ndembu experience. Other Ndembu symbols, at their sensory poles of meaning, represent such themes as blood, male and female genitalia, semen, urine and faeces. The *same* symbols, at their ideological poles of meaning, represent the unity and continuity of social groups, primary and associational, domestic and political.

Reference and Condensation

It has long been recognised in anthropological literature that ritual symbols are stimuli of emotion. Perhaps the most striking statement of this position is that made by Edward Sapir in the *Encyclopaedia of the Social Sciences* (XIV, 492-3 [1930-5]). Sapir distinguishes, in a way which recalls Jung's distinction, between two principal classes of symbols. The first he calls *referential* symbols. These include such forms as oral speech, writing, national flags, flag signalling, and other organisations of symbols which are agreed upon as economical devices for purposes of reference. Like Jung's 'sign', the referential symbol is predominantly cognitive and refers to known facts. The second class, which includes most ritual symbols, consists of *condensation* symbols, which Sapir defines as 'highly condensed forms of substitutive behaviour for direct expression, allowing for the ready release of emotional tension in conscious or unconscious form'. The condensation symbol is 'saturated with emotional quality'. The chief difference in development between these types of symbolism, in Sapir's view, is that 'while referential symbolism grows with formal elaboration in the conscious, condensation

161

symbolism strikes deeper and deeper roots in the unconscious, and diffuses its emotional quality to types of behaviour and situations apparently far removed from the original meaning of the symbol'.

Sapir's formulation is most illuminating. He lays explicit stress on four main attributes of ritual symbols: (1) the condensation of many meanings in a single form; (2) economy of reference; (3) predominance of emotional or orectic quality; (4) associational linkages with regions of the unconscious. But he tends to underestimate the importance of what I have called the ideological (or, I would add, normative) pole of meaning. Ritual symbols are at one and the same time referential and condensation symbols, though each symbol is multi-referential rather than uni-referential. Their essential quality consists in their juxtaposition of the grossly physical and the structurally normative, of the organic and the social. Such symbols are coincidences of opposite qualities, unions of 'high' and 'low'. We do not need a detailed acquaintance with any of the current depth-psychologies to suspect that this juxtaposition, and even interpenetration, of opposites in the symbol is connected with its social function. Durkheim was fascinated by the problem of why many social norms and imperatives were felt to be at the same time 'obligatory' and 'desirable'. Ritual, scholars are coming to see, is precisely a mechanism which periodically converts the obligatory into the desirable. The basic unit of ritual, the dominant symbol, incapsulates the major properties of the total ritual process which brings about this transmutation. Within its framework of meanings, the dominant symbol brings the ethical and jural norms of society into close contact with strong emotional stimuli. In the action situation of ritual, with its social excitement and directly physiological stimuli, such as music, singing, dancing, alcohol, incense, and bizarre modes of dress, the ritual symbol, we may perhaps say effects an interchange of qualities between its poles of meaning. Norms and values, on the one hand, become saturated with emotion, while the gross and basic emotions become ennobled through contact with social values. The irksomeness of moral constraint is transformed into the 'love of virtue'.

Before proceeding any further with our analysis, it might

be as well to restate the major empirical properties of dominant symbols derived from our classification of the relevant descriptive data: (1) condensation; (2) unification of disparate meanings in a single symbolic formation; (3) polarisation of meaning.

Dominant and Instrumental Symbols

Certain ritual symbols, as I have said, are regarded by Ndembu as 'dominant'. In rituals performed to propitiate ancestor spirits who are believed to have afflicted their living kin with reproductive disorders, illness, or bad luck at hunting, there are two main classes of dominant symbols. The first class is represented by the first tree or plant in a series of trees or plants from which portions of leaves, bark or roots are collected by practitioners or adepts in the curative cult. The subjects of ritual are marked with these portions mixed with water, or given them, mixed in a potion, to drink. The first tree so treated is called the 'place of greeting' *(ishikenu)*, or the 'elder' *(mukulumpi)*. The adepts encircle it several times to sacralise it. Then the senior practitioner prays at its base, which he sprinkles with powdered white clay. Prayer is made either to the named spirit, believed to be afflicting the principal subject of ritual, or to the tree itself, which is in some way identified with the afflicting spirit. Each *ishikenu* can be allotted several meanings by adepts. The second class of dominant symbols in curative rituals consists of shrines where the subjects of such rituals sit while the practitioners wash them with vegetable substances mixed with water and perform actions on their behalf of a symbolic or ritualistic nature. Such shrines are often composite, consisting of several objects in configuration. Both classes of dominant symbols are closely associated with non-empirical beings. Some are regarded as their repositories; others, as being identified with them; others again, as representing them. In life-crisis rituals, on the other hand, dominant symbols seem to represent not beings but non-empirical powers or kinds of efficacy. For example, in the boys' circumcision ritual, the dominant symbol for the

163

whole ritual is a 'medicine' *(vitumbu)*, called *nfunda,* which is compounded from many ingredients, e.g., the ash of the burnt lodge which means 'death', and the urine of an apprentice circumciser which means 'virility'. Each of these and other ingredients has many other meanings. The dominant symbol at the camp where the novices' parents assemble and prepare food for the boys is the *chikoli* tree, which represents, among other things, an erect phallus, adult masculinity, strength, hunting prowess, and health continuing into old age. The dominant symbol during the process of circumcision is the milk-tre, beneath which novices are circumcised. The dominant symbol in the immediate post-circumcision phase is the red *mukula* tree, on which the novices sit until their wounds stop bleeding. Other symbols are dominant at various phases of seclusion. Each of these symbols is described as *mukulumpi* ('elder', 'senior'). Dominant symbols appear in many different ritual contexts, sometimes presiding over the whole procedure, sometimes over particular phases. The meaning-content of certain dominant symbols possesses a high degree of constancy and consistency throughout the total symbolic system, exemplifying Radcliffe-Brown's proposition that a symbol recurring in a cycle of rituals likely to have the same significance in each. Such symbols also possess considerable autonomy with regard to the aims of the rituals in which they appear. Precisely because of these properties, dominant symbols are readily analysable in a cultural framework of reference. They may be regarded for this purpose as what Whitehead would have called 'eternal objects'.[6] They are the relatively fixed points in both the social and cultural structures, and indeed constitute points of junction between these two kinds of structure. They may be regarded irrespective of their order of appearance in a given ritual, as ends in themselves, as representative of the axiomatic values of the widest Ndembu society. This does not mean that they cannot also be studied, as we have indeed studied them, as factors of social action, in an action frame of reference. But their social properties make them more appropriate objects of morphological study than the class of symbols we will now consider.

These symbols may be termed 'instrumental symbols'. An

164

instrumental symbol must be seen in terms of its wider context, i.e. in terms of the total system of symbols which makes up a given kind of ritual. Each kind of ritual has its specific mode of interrelating symbols. This mode is often dependent upon the ostensible purposes of that kind of ritual. In other words, each ritual has its own teleology. It has its explicitly expressed goals, and instrumental symbols may be regarded as means of attaining those goals. For example, in rituals performed for the overt purpose of making women fruitful, among the instrumental symbols used are portions of fruit-bearing trees, or of trees which possess innumerable rootlets. These fruits and rootlets are said by Ndembu to represent children. They are also thought of as having efficacy to make the woman fruitful. They are means to the main end of the ritual. Perhaps such symbols could be regarded as mere signs or referential symbols, were it not for the fact that the meanings of each are associated with powerful conscious and unconscious emotions and wishes. At the psychological level of analysis, I suspect that these symbols too would approximate to the condition of condensation symbols. But here we touch upon the present limits of competence of anthropological explanation, a problem which we will shortly discuss more fully.

The Limits of Anthropological Interpretation

We now come to the most difficult aspect of the scientific study of ritual symbolism: analysis. How far can we interpret these enigmatic formations by the use of anthropological concepts? At what points do we reach the frontiers of our explanatory competence? Let us first consider the case of dominant symbols. I have suggested that these have two poles of meaning, and sensory and an ideological pole. I have also suggested that dominant symbols have the property of unifying disparate *significata*. I would go so far as to say that at *both* poles of meaning are clustered disparate and even contradictory *significata*. In the course of its historical development, anthropology has acquired techniques and concepts which enable it to handle fairly adequately the kind of data which we have classified as falling around the

165

ideological pole. Such data, as we have seen, include components of social structure, and cultural phenomena, both ideological and technological. I believe that study of these data in terms of the concepts of three major sub-divisions of anthropology, cultural anthropology, structuralist theory and social dynamics, would be extremely rewarding. I shall shortly outline how I think such analyses might be done, and how the three frameworks might be interrelated. But first we must ask, how far and in what respects is it relevant to submit the sensory pole of meaning to intensive analysis, and, more importantly, how far are we, as anthropologists, qualified to do so? For it is evident, as Sapir has stated, that ritual symbols, like all condensation symbols, 'strike deeper and deeper roots in the unconscious'. Even a brief acquaintance with depth-psychology is enough to show the investigator that ritual symbols, with regard to their outward form, to their behavioural context, and to several of the indigenous interpretations set upon them, are partially shaped under the influence of unconscious motivations and ideas. The interchange of clothes between mother and daughter at the Nkang'a ritual; the belief that a novice would go mad if she saw the milk-tree on the day of her separation ritual; the belief that if a novice lifts up the blanket with which she is covered during seclusion, and sees her village, her mother would die: all these are items of symbolic behaviour for which the Ndembu themselves can give no satisfactory interpretation. For these beliefs suggest an element of mutual hostility in the mother–daughter relationship which runs clean counter to orthodox interpret-ations of the milk-tree symbolism, in so far as it refers to the mother–daughter relationship. One of the main character-istics of ideological interpretations is that they tend to stress the harmonious and cohesive aspect of social relationships. The exegetic idiom feigns that persons and groups always act in accordance with the ideal norms of Ndembu society.

Depth Psychology and Ritual Symbolism

When psycho-analysts like Theodore Reik, Ernest Jones or Bruno Bettelheim analyse the ritual symbolism of primitive
166

and ancient society, they tend to regard as irrelevant the ideological pole of meaning, and to focus their attention on the outward form and sensory meanings of the symbols. They regard most indigenous interpretations of symbols, which form the main component of the ideological pole, almost as though they were identical with the rationalisations by which neurotics explain and justify their aberrant behaviour. Furthermore, they tend to look upon ritual symbols as identical with neurotic and psychotic symptoms or as though they had the same properties as the dream symbols of Western European individuals. In effect, their procedure is the exact reverse of that of the social anthropologists who share the views of Nadel and Wilson. This school of anthropologists, it will be remembered, considers that *only* conscious, verbalised, indigenous interpretations of symbols are sociologically relevant. The method of the psycho-analysts, on the other hand, is to examine the form, content and mode of interconnection of the symbolic acts and objects described by ethnographers, and to interpret these by means of concepts formulated in Western European clinical practice. Such psycho-analysts claim to recognise, in the structure and action-context of ritual symbols, material derived from what they consider to be the universal experiences of human infancy in the family situation. For example, Fenichel states that two contrary psychic tendencies exist universally in the father—son relationship, i.e., submission and rebellion, and that both derive from the Oedipus complex. He then goes on to argue that

> since most patriarchal religions also veer between submission to a paternal figure, and rebellion (both submission and rebellion being sexualised), and every god, like a compulsive super-ego, promises protection on condition of submission, there are many similarities in the manifest picture of compulsive ceremonials and religious rituals, due to the similarity of the underlying conflicts.[7]

As against this point of view, we have already shown how the successive symbolic acts of many Ndembu rituals are given order and structure by the explicitly stated purposes of those rituals. We do not need to invoke the notion of underlying

167

conflicts to account for their conspicuous regularity. Psycho-analysts might argue that in patriarchal societies ritual might exhibit a greater rigidity and compulsive quality than among the Ndembu, who are matrilineal. In other words, the formal pattern might be 'over-determined' by the unconscious father—son conflict. But ethnographic comparison would seem to refute this view, for the most rigid formalism known to students of comparative religion is found among the Pueblo Indians, who are more strongly matrilineal than the Ndembu, while the Nigerian Nupe, a strongly patrilineal society, possess rituals with a 'fluid' and 'not over-strict' form.[8]

Other psycho-analysts profess to find in symbolic forms traces of 'orally aggressive', 'orally dependent', 'anal-sadistic' and 'masochistic' ideas and drives. Indeed, several anthro-pologists, after reading psycho-analytical literature, have been tempted to 'explain' ritual phenomena in this way.

Perhaps the most spectacular recent attempt to make a comprehensive interpretation of ritual symbolism by using psycho-analytical concepts is Bruno Bettelheim's book *Symbolic Wounds*. Bettelheim, after observing the behaviour of four schizoid adolescent children, who formed a secret society, considered that in this behaviour lay the clue to an understanding of many features of primitive initiation ritual. From his schizoids, he inferred that one of the (unconscious) purposes of male initiation rites may be to assert that men too can bear children, and that 'through such operations as subincision men may try to acquire sexual apparatus and functions equal to women's'.[9] Womb-envy, and an unconscious infantile identification with the mother, in Bettelheim's opinion, were powerful formative factors, both in the *ad hoc* ritual of his four schizoids, and in male circumcision rituals all over the world.

Bettelheim's veiwpoint is in important respects opposed to that of many orthodox Freudians, who hold that the symbolic events comprising these rituals result principally from the fathers' jealousy of their sons, and that their purpose is to create sexual (castration) anxiety and to make the incest taboo secure. Where psycho-analysts disagree, by what criterion can the hapless social anthropologist judge between their interpretations, in a field of inquiry in which

168

he has neither received systematic training nor obtained thorough practical experience?

Provinces of Explanation

I consider that if we conceptualise a dominant symbol as having two poles of meaning, we can more exactly demarcate the limits within which anthropological analysis may be fruitfully applied. Psycho-analysts, in treating most indigenous interpretations of symbols as irrelevant, are guilty of a naïve and one-sided approach. For those interpretations which show how a dominant symbol expresses important components of the social and moral orders are by no means equivalent to the 'rationalisations', and the 'secondary elaborations' of material deriving from endopsychic conflicts. They refer to social facts which have an empirical reality exterior to the psyches of individuals. On the other hand, those anthropologists who regard only indigenous interpretations as relevant are being equally one-sided. This is because they tend to examine symbols within two analytical frameworks only, the cultural and the structural. This approach is essentially a static one, and it does not deal with processes involving temporal changes in social relations.

But the crucial properties of a ritual symbol involve these dynamic developments. Symbols instigate social action. In a field context they may even be described as 'forces' in that they are determinable influences inclining persons and groups to action. It is in a field context, moreover, that the properties we have described, namely, polarisation of meanings, transference of affectual quality, discrepancy between meanings, and condensation of meanings, become most significant. The symbol as a unit of action, possessing these properties, becomes an object of study both for anthropology and for psychology. Both disciplines, in so far as they are concerned with human actions, must conceptualise the ritual symbol in the same way.

The techniques and concepts of the anthropologist enable him to analyse competently the interrelations between the data associated with the ideological pole of meaning. They also enable him to analyse the social behaviour directed upon the total dominant symbol. But he cannot, with his present skills, discriminate between the *precise sources* of unconscious feeling and wishing, which shape much of the outward form of the symbol; select some natural objects rather than others to serve as symbols; and account for certain aspects of the behaviour associated with symbols. For him, it is enough that the symbol should evoke 'emotion'. He is interested in the fact that emotion is evoked and not in the specific qualities of its constituents. He may indeed find it situationally relevant for his analysis to distinguish whether the emotion evoked by a specific symbol possesses the gross character, say, of aggression, fear, friendliness, anxiety or sexual pleasure. But he need go no further than this. For him the ritual symbol is primarily a factor in *group* dynamics, and as such its references to the groups, relationships, values, norms and beliefs of a society are his principal items of study. In other words, the anthropologist treats the sensory pole of meaning as a constant, and the social and ideological aspects as variables whose interdependencies he seeks to explain.

The psycho-analyst, on the other hand, must, I think, attach greater significance than he now does to social factors in the analysis of ritual symbolism. He must cease to regard interpretations, beliefs and dogmas as mere rationalisations when, often enough, these refer to social and natural realities. For, as Durkheim wrote, 'primitive religions hold to reality and express it. One must learn to go underneath the symbol to the reality which it represents and which gives it its meaning. No religions are false, all answer, though in different ways, to the given conditions of human existence.'[10] Among those given conditions, the arrangement of society into structured groupings, discrepancies between the principles which organise these groupings, economic collaboration and competition, schism within groups and opposition between groups — in short, all those things which th social aspect of ritual symbolism is concerned — are surely of at least equal importance with biopsychical drives and early conditioning in the elementary family. After all, the ritual symbol has, in common with the dream symbol, the characteristic, discovered by Freud, of being a compromise-formation between two main opposing tendencies. It is a

170

compromise between the need for social control, and certain innate and universal human drives whose complete gratification would result in a breakdown of that control. Ritual symbols refer to what is normative, general and characteristic of unique individuals. Thus Ndembu symbols refer, among other things, to the basic needs of social existence (hunting, agriculture, female fertility, favourable climatic conditions, and so forth), and to shared values on which communal life depends (generosity, comradeship, respect for elders, the importance of kinship, hospitality, and the like). In distinguishing between ritual symbols and individual psychic symbols, we may perhaps say that while ritual symbols are gross means of handling social and natural reality, psychic symbols are dominantly fashioned under the influence of inner drives. In analysing the former, attention must mainly be paid to relations between data external to the psyche; in analysing the latter, to endopsychic data.

For this reason, the study of ritual symbolism falls more within the province of the social anthropologist than that of the psychologist or psycho-analyst, although the latter can assist the anthropologist by examining the nature and interconnections of the data clustered at the sensory pole of ritual symbolism. He can also, I believe, illuminate certain aspects of the stereotyped behaviour associated with symbols in field contexts, which the actors themselves are unable to explain. For, as we have seen, much of this behaviour is suggestive of attitudes which differ radically from those deemed appropriate in terms of traditional exegesis. And indeed certain conflicts would appear to be so basic that they totally block exegesis.

The Interpretation of Observed Emotions

But can we really say that behaviour portraying conflict between persons and groups, who are represented by the symbols themselves as being in harmony, is in the full Freudian sense *unconscious* behaviour? For the Ndembu themselves in many situations outside Nkang'a, both secular and ritual, are perfectly aware of and ready to speak about hostility in the relationships between particular mothers and daughters, between particular sub-lineages, and between particular young girls and the adult women in their villages. It is rather as though there existed in certain precisely defined public situations, usually of a ritual or ceremonial type, a norm obstructing the verbal statement of conflicts in any way connected with the principle and rules celebrated or dramatised in those situations. Evidences of human passion and frailty are just not spoken about when the occasion is given up to the public commemorations, and reanimation, of norms and values in their abstract purity.

Yet, as we have seen, recurrent kinds of conflict may be *acted* out in the ritual or ceremonial form. For on great ritual occasions common practice, as well as highest principle, receives its symbolic or stereotyped expression. But practice, which is dominantly under the sway of what all societies consider man's 'lower nature', is rife with expression of conflict. Selfish and factional interests, oath-breaking, disloyalty, sins of omission as well as sins of commission, pollute and disfigure those ideal prototypes of behaviour which in precept, prayer, formula and symbol are held up before the ritual assembly for its exclusive attention. In the orthodox interpretation of ritual it is pretended that common practice has no efficacy and that men and women really are as the ideally should be. Yet, as I have argued above, the 'energy' required to reanimate the values and norms enshrined in dominant symbols and expressed in various kinds of verbal behaviour is 'borrowed', to speak metaphorically in lieu at the moment of a more rigorous language, from the miming of well-known and normally mentionable conflicts. The raw energies of conflict are domesticated into the service of social order.

I should say here that I believe it possible, and indeed necessary, to analyse symbols in a context of observed emotions. If the investigator is well acquainted with the common idiom in which a society expresses such emotions as friendship, love, hate, joy, sorrow, contentment and fear, he cannot fail to observe that these are experienced in ritual situations. Thus in Nkang'a, when the women laugh and jeer at the men, tease the novice and her mother, fight one another for the 'porridge of *chipwampwilu*', and so on, the observer can hardly doubt that emotions are really aroused in

172

the actors as well as formally represented by ritual custom. ('What's Hecuba to him or he to Hecuba, that he should weep for her?')

These emotions are portrayed and evoked in close relation with the dominant symbols of tribal cohesion and continuity, often by the performance of instrumentally symbolic behaviour. But since they are often associated with the mimesis of inter-personal and inter-group conflict such emotions and acts of behaviour obtain no place among the official, verbal meanings attributed to such dominant symbols.

The Situational Suppression of Conflict from Interpretation

Emotion and praxis, indeed, give life and colouring to the values and norms: but the connection between the behavioural expression of conflict and the normative components of each kind of ritual, and of its dominant symbols, is seldom explicitly formulated by believing actors. Only if one were to personify a society, regarding it as some kind of supra-individual entity, could one speak of 'unconsciousness' here. Each individual participant in the Nkang'a ritual is well aware that kin quarrel most bitterly over rights and obligations conferred by the principle of matriliny. But that awareness is situationally held back from verbal expression: the participants must behave *as if* conflicts generated by matriliny were irrelevant.

This does not mean, as Nadel considers, that what is not verbalised is *in fact* irrelevant either to the participants or to the anthropologist. On the contrary, in so far as the anthropologist considers problems of social action to fall within his purview, the suppression from speech of what might be termed 'the behavioural meaning' of certain dominant symbols is highly relevant. The fact is that any kind of coherent, organised social life would be impossible without the assumption that certain values and norms, imperatives and prohibitions, are axiomatic in character, ultimately binding on everyone. But for many reasons, the axiomatic quality of these norms is difficult to maintain in practice,

173

since the endless variety of real situations norms considered equally valid in abstraction are frequently found to be inconsistent with one another, and even mutually to conflict.

Furthermore, social norms, by their very nature, impose unnatural constraints on those whose biopsychical dispositions impel them to supranormal or abnormal behaviour, either fitfully or regularly. Social life in all organised groups appears to exhibit a cyclicality or oscillation between periods when one set of axiomatic norms are observed and periods when they give way to the dominance of another set. Thus since different norms govern different aspects of sectors of social behaviour, and, more importantly, since the sectors overlap and interpenetrate in reality, causing norm-conflict, the validity of several major norms has to be reaffirmed in isolation from others, and outside the contexts in which struggles and conflicts arise in connection with them. This is why one so often finds in ritual that dogmatic and symbolic emphasis is laid on a single norm or on a cluster of closely, and on the whole harmoniously, interrelated norms in a single kind of ritual.

And yet, since at major gatherings of this sort people assemble not as aggregates of individuals but as social personalities arrayed and organised by many principles and norms of grouping, it is by no means a simple matter to assert the clear situational paramountcy of the norms to be commemorated and extolled. Thus, in the Ndembu boys' circumcision ritual, relationships between social categories, such as men and women, old men and young men, circumcised and uncircumcised, and the norms governing such relationships, are given formal representation. But the members of the ritual assembly come as members of corporate groups, such as villages and lineages, which in secular life are in rivalry with one another. That this rivalry is not mysteriously and wonderfully dispelled by the circumcision ritual becomes abundantly clear from the number of quarrels and fights that can be observed during public dances and beer drinks in the intervals between phases of the ritual proper. Here people quarrel as members of groupings which are not recognised in the formal structure of the ritual.

It may be said that any major ritual which stresses the importance of a single principle of social organisation only does so by blocking the expression of other important principles. Sometimes the submerged principles, and the norms and customs through which they become effective, are given veiled and disguised representation in the symbolic pattern of the ritual: sometimes, as in the boys' circumcision ritual, they break through to expression in the spatial and temporal interstices of the procedure. In this essay we are concerned principally with the effects of the suppression on the meaning-structure of dominant symbols.

For example, in the frequently performed Nkula ritual, the dominant symbols are a cluster of red objects, notably red clay (*mukundu*) and the *mukula* tree mentioned previously. In the context of Nkula, both of these are said to represent menstrual blood, and the 'blood of birth', which is the blood that accompanies the birth of a child. The ostensible goal of the ritual is to coagulate the patient's menstrual blood, which has been flowing away in menorrhagia, around the foetus in order to nourish it. A series of symbolic acts are performed to attain this end. For example, a young *mukula* tree is cut down by male doctors and part of it carved into the shape of a baby, which is then inserted into a round calabash medicated with the blood of a sacrificed cock, with red clay and with a number of other 'red' ingredients. The red medicines here, say the Ndembu, represent wished-for coagulation of the patient's menstrual blood, and the calabash is a symbolic womb. At the ideological pole of meaning, the *mukula* tree and the medicated calabash both represent (as the milk-tree does) the patient's matrilineage and, at a higher level of abstraction, the principle of matriliny itself. This is also consistent with the fact that *ivumu*, the term for 'womb', also means 'matrilineage'. In this symbolism the procreative, rather than the nutritive, aspect of motherhood is stressed. But Ndembu red symbolism, unlike the white symbolism of which the milk-tree symbolism is a species, nearly always has explicit reference to violence, to killing, and, at its most general level of meaning, to breach, both in the social and natural orders. Although informants, when discussing this Nkula ritual specifically, tend to stress the positive, feminine aspects of parturition and reproduction, other meanings of the red symbols, stated explicitly in other ritual contexts, can be shown to make their

175

influence felt in Nakula. For example, both red clay and the *mukula* tree are dominant symbols in the hunter's cult, where they mean the blood of animals, the red meat of game, the inheritance through either parent of hunting prowess, and the unity of all initiated hunters. It also stands for the hunter's power to kill. The same red symbols, in the context of the Wubanji ritual performed to purify a man who has killed a kinsman, or a lion or leopard (animals which are believed to be reincarnated hunter kin of the living), represent the blood of homicide. Again, in the boys' circumcision ritual, these symbols stand for the blood of circumcised boys. More seriously still, in divination and in anti-witchcraft rituals, they stand for the blood of witches' victims that is exposed in necrophagous feasts.

Most of these meanings are implicit in Nkula. For example, the female patient, dressed in skins like a male hunter, and carrying a bow and arrow, at one phase of the ritual performs a special hunter's dance. Moreover, while she does this, she wears in her hair, just above the brow, the red feather of a lourie bird. Only shedders of blood, such as hunters, man-slayers and circumcisers, are customarily entitled to wear this feather. Again, after the patient has been given the baby figurine in its symbolic womb, she dances with it in a style of dancing peculiar to circumcisers when they brandish aloft the great *nfunda* medicine of the circumcision lodge. Why then is the woman patient identified with male bloodspillers? The field context of these symbolic objects and items of behaviour suggests that the Ndembu feel that the woman, in wasting her menstrual blood and in failing to bear children, is actively renouncing her expected role as a mature married female. She is behaving like a male killer, not like a female nourisher. The situation is analogous, though modified by matriliny, to the following pronouncement in the ancient Jewish Code of Qaro: 'Every man is bound to marry a wife in order to beget children, and he who fails of this duty is as one who sheds blood.'

One does not need to be a psycho-analyst, one only needs sound sociological training, acquaintance with the total Ndembu symbolic system, plus ordinary common sense, to see that one of the aims of the ritual is to make the woman accept her lot in life as a child-bearer and rearer of children

176

for her lineage. The symbolism suggests that the patient is unconsciously rejecting her female role, that indeed she is guilty: indeed, *mbayi*, one term for menstrual blood, is etymologically connected with *ku-baya* (to be guilty). I have not time here to present further evidence of symbols and interpretations, both in Nkula and in cognate rituals, which reinforce this explanation. In the situation of Nkula, the dominant princples celebrated and reanimated are those of matriliny, the mother—child bond, and tribal continuity through matriliny. The norms in which these are expressed are those governing the behaviour of mature women, which ascribed to them the role appropriate to their sex. The suppressed or submerged principles and norms, in this situation, concern and control the personal and corporate behaviour deemed appropriate for men.

The analysis of Nkula symbolism throws into relief another major function of ritual. Ritual adapts and periodically re-adapts the biopsychical individual to the basic conditions and axiomatic values of human social life. In redressive rituals, the category to which Nkula belongs, the eternally rebellious individual is converted for a while into a loyal citizen. In the case of Nkula, a female individual whose behaviour is felt to demonstrate her rebellion against, or at least her reluctance to comply with, the biological and social life-patterns of her sex, is both induced and coerced by means of precept and symbol to accept her culturally pre-scribed destiny.

Modes of Inference in Interpretation

Each kind of Ndembu ritual, like Nkula, has several meanings and goals which are not made explicit by informants, but must be inferred by the investigator from the symbolic pattern and from behaviour. He is able to make these inferences only if he has previously examined the symbolic configurations, and the meanings attributed to their component symbols by skilled informants, of many other kinds of ritual in the same total system. In other words, he must examine symbols not only in the context of each specific kind of ritual, but in the *context of the total system*.

177

He may even find it profitable, where the same symbol is found throughout a wide culture area, to study its changes of meaning in different societies in that area.

There are two main types of contexts, irrespective of size. There is the action-field context, which we have discussed at some length. There is also the cultural context in which symbols are regarded as clusters of abstract meanings. By comparing the different kinds and sizes of contexts in which a dominant symbol occurs, we can often see that the meanings, 'officially' attributed to it in a particular kind of ritual may be mutually consistent. But there may be much discrepancy and even contradiction between many of the meanings given by informants, when this dominant symbol is regarded as a unit of the total symbolic system. I do not believe that this discrepancy is the result of mere carelessness and ignorance, or variously distributed pieces of insight. I believe that discrepancy between *significata* is a quintessential property of the great symbolic dominants in all religions. Such symbols come in the process of time to absorb into their meaning-content most of the major aspects of human social life, so that, in a sense, they come to represent 'human society' itself. In each ritual they assert the situational primacy of a single aspect or a few aspects only, but by their mere presence they suffuse those aspects with the awe that can only be inspired by the human total. All the contradictions of human social life, between norms and drives, between different drives and between different norms, between society and the individual, and between groups, are condensed and unified in a single representation, the dominant symbols. It is the task of analysis to break down this amalgam into its primary constituents.

The Relativity of 'Depth'

Perhaps this can best be done within different analytical frameworks. I was formerly in favour of talking about 'different levels of analysis', but the term 'level' contains an implication of depth which I now find misleading, unless we can agree to take 'level' to mean any class of abstraction whatsoever. The question of the relative depth of different

178

ways of interpreting symbols is still very much under dispute. For example, psycho-analysts assert that their interpretations of ritual symbols are 'deeper' than those of social anthropologists. On the other hand, anthropologists like Monica Wilson hold that at their 'deepest level' rituals reveal values, which are socio-cultural facts.

I have suggested in this essay that different aspects of ritual symbolism can be analysed within the framework of structuralist theory and of cultural anthropology respectively. As I have said, this would be to treat ritual symbols as timeless entities. Many useful conclusions can be arrived at by these methods. But the essential nature, both of dominant symbols and of constellations of instrumental symbols, is that they are dynamic factors. Static analysis would here presuppose a corpse, and, as Jung says, 'a symbol is alive'. It is alive only in so far as it is 'pregnant with meaning' for men and women, who interact by observing, transgressing and manipulating for private ends the norms and values which the symbol expresses. If the ritual symbol is conceptualised as a force in a field of social action, its critical properties of condensation, polarisation, and unification of disparities become intelligible and explicable. On the other hand conceptualising the symbol as if it were an object, and neglecting its role in action, often lead to a stress on only those aspects of symbolism which can be logically and consistently related to one another to form an abstract unitary system. In a field situation, the unity of a symbol or a symbolic configuration appears as the resultant of many tendencies converging towards one another from different areas of biopsychical and social existence. The symbol is an independent force which is itself a product of many opposed forces.

Conclusion: The Analysis of Symbols in Social Processes

Let me briefly outline the way in which I think ritual symbols may fruitfully be analysed. Performances of ritual are phases in broad social processes, the span and complexity of which are roughly proportional to the size and degree of differentiation of the groups in which they occur. One class

179

of ritual is situated near the apex of a whole hierarchy of redressive and regulative institutions which correct deflections and deviations from customarily prescribed behaviour. Another class anticipates deviations and conflicts. This class includes periodic rituals and life-crises rituals. Each kind of ritual is a patterned process in time, the units of which are symbolic objects and serialised items of symbolic behaviour.

The symbolic constituents may themselves be classed into structural elements, or 'dominant symbols', which tend to be ends in themselves, and variable elements, or 'instrumental symbols', which serve as means to the explicit or implicit goals of the given ritual. In order to give an adequate explanation of the meaning of a particular symbol it is necessary first to examine the widest action-field context, that, namely, in which the ritual itself is simply a phase. Here one must consider what kinds of circumstances give rise to a performance of ritual, whether these are concerned with natural phenomena, economic and technological processes, human life-crises, or with the breach of crucial social relationships. The circumstances will probably determine what sort of ritual is performed. The goals of the ritual will have overt and implicit reference to the antecedent circumstances and will in turn help to determine the meaning of the symbols. Symbols must now be examined within the context of the specific ritual. It is here that we enlist the aid of indigenous informants. It is here also that we may be able to speak legitimately of 'levels' of interpretation, for laymen will give the investigator simple and exoteric meanings, while specialists will give him esoteric explanations and more elaborate texts. Next, behaviour directed towards each symbol should be noted, for such behaviour is an important component of its total meaning.

We are now in a position to exhibit the ritual as a system of meanings. But this system acquires additional richness and depth if it is regarded as itself constituting a sector of the Ndembu ritual system, as interpreted by informants and as observed in action. It is in comparison with other sectors of the total system, and by reference to the dominant articulating principles of the total system, that we often become aware that the overt and ostensible aims and purposes of a

180

given ritual conceal unavowed, and even 'unconscious', wishes and goals. We also become aware that a complex relationship exists between the overt and the submerged, and the manifest and latent patterns of meaning. As social anthropologists we are potentially capable of analysing the social aspect of this relationship. We can examine, for example, the relations of dependence and independence between the total society and its parts, and the relations between kinds of parts, and between different parts of the same kind. We can see how the same dominant symbol, which in one kind of ritual stands for one kind of social group, or for one principle of organisation, in another kind of ritual stands for another kind of group or principle, and in its aggregate of meanings stands for unity and continuity of the widest Ndembu society, embracing its contradictions.

The Limits of Contemporary Anthropological Competence

But our analysis must needs be incomplete when we consider the relationship between the normative elements in social life and the individual. For this relationship, too, finds its way into the meaning of ritual symbols. Here we come to the confines of our present anthropological competence, for we are now dealing with the structure and properties of psyches, a scientific field traditionally studied by other disciplines than ours. At one end of the symbol's spectrum of meanings we encounter the individual psychologist and the social psychologist, and even beyond them (if one may make a friendly tilt at an envied friend), brandishing his Medusa's head, the psycho-analyst, ready to turn to stone the foolhardy interloper into his caverns of terminology.

We shudder back thankfully into the light of social day. Here the significant elements of a symbol's meaning are related to what it does, and what is done to it by and for whom. And these aspects can only be understood if one takes into account from the beginning, and represents by appropriate theoretical constructs, the total field situation in which the symbol occurs. This situation would include the structure of the group which performs the ritual we observe,

181

its basic organising principles and perdurable relationships, and, in addition, its extant division into transient alliances and factions on the basis of immediate interest and ambitions. For both abiding structure and recurrent forms of conflict and selfish interest are stereotyped in ritual symbolism. Once we have collected informants' interpretations of a given symbol, our work of analysis has indeed just begun. We must gradually approximate to the action-meaning of our symbol by way of what Lewin calls 'a stepwise increasing specificity'[11] from widest to narrowest significant action-context. Informants' 'meanings' only become meaningful as objects of scientific study in the course of this analytical process.

NOTES

1. 'Muchidi' also means 'category', 'kind', 'species', and 'tribe' itself.
2. S. F. Nadel, 'Nupe Religion' (1954) p. 108.
3. M. Wilson, 'Rituals of Kinship among the Nyakyusa' (1957) p. 6.
4. C. G. Jung, 'Psychological Types' (1949) p. 601.
5. Lewin, 'Field Theory in Social Science', p. 200.
6. I.e. objects not of indefinite duration but to which the category of time is not applicable.
7. O. Fenichel, 'The Psychoanalytic Theory of Neuroses' (1949) p. 302.
8. Nadel, 'Nupe Religion' (1954) p. 101. Nadel writes: 'We might call the very fluidity of the formalism part of the typical form of Nupe ritual.'
9. B. Bettelheim, 'Symbolic Wounds: Puberty Rites and the Envious Male' (1954) pp. 105-23.
10. E. Durkheim, 'Elementary Forms of Religious Life' (1954) pp. 2-3.
11. Lewin, 'Field Theory in Social Science', p. 149.

9 Telstar and the Aborigines or *La pensee sauvage**

Edmund Leach

Lévi-Strauss's book is like a Chinese puzzle box in which a number of bits of wood of seemingly random and eccentric shape can with ingenuity and patience be fitted together to form a perfect cube. Turn the whole thing upside down; the total shape is the same but the combination seems quite different. I have now read *La pensée sauvage* from beginning to end at least three times and on each occasion I have obtained a very different impression of how it all fits together. It all depends on what you take to be the leading theme. In this essay I am writing with the prejudices of an English social anthropologist and it could be that, from the author's point of view, I have altogether missed the point. The considerable section of the final chapter which is taken up with a commentary upon Jean-Paul Sartre's *Critique de la raison dialectique* is certainly quite outside my comprehension.

I will start with two quotations. The first comes from an article published in 1917, in which A. L. Kroeber reaffirmed his scepticism as to whether the category systems implicit in kinship terminologies could be expected to 'make sense' in terms of the wider social system. To clinch his argument Kroeber used the following linguistic analogy:

We have in English the curious habit of designating an oyster or a lobster as a 'shell fish'. The word 'fish' unquestionably calls up a concept of a smooth elongated free-swimming water animal with fins. The only conceivable reason why a flat and sessile mollusk without any of the appendages of a fish or a legged and crawling animal of utterly different appearance should be brought in terminology into the class of fishes is the fact that they

* English version of 'Telstar et les Aborigènes ou "La pensée sauvage" ', 'Annales (Economies, Sociétés, Civilisations', Nov.-Dec. 1964).

both live in the water and are edible. Now these two qualities are only a small part of those which attach to the generic concept that the word 'fish' carries in English; and yet the wide discrepancy has not prevented the inclusion of the other two animals under the term. All speech is full of just such examples, and no one dreams of explaining the multitudinous phenomena of this kind by reference to social institutions, former philosophies, or other formulated manifestations of non-linguistic life, or of reconstructing the whole of a society from a vocabulary (Kroeber, 1917, p. 391)

One way of describing the subject matter of *La pensée sauvage* would be to say that Lévi-Strauss is setting out to do precisely that which Kroeber held to be absurd.

My second quotation comes from Professor Gilbert Ryle's *Concept of Mind* (1949):

This trick of talking to oneself in silence is acquired neither quickly nor without effort: and it is a necessary condition of our acquiring it that we should have previously learned to talk intelligently aloud and have heard and understood other people doing so. Keeping our thoughts to ourselves is a sophisticated accomplishment. It was not until the Middle Ages that people learned to read without reading aloud . . . (p. 27)

More briefly, Ryle's view is that: 'thinking is talking'. Lévi-Strauss carries the argument one stage further back; words are just sound patterns conjured out of the air, they are sound patterns which relate to objects and categories in the external world. Even more basic to logical thought than the operation of words is the operation of the concrete entities to which the words correspond. Arithmetic begins with the manipulation of an abacus rather than with simply 'saying' 'two plus two equals four'. Ryle was concerned to demolish the Cartesian distinction between abstract mind and concrete body — 'the dogma of the Ghost in the Machine'; Lévi-Strauss is similarly concerned to break down the conventional distinction between verbal and non-verbal aspects of culture, his argument being that both are equally a means of communication, a language. In recent years theoretical studies in structural linguistics and the closely related applied studies of communication engineers have enormously advanced our understanding of the way in which verbal forms of language actually operate as a means of communication. Lévi-Strauss is suggesting that we apply strictly comparable forms of analysis to the 'language' aspect of non-verbal culture.

Two propositions are crucial. The first, as stated on the dust cover, is that the subject-matter of the book is 'La pensée sauvage' and not 'la pensée des sauvages'. The fact that the author draws many of his examples from the ethnography of exotic peoples does not mean that he supposes that the thought processes of Australian aborigines are in any fundamental way different from our own. If we exclude from consideration the specialised technical languages exployed by modern intellectuals and scientists of various kinds then the generalisations which Lévi-Strauss derives from the speech patterns and beliefs of the Menomini Indians apply equally to a Chinese or to a Western European. He is concerned with the elementary principles common to all thinking, and not simply with the thoughts of 'primitive peoples'. Generalisations on such a grandiose scale are likely to provide many easy targets for the hostile critic and there are some weak patches in Lévi-Strauss's argument but I cannot see that this really matters. In a comparable way it is easy to show that Freud was very often wrong on points of detail; this does not detract from the massive validity of Freud's major generalisations. Even if time should show that some of the items of evidence have been misplaced, the fundamental method of Lévi-Strauss's analysis is an innovation from which there can be no retreat.

The second essential proposition is that which I have mentioned already. The non-verbal content of human culture is to be understood as a system of communication to which the principles of a general theory of communication may be applied. The elements of culture constitute a language full of redundancies by means of which 'senders' transmit 'information' to 'receivers' against a background of 'noise'. Lévi-Strauss is not the first to draw an analogy between 'culture' and 'language' but he takes the argument much further than his predecessors.

In presenting his case he hangs a great deal of the discussion around the class of institutions which anthropologists have been accustomed to group together under the label 'totemism' — a system of belief in which real components of the universe external to man (e.g. animal species) appear to be drawn into and merged with human society itself. The implied equation might be represented thus:

things in the external world	words in the verbal language	the operations of human 'thought'
categories of things in the external world (e.g. totems)	beliefs as expressed in mythology	the operations of culturally defined behaviour

This is an immensely difficult and intricate theme. For centuries past sophisticated societies have sustained their superiority by maintaining a store of information in the form of written documents, which are a special category of material things subject to human manipulation. It is a common assumption that this ability to communicate by means of the written word is a unique cultural phenomenon peculiar to 'civilised' societies. But Lévi-Strauss denies that this is so. 'Uncivilised' societies likewise have their categories of material things which serve as a store of knowledge and a means of communication. Indeed in primitive thought 'the universe consists of messages' ('l'univers des primitifs consiste principalement en messages'). The categories into which the primitive world is ordered have the same function as the words of a sentence. Only a short while ago it would have seemed purely fanciful to argue in this way but now, in the age of electronics, it is much easier to understand that written documents are only one specialised and very inefficient device for storing information.

The combinations of binary oppositions which make up the universe of a totemic society might seem to constitute a very crude and restricted vocabulary yet the latest miracles of the communication engineer operate within the precisely similar restrictions. In a delightful passage Lévi-Strauss recalls

186

the poetic evocation of a time

> ... où le ciel sur la terre
> Marchait et respirait dans un peuple de dieux.
> (L.-S. 1962 b, 354.)

Is this the golden age of the primitive past or the vital age of the electronic present? 'This time is now restored to us, thanks to the discovery of a universe of information where the laws of savage thought reign once more: "heaven" too "walking on earth" among a population of transmitters and receivers whose messages, while in transmission, constitute objects of the physical world and can be grasped both from without and from within' (p. 267).[1]

This particular passage illustrates in an extreme form a not infrequent feature of Lévi-Strauss's method. His most telling generalisations are often achieved by opposing the characteristics of sharply contrasted cultural situations. Earlier exponents of the 'comparative method' in anthropology (e.g. Sir James Frazer) illustrated their *a priori* propositions by pointing out obvious superficial similarities between spatially dispersed customs; in contrast Lévi-Strauss demonstrates *structural* similarity by comparing clusters of custom which are not only spatially separate but also, in a superficial sense, totally dissimilar. In my quotation the unstated opposition seems to be between Telstar and the Aborigines. Elsewhere in the book one of the most effective chapters is that in which the author discusses structural parallels between Australian totemism and the Indian caste system, two modes of social organisation which, by any conventional taxonomy, would appear as different as chalk from cheese.

The effect of such work is to break up the traditionally accepted categories of anthropological analysis including totemism itself. This is salutary, for we are thereby reminded of an essential fact which is very easily forgotten. *Any* taxonomy in any academic discipline is only a heuristic device; it is an aid to clear thinking, not a permanent fact of nature.

This aspect of Lévi-Strauss's argument is very much in line with current developments in many of the natural sciences.

Botanists, zoologists, bacteriologists, soil scientists and many others are all searching for structural identities which cross-cut the neat discrimination of conventional taxonomic systems (Aslib 1962). Linnaeus's concept of 'species' is suddenly very much out of fashion. It is easy to see how this has come about. Increasing familiarity with the programming requirements of digital computers has made the ordinary scientific worker familiar with the notion that 'similarity' may be thought of in statistical terms as representing a clustering rather than an identity of characteristics. Such similarities, which show up in a matrix computation, are often very different from those which might be inferred from direct inspection. Traditional taxonomies have necessarily depended upon the presence or absence of a small number of 'obvious' characteristics. This has meant that a very large number of apparently minor yet possibly significant variables have been excluded from all consideration. Until the coming of computers any other routine would have proved impossibly cumbersome. But now, in the computer era, it is the previously neglected variables which are receiving priority attention. In the long run this reaction may prove to have been exaggerated but, for the time being, the taxonomic 'shake-up' is proving most invigorating.

What has all this to do with the thinking of Lévi-Strauss? The particular system of factorial analysis which has influenced Lévi-Strauss most directly is that of the structural linguists (especially R. Jakobson and M. Halle, *Fundamentals of Language* (The Hague, 1956)), and the particular feature of general communication theory which he finds best adapted to his purposes is that of binary discrimination. The most fundamental proposition here is that, in any kind of code, every 'message' may be analysed into a series of cross-cutting binary discriminations such that:

Any x may be slotted as
    (i) either 'p' or 'not p'
    (ii) if 'p' then either 'q' or 'not q'
        if 'not p' then either 'q' or 'not q'
    (iii) if 'p and q' then either 'r' or 'not r'
        if 'p and not q' then either 'r' or 'not r'
        if 'not p and q' then either 'r' or 'not r'

if 'not p and not q' then either 'r' or 'not r'

(iv) if 'p and q and r' then either 's' or 'not s'

if p and q and not r' then either 's' or 'not s'

and so on.

For the communication engineer the importance of this highly cumbersome way of arriving at the facts is that any message can be encoded as a series of positive and negative impulses. For the linguist the same kind of argument implies that any sound pattern which adds up to a piece of meaningful speech can be analysed into a series of phonemic 'distinctive features' which are distinguished as binary opposites: e.g. vocalic/non-vocalic, consonantal/non-consonantal, compact/diffuse, tense/lax (Jakobson and Halle, *Fundamentals of Language*, pp. 29 ff). Lévi-Strauss looks for comparable 'distinctive features' in non-verbal patterns of culture which will likewise sort out the facts by means of binary discriminations.

In practice, Lévi-Strauss has used these ideas in a great many different ways with increasing sophistication. In *Les structures élémentaires de la parenté* (1949) the principle of binary discrimination is present in the notions of harmonic versus disharmonic organisation and also in the opposition between *échange restreint* and *échange généralisé*. But at this stage Lévi-Strauss had made no radical break with conventional procedures; the argument was a fairly straightforward development from themes already present in the writings of Durkheim and his pupils, Mauss and Hertz in particular.

In the various essays on myth, the earliest of which appeared in 1953, the influence of linguistic analysis is much more obvious; in the present volume it is dominant. A striking example occurs at pp. 140-9 where a vast body of ethnography relating to the Osage, an American Indian tribe, is tentatively reduced to a three-dimensional matrix so as to form at least the outline of an explicit computer programme.

This merging of linguistics and social anthropology is something far more important than merely 'bringing Mauss up to date', and we need to understand clearly just what is entailed.

It is widely accepted that the specifically human

189

characteristic which differentiates man from all other living creatures is the inferiority of his instinctive apparatus and his consequent total dependence upon culture, that is, upon patterns of behaviour which are learned from others. The humanity of man does not rest in the *capacity* to communicate but in the *necessity* to do so. A mere dependence upon communication is in itself a limiting factor; the circumstance which makes man superior to all other creatures is not the faculty to communicate but the faculty to operate with the symbols through which he communicates.

The mathematical transformation by means of which a particular sound pattern, 'man kills dog', is made to mean precisely the opposite to another sound pattern. 'dog kills man', is a characteristic which appears in all kinds of human communication systems. No non-human creature, so far as we are aware, can 'play games' with the elements of its communication system in this way.

Now this seems highly paradoxical. I am saying that the uniquely human characteristic is a capacity to perform logical transformations, to perform such mental exercises as:

$$\text{if } a+b=c \quad \text{then } c-a=b$$

But if this is really true, if it is its *mathematical* quality which differentiates Culture from Nature, how can it begin? How does mathematical (logical) thinking first grow in the minds of unsophisticated man? This, it seems to me, is the core of Lévi-Strauss's problem.

It is a basic part of the argument that mathematical relations, linguistic relations, kinship relations and transactional relations of all types are really 'all of the same kind'. Mauss's 'essai sur le don' (Mauss 1924) is here of cardinal significance. Mauss lived before the coming of computers and matrix algebra, but he perceived a very fundamental truth. Individuals communicate with one another by 'giving'. The 'gifts' may be words or things, services or women, but in every case the act of giving sets up a 'relationship', and patterns of giving establish whole structures of relationship, networks of debtors and creditors, of rights and obligations. When an anthropologist studies a social system he is concerned with individuals whose lives are governed by a system of relationships and who conduct their mutual affairs by means of strategies defined by rules, as if all concerned were engaged in a multidimensional cosmic game of chess. In such a context, the rules of the game, the system of relationships, the network of exchange, the total system of communication are all aspects of the same 'thing' — the Culture of Society.

But here we face a problem. When we describe the ordering of society as a 'system of relationships' we are using the special technical language of the professional anthropologist. What is the objective reality to which this description refers? The anthropologist's notion of relationship is highly abstract; how are such 'relationships' perceived to be by those who employ them in their most rudimentary form?

It is not just a question of perceiving the nature of the relationships between man and man, there is also the question of the relations between man and his environment. To become aware of himself, Man must differentiate himself from Nature. But, furthermore, if man is to have a position in the order of the universe, the universe must at the same time itself be given a sense of order. How is this done? Whence does the orderliness spring?

Scholars who are unfamiliar with ethnographic literature commonly suppose that the formulation of taxonomies is a peculiar mark of the true scientist: indeed there are eminent anthropologists who have themselves held this to be the case (e.g. A. R. Radcliffe-Brown, *A Natural Science of Society*, 1957). But this is a fundamental error. Modern ethnographic research has shown that even the most 'primitive' peoples are prone to discriminate the elements of their environment by means of extremely elaborate, logically ordered taxonomies. Although the 'species' categories which result are different from those of modern science, the procedures by which a particular species is distinguished are the same as those which an orthodox scientist would employ:

Many times I have seen a Negrito, who, when not being certain of the identification of a particular plant, will taste the fruit, smell the leaves, break and examine the stem, comment upon its habitat, and only after all of this, pronounce whether he did or did not know the plant. (R. B. Fox, quoted by Lévi-Strauss, p. 4.)

191

The comprehensiveness of this kind of classification may be formidable. Conklin has observed that the Hanonoo of Mindanao discriminate 1800 mutually exclusive botanical species among a range of plants in which orthodox botany finds only 1300 taxa.

I have already noted how Western scientists have been tending to lose their confidence in the absolute validity (or utility) of conventional taxonomies. It is more and more widely recognised that a taxonomy simply represents a convenient (though sometimes misleading) summary of information which could more satisfactorily be presented in matrix form in a shape which could be digested by a digital computer. It is part of Lévi-Strauss's argument that the 'non-scientific yet logical' taxonomies of primitive peoples are likewise summaries of information which could very well be presented in matrix form.

One of our difficulties here is that we have got so used to thinking of the concept of 'species' as corresponding to a true fact of nature that it is now difficult to recognise that the word means no more than 'kind' or 'sort'. The statement: 'a kangaroo is a different species of mammal from a wallaby' is really just the same type of statement as: 'a Parisian is a different kind of man from a Lyonnais'. Thus we might merge the two formulae and say 'a kangaroo-Parisian is a different species of man-mammal from a wallaby-Lyonnais'. This makes nonsense in conventional French or English but is just the kind of statement that has repeatedly been reported by the ethnographers of Australian aborigines under the heading of 'totemism'.

Lévi-Strauss argues that the reason that anthropologists have discerned a mystery in the phenomena which they lump together under the label 'totemism' is that they have been inhibited by the special conventions of syntax customary in modern Western European languages. 'Totemism', according to Lévi-Strauss, is really just one aspect of a more complex and more important phenomenon, the general classificatory process which is essential for all thought. 'Totemism' seems mysterious to us because it merges into one taxonomy (a) a system of classification of natural things external to human society and (b) a system of classification of categories of human being internal to human society. We find this absurd because our own equally arbitrary linguistic conventions imply that (*a*) and (*b*) are, self-evidently, of 'different kinds'.

Though such conventions vary as between one language system and another, a classification of type (*b*) is a necessity for any ordered society. Lévi-Strauss's novel insight is to perceive that, at the level of 'la pensée sauvage', the linguistic apparatus in terms of which categories of human grouping are arranged *must* be integral with, and in certain respects derivative from, the linguistic apparatus which is employed for establishing a description of the world. This comes about because the 'stuff' of which messages are made as they pass from one human being to another is itself a material stuff, a part of the external world:

> Above all, during the period of their transmission, when they have an objective existence outside the consciousness of transmitters and receivers, messages display properties which they have in common with the physical world. (p. 268)

As Lévi-Strauss has himself recognised, his view that the essence of totemism is to be seen in the ordering of the world into logical categories has some resemblance to the view propounded many years ago by the British functionalist anthropologists. The latter tended to argue that the constituent objects distinguished by any cultural system are intrinsically valuable because of their utility. Totemism serves not only to classify but also to express the value of useful things, especially foodstuffs. Lévi-Strauss has shifted the emphasis. In his view things have value in themselves because of the requirements of logic; utility is a secondary matter. Totems he says are 'bonnes à penser' rather than 'bonnes à manger' (*Le Totémisme aujourd'hui*, p. 128).

I believe that Lévi-Strauss may here have evaded some issues of importance, but certainly his insistence that all systems of classification are essentially similar in that they imply a logically ordered set of binary discriminations has far-reaching implications for the anthropologist. As an example let me cite one particular case where Lévi-Strauss applies his argument to a problem of ethnographic analyses. At some stage Lévi-Strauss seems to have asked himself: By what criteria do the aborigines of central Australia feel themselves to be of different kinds (tribes) (e.g. Arabanna, Aranda, Kaitish, Warramunga)? According to his interpretation of the ethnography, these distinctions depend upon a variety of factors (distinctive features) involving patterns of belief, marriage, ritual, and temporal periodicity. These factors can be displayed on a matrix as follows (p. 87):

Factor	Arabanna	'Tribe' Aranda	Kaitish	Warramunga
A	+	−	−	+
B		+		−
C	+	−		+
D		+	−	+
E			+	−
F		+		−
G		+		−

Presumably, if the ethnography were more complete and the patience of the analyst more enduring, the empty spaces in the matrix could be filled in and the list of distinctive features further extended. This is not just an example of anthropological cleverness; it is, in Lévi-Strauss's view, a true key to the way in which the native aborigines think about themselves.

I find an unexpected convergence here between Lévi-Strauss's work and that of some of his English colleagues. The English 'structuralist' anthropologists, notable Evans-Pritchard in *The Nuer* (1940), have made extended use of an argument already implicit in Durkheim's *De la division du travail social* (1893). In that book Durkheim's discussion of mechanical solidarity amounts to a thesis that the binary discrimination between *we* and *they* depends upon context; those who are members of 'our group' at one level of (lineage) segmentation will be felt to be members of the 'other group' at a different level of (lineage) segmentation. Since 1940, English social anthropologists have applied these ideas very extensively to the dimension of political relations, and, latterly, some have attempted to link up the political frame of reference with other dimensions. To this end Gluckman has coined the expression 'multiplex relationships' (Gluckman 1955, p. 156; 1962, p. 40), a notion which implies that we/they discriminations can simultaneously manifest themselves within many different fields which are not necessarily co-extensive. Even at one specific level of group segmentation the we/they discrimination which is derived from ritual relations may be quite different from the we/they distinctions which emerge from political, or economic, or kinship obligations. In Gluckman's view the sum of such binary distinctions is always cohesive in effect because of the resultant inconsistency of mutual obligations.

This no doubt somewhat distorts Gluckman's thesis but I have twisted it into this form merely to show that there is some convergence between Lévi-Strauss's argument and the superficially quite different British view. The differences also deserve attention. The British remain crudely empirical — their problem is: 'How does society work' ('function')? Lévi-Strauss's interest is much more that of the philosopher: 'How does man perceive himself to be in relation to the world and to society?'

But now let me raise certain objections. I was myself first attracted to Lévi-Strauss's work by the circumstance that the ethnography of the Kachins of North Burma is of central importance for the argument of *Les structures élémentaires de la parenté*, and I happened to have first-hand knowledge of the Kachin facts. What amazed me at the time was that Lévi-Strauss had somehow perceived much more clearly than I had myself certain essential features of the structure of Kachin society, but that he had done so on the basis of a very cursory and sometimes quite misleading review of the ethnographic evidence.

Something of the same problem troubles me now. The range of Lévi-Strauss's ethnographic reading is vast, and his use of ethnographic evidence is extremely ingenious but it is also very selective, and, in particular cases, the selectivity produces a bad fit between the analysis and the evidence.

One example of this occurs at pp. 191-8, where Lévi-Strauss claims to resolve the logical puzzle presented by the extremely complex material relating to Penan teknonyms and 'death-names' (necronyms). Lévi-Strauss's discussion here is a

195

profoundly illuminating contribution to the general theory of naming procedures but it does not satisfy me as a solution to the particular problem provided by the Penan ethnography. (If this comment seems unduly curt the interested reader may compare Lévi-Strauss's remark, p. 259: 'The proper name is the reverse of the necronym' with the original evidence provided by ̄Needham (1954), pp. 422-3, which shows that a 'proper name' and a 'necronym' are commonly held by the same individual at the same time either as alternatives or in combination.) Or again there is the material at pp. 204-8 which presents a fascinating discussion of 'our' customs regarding the naming of birds and dogs and race-horses and cattle. Fascinating as an illustration of the way in which 'species of words may correspond to categories of social origin, but somehow doubtful as an interpretation of the evidence? Presumably English naming customs are sufficiently different from the French to spoil the bite of the argument as soon as it crosses the Channel.

Details of this kind are liable to exasperate the specialist but they should not be overrated. Lévi-Strauss has been engaged in a reconnaissance of largely unexplored territory. When a cadastral survey comes to be made, some of the finer points are bound to need revision.

But there are more serious difficulties, and I propose to consider one of these in some detail.

There is a sense in which the central theme of the book is the grandiose problem of the Nature of Man. What distinguishes Man from non-Man? Lévi-Strauss claims that his answer to this problem is akin to that of Rousseau. The *Discours sur l'origine et les fondéments de l'inégalité parmi les hommes* distinguishes the characteristics of man by means of a three-dimensional binary opposition:

      (i) *animalité* /   *humanité*
     (ii) *nature*   /   *culture*
    (iii) *affectivité*/   *intellectualité*
         (Le Totémisme aujourd'hui, p. 144.)

The first of these distinctions is that which is involved in the concept of 'totemism'. Lévi-Strauss argues that the anthropologists have erred in trying to isolate totemism as a one-dimensional phenomenon; Rousseau's larger frame of reference needs to be taken into account. Despite the amount of space which he devotes to its consideration, Lévi-Strauss takes the view that totemism does not deserve to be classed as a special category of behaviour because it is only one facet of something much wider and more fundamental — the *total* process by which man uses categories of words and categories of objective things to place himself in an ordered world. For Lévi-Strauss totemic species are simply logical operators.

I grant that Lévi-Strauss demonstrates in a most brilliant and convincing way that totems are in fact used as the 'stuff of thinking' and this previously neglected aspect of totemism is of great importance. But that is not the whole of the matter. This treatment of the ethnographic facts seems to evade the central problem (as it has formerly been understood) which is: Why are totemic species held to be sacred?

I agree that the earlier functionalist theories of the British anthropologists which Lévi-Strauss criticises were inadequate, but to this particular question they provided some sort of answer. They suggested that totems are sacred because they are useful, that they are, to use Lévi-Strauss's phrase 'bonnes à manger'. But here it seems to me Lévi-Strauss has been trapped by his fondness for binary discriminations. He distinguishes things which are 'bonnes à manger' from things which are 'bonnes à penser' as opposite categories, and opts for the latter rather than the former. But surely totems may very well be both at once?

Binary discrimination is a very powerful tool of analysis. Any kind of information whatsoever *can* be discriminated in this way. But binary analysis is a possible rather than a necessary procedure. It has important disadvantages. One of these is that it tends to minimise problems of value. Lévi-Strauss's use of the communication theory analogy is very illuminating, but he seems to have overlooked the fact that there are types of communication problem which are more conveniently handled by analog computers (which answer questions in terms of *more* or *less*) than by digital computers (which can only answer *yes* or *no*). Lévi-Strauss's treatment hardly allows for the fact that in a society which orders living creatures into sets of 'species' which serve as a paradigm for corresponding sets of human groups, the individual members of any set may be valued in very different ways. The distinction is not just a binary matter of tame/wild, sacred/profane, prohibited/allowed, but of a subtle and many-sided graduation between 'more sacred' and 'less sacred', and this may bring into consideration factors which have so far escaped Lévi-Strauss's attention.

As I have remarked above, Lévi-Strauss argues that totemic species are 'bonnes à penser' rather than 'bonnes à manger'. Food preferences and food taboos are simply logical counters, 'bits' of information (p. 103: 'Eating prohibitions and obligations thus seem to be theoretically equivalent means of "denoting significance" in a logical system some or all of whose elements are edible species'). So also in the discussion of caste, food taboos, exogamy, endogamy are treated simply as digital indicators like the plus and minus signs on a computer tape.

Here again the point of my criticism is not that Lévi-Strauss is wrong but that he does not pursue the implications of his insights far enough. Thus in the chapter entitled 'Totem et Caste' he demonstrates with superlative elegance how a structure of categories composed of endogamous sub-castes which are interdependent by virtue of their specialised cultural activities may resemble a structure of categories composed of exogamous totemic groups which are made interdependent through the pattern of marriage and which are differentiated because of the natural differences between the totemic species with which they are identified (pp. 123-5), a dialectic which leads to the generalisation (p. 128) that: 'the "system of women" is, as it were, a middle term between the system of (natural) living creatures and the system of (manufactured) objects' — a statement from which I personally can derive immense illumination.

In this discussion Lévi-Strauss very naturally takes note of the 'food prohibitions' which are commonly associated with totemism and he even notes (p. 126) that in caste systems the rules regarding 'culinary operations and utensils' are in some degree the 'equivalent' of such food taboos. Nevertheless he consistently plays down the importance of food customs as cultural indicators. 'Systems of names deriving from the natural kingdoms are not always accompanied by food prohibitions: they can be "stressed" (*marqués*) in diverse

198

fashions' (p. 129). This is true but it leads Lévi-Strauss to overlook the fact that the food customs of Indian castes fit superbly well with his general argument.

Beals (1962) gives the following chart to show the interrelations of the caste groups in a South Indian village. It seems clear from column 1 that, in this instance at least, 'bonnes à manger' are also 'bonnes à penser'.

Economic status

Ceremonial rank	Landlord	Middle class	Landless
Vegetarian	Brahmin	Lingayat Priest Carpenter Blacksmith	Lingayat Farmer
Mutton no beer		Saltmaker	Saltmaker
Mutton and beer		Farmer Shepherd Barber	Farmer Shepherd
Beef no pork		Muslim Priest Muslim Butcher Muslim Weaver	
Pork no beef		Stoneworker	Stoneworker Basketweaver
Beef and pork			Leatherworker

(After Alan R. Beals (1962), p. 38.)

Let me repeat: I do not disagree with what Lévi-Strauss

says on this theme but I feel he is leaving something out.

He observes, for example, that there is a world-wide tendency to make some kind of verbal equation between eating and sexual intercourse. As a consequence the ritual attitudes evoked by food taboos and by sex taboos are inter-related. The linkage he asserts is metaphorical rather than causal (p. 105). The human mind perceives a logical similarity between the acts of eating and copulation — 'the lowest common denominator of the union of the sexes and union of eater and eaten is that they both effect a conjunction by complementarity' (pp.105-6). I understand what he means. I can accept the proposition. But it seems to me to miss the point.

For most anthropologists the most interesting aspect of taboo is its relation to sacredness. A taboo has a qualitative value; it is not just a trap door that is either open or shut.

Lévi-Strauss wants to use the rules of sex and the rules of eating as binary discriminators which say 'yes' or 'no'.

Item A is allowed. The answer is 'yes'. The sign is +

Item B is prohibited. The answer is 'no'. The sign is —

But, what about item C which is also prohibited but against which the sanctions are of quite a different kind and strength from those that are raised against item B?

It is here that I would bring in the issue of edibility.

It is surely always true that the edibility is a very important factor in determining the way any particular animal species is categorised. But such categories are intricate. Lévi-Strauss (p. 205) notes that there is a food taboo which inhibits us from eating pet dogs. True, but the matter is complicated. The rule which prevents us from eating dog is tacit, unstated; the rule which prevents a Jew from eating pork is explicit. The valuations are quite different and these valuations deserve attention.

The complexity of the problem is obvious. Clearly the environment of any society contains a vast number of plants and living things which are dietetically nourishing but which are nonetheless treated as inedible. Taboo establishes dis-criminations but not in any simple fashion. Europeans do not eat rats; Hindus do not eat beef. There are similarities between the two cases but also radical differences, and Lévi-Strauss has, as yet, scarcely suggested how we should investigate such matters.

Goody (1956) has pointed out that a satisfactory analysis of the rules of incest calls for a consideration of the whole system of permissible, prohibited and undesirable sex relations, and in a comparable way Lévi-Strauss is himself insisting that totemism needs to be considered within the setting of a wider set of categories. So far so good. But if we are considering the relationships of man to animals — and that after all is what totemism is all about — then the edibility of the animals from the viewpoint of man is a very important part of the story. We need to consider the whole range of dietetic possibilities; every society distinguishes not only between food and non-food but also between food that is good and food that is bad and between food that is pleasant and food that is unpleasant. For such an ordering of materials the binary discriminations of which Lévi-Strauss is so fond seem clumsy and inappropriate. Indeed, it seems to me that the limitations of binary analysis have infected Lévi-Strauss's own thinking in a rather serious way. He has been engaged in expounding to us the logic of religious categories, but in the process he has come to ignore precisely those aspects of the matter which are most specifically religious.

Sir James Frazer's first study of totemism (Frazer 1887) might have been criticised on somewhat similar grounds. Frazer in that book distinguishes between 'The Religious side of Totemism' and 'The Social Side of Totemism' but does not succeed very well in tying the two together. In discussing 'the Social Side of Totemism' Frazer recognises that the totemic categories might be expected to reflect in some way the segmentary structure of the society with which they are associated, but he despairs of discovering the logical key to the system.

Lévi-Strauss's analysis shows us that logical ordering of categories may after all be embedded in even the most confusing ethnographic evidence, and it is a further great step forward to be able to recognise that this 'totemic style' of logic can be discerned not only in systems composed of exogamous unlineal descent groups but also in the converse type of segmentary structure represented by an endogamous caste system. But this leaves out of account those social structures which are not 'segmentary' in any straightforward sense and which, on that account, do not readily lend themselves to binary analysis. Where, for example, do we meet with a totemic style of logic in the collective representations of societies which have a bilateral (cognatic) pattern of kinship organisation?

I believe that Lévi-Strauss's theory can be developed so as to provide an answer to this question which will at the same time tie in the 'sacred' aspect of totemism with its 'category-forming' aspect. But in the present volume this synthesis has not been achieved.

Professor Lévi-Strauss might well reply that I should confine my attention to what he has written and not concern myself with hypothetical missing chapters. But that is just my point. I consider that *La pensée sauvage* is one of the most illuminating and potentially germinal contributions to anthropology that has been published within the last forty years, but its importance lies in its innovations and beginnings, not in its conclusions. That surely is the best kind of merit that any book can ever have?

REFERENCES

Aslib, 1962: 'Symposium on Classification', 'Aslib Proceedings', xiv 8 (London).

Alan R. Beals, 1962: 'Gopalpur. A South Indian Village' (New York).

Emile Durkheim, 1893: 'De la division du travail social' (Paris).

R. B. Fox, 1952: 'The Pintubo Negritos : their useful plants and material culture', 'The Philippines Journal of Science', lxxxi 3-4 (Manila).

J. G. Frazer, 1887: 'Totemism' (Edinburgh).

Max Gluckman, 1955: 'The Judicial Process among the Barotse of Northern Rhodesia' (Manchester).

Max Gluckman (ed), 1962: 'Essays on the Ritual of Social Relations' (Manchester).

J. R. Goody, 1956: 'A Comparative Approach to Incest and Adultery', British Journal of Sociology, vii 286-305.

R. Jakobson and M. Halle, 1956: 'Fundamentals of

Language' (The Hague).

A. L. Kroeber, 1917: 'California Kinship Terms', 'University of California: Publications in American Archaeology and Ethnology', xii 9 pp. 339-396.

C. Lévi-Strauss, 1949: 'Les Structures élémentaires de la parenté' (Paris).

—— 1962 a : 'Le Totémisme aujourd'hui' (Paris).

—— 1962 b : 'La Pensée Sauvage' (Paris).

—— 1966 : 'The Savage Mind' (London).

M. Mauss, 1924: 'Essai sur le don : forme et raison de l'échange dans les sociétés archaiques', 'L'Année Sociologique', 1923-24 (Paris).

R. Needham, 1954: 'The System of Teknonyms and Death-Names of the Penan', 'Southwestern Journal of Anthropology', x 4 (Albuquerque).

A. R. Radcliffe-Brown, 1957: 'A Natural Science of Society' (Glencoe).

G. Ryle, 1949: 'The Concept of Mind' (London).

J.-J. Rousseau, 1755: 'Discours sur l'origine et les fondements de l'inégalité parmi les hommes' (Amsterdam).

Max Weber, 1947: 'The Theory of Social and Economic Organization', trans A. R. Henderson-Talcott Parsons (London).

L. Wittgenstein, 1922: 'Tractatus Logico-Philosophicus' (London).

NOTE

1. Unless otherwise stated, page references for Lévi-Strauss's work are to Lévi-Strauss 1966.

10 Groote Eylandt Totemism and *Le Totémisme aujourd'hui**

Peter Worsley

'Thought which is totally unscientific and even which contradicts experience may yet be entirely coherent in that there is a reciprocal dependence between its ideas. Thus I may instance the writings of medieval divines and political controversialists as examples of mystical thought which, far from being chaotic, suffers from a too rigid application of syllogistic rules. Also the thought of many insane persons (monomaniacs, paranoiacs) presents a perfectly organized system of interdependent ideas.'

E. E. Evans-Pritchard (1934)

'The insane have a terrific obsession for logic and order, as have the French.'

Henry Miller (1936)

The two quotations at the head of this article only refer obliquely — and most affectionately — to the writing of that most respected and creative of colleagues, Claude Lévi-Strauss; they bear more centrally upon the thinking of the Australian aborigines. I have no desire, that is, to be cast in the role of a simple-minded English empiricist breaking a lance for God, Harry and the Cult of the Fact against the dragon of Gallic systematics. Even though the orientation of this paper was originally suggested to me as the presentation of Australian aboriginal totemism 'as it really is', such a 'pure' empiricist brief is logically impossible, for 'as it really is' (shades of Ranke!) has to be translated 'as it really is *in contradistinction to Lévi-Strauss's interpretations*'. As Lévi-Strauss would no doubt be the first to observe, an analysis of totemism 'as it really is' cannot exist 'in itself', but implies its opposite.

* 'The Structural Study of Myth and Totemism' (Tavistock Publications, 1967) pp. 141-59. © Association of Social Anthropologists of the Commonwealth.

Yet I may 'revise' the Marxian dialectic this far: that I do not conceive of my arguments as being any kind of 'antithesis' to Lévi-Strauss's 'thesis'. The analysis here develops, not in negative *o*pposition to his approach, but in *a*pposition to it. Any discussion of totemism must be conditioned by his significant contribution to our understanding of the phenomenon: it must extend his insights.

Simple empiricism, indeed, invites the kind of criticism that Lévi-Strauss develops in discussing Elkin's fragmentation of 'totemism' into various 'totemisms': sex totemism, moiety totemism, clan totemism, dream totemism, local totemisms, section totemism, subsection totemism, etc. (Elkin, 1933). The problem is merely rephrased, not eliminated: now it becomes 'What is the sociological significance of totemism*s*', instead of 'What is the sociological significance of totemism?'

Or, as Lévi-Strauss wittily puts it, Elkin, 'instead of helping to slay the hydra [of totemism] . . . has dismembered it and made peace with the bits' (Lévi-Strauss, 1962*a*, p.66).

For Lévi-Strauss, indeed, the problem is not to understand totemism, but to abolish it. Totemism is not a separable 'ethnographic' specimen peculiar to the Australians and some other peoples, but a particular instance of a much more general phenomenon, one indeed that all societies have to face in one way or another: the problem of how men perceive, select, intellectually order and socially structure the similarities and differences in both the natural and cultural realms respectively, and how connections are established between these two orders. It is not that there is a 'natural' order in Nature, which, as in seventeenth-century theories of consciousness, somehow 'orders' or registers itself automatically within brains which passively 'receive' these already-processed sense impressions. Nature itself is ordered by the *active* organising intervention of the brain, as the eighteenth-century idealists, notably Kant, correctly told us. The order of Nature is not mechanically registered, but is created by human agency. It is an ordering achieved via human consciousness, not an order 'in itself'.[1] The ordering of Nature is thus as much a human product, the outcome of human activity within Nature, as is (more obviously) the ordering of society. The gulf between verbal and non-verbal aspects of culture, between the ordering of cultural experience through the medium of written documents and ordering via the classification of other objects in the environment is thus bridged in Lévi-Strauss's analysis. The totemic 'objects are not just *objects*; they are messages'[2] (Lévi-Strauss, 1962*b*, p.355). In classifying, man organises his experience, and locates the classified raw materials of his experience within a framework of *meaning*; the imputation of meaning rests upon an underlying set of values. Thus the worlds of natural objects and cultural objects are brought into relationship with each other. In Lévi-Strauss's paradoxical formulation, the problem then consists in analysing how these *differences* between the two areas, Nature and Culture, 'resemble' each other (or perhaps, more accurately, 'are brought into relationship'), since there may not be — as we shall see — that closeness of fit between different classificatory schemes within the same culture which alone would permit us, legitimately, to speak of 'resemblance', 'congruence', etc.[3]

One possible type of explanation of totemism rejected by Lévi-Strauss (1962*a*, ch. 5) is the naturalistic or utilitarian type, which asserts that the objects selected as totems are so selected because of their usefulness, normally as food or in terms of some other economic 'good' (e.g. as raw materials, etc.). This he rejects, since, on the one hand (to take animals used as totems), many animals found in the totemic schemata are not necessarily of much (if any) economic importance, and, moreover, by no means occupy a place in the ritual hierarchy which would correspond to their degree of importance from a utilitarian point of view. Thus, to take illustrations from the totems of one single clan of the Wanindiljaugwa tribe of Groote Eylandt, Northern Territory of Australia — whom I studied in 1953 as a Research Scholar of the Australian National University — parrot fish, dugong, paperbark, and cypress pine are all valued either as foods or as raw material, but the echidna, scrub fowl, goose or crow are not so valued, either because they are not regarded as edible, or because they are rarely encountered. The presence of the Northwest wind as a further totem of this clan raises a problem, however, for clearly it is not used either for food or for raw material. One can argue that it is of 'economic' significance, either because it fills the sails of the aborigines'

206

canoes, or — more convincingly — because this wind symbolises the wet season of the year. But this argument involves such a radical extension of the notion of 'economic interest' from simple, specific and direct utility in production and consumption, to diffuse and symbolic 'social value', that it could be used to rationalise *anything* as having 'social value' (it also assumes what has to be proved — that the totemic entities are adopted *because* they 'reflect' some underlying concern with the utilitarian). The ultimate absurdity of this position is reached when we find things like diarrhoea, vomit or the mosquito used as totems. How are these of 'social value'? The only possible way out of this is to argue that they are of 'negative social value', i.e. they are important because they are noxious. By this stage, since practically everything in society and Nature has either a positive or negative social value, we are still left with the problem of why *this* (often minor) item has been selected, and not that. Normally, however, it is not necessary to fall back on the argument from 'negative social value'. Since the aborigine has a prodigious knowledge of natural species, and uses hundreds of plants and animals, nearly every plant or animal which can possibly occur in a totemic collection can be shown to have at least some, partial or occasional, utility value.

The totems, then, are not necessarily of greater economic importance than are species of animals and plants which do not figure as totems. Many totems are not natural species at all; some of them are noxious; or, like the 'sleep' totem reported from one tribe, could perhaps be regarded as neutral, rather than either positive or negative.

Durkheim himself had originally pointed out that it was erroneous to interpret the function of totemism as the maintenance of valued plants and animals, when he observed that the so-called 'increase' rituals were also performed within the context of initiation (Durkheim, 1957, p. 384). Moreover, since the environment of the aborigines contains only an exiguous man-made culture, natural species are bound to predominate, merely because they are plentiful and accessible (though heavenly bodies, inorganic substances such as stones, and geographical features are all totems which are natural, but not species).

207

If, then, certain animal and plant species (though, to be precise, aboriginal taxonomic divisions do not necessarily coincide with the biologist's *species*) are used as totems, it is not because these species are 'choses bonnes à manger'. But are they any less good to 'think with' than other 'failed' totems? Are they, in fact, just arbitrary symbols, only connected to the social units that bear them in a purely contingent way – say, through historical accident – which then become 'fixed', or as they more systematically distributed among the component social units according to consistent principles of distribution?

For some totemic systems, as in the analysis of Tallensi totemism by Fortes (1945, pp.141-5), a peculiar appropriateness has been suggested for the animals used as totems (tooth-bearing animals which symbolise the potential aggressiveness of the ancestors). Malinowski and Firth, earlier, had suggested that animals were inherently more suitable totemic material than plants, because of their distinctive differences in motility, form, colour, sound, etc. (Lévi-Strauss, 1962a, pp. 82-3, 108-9).

But these modes of analysis, even if accepted as valid for the Tallensi and Tikopia, are not extensible beyond these societies. What is common to both types of explanation, however – which is extensible generally – is the observation which Lévi-Strauss found foreshadowed in Bergson (1958): that it is not the individual characteristics of particular animals that are highlighted in totemic classifications, but the *generic* characteristics of whole classes of animals.

Even this, however, is only relevant in so far as specifically *animal* totems are concerned. But not all totems are animal totems. And even among animal totems, in Australian totemism, species possess negative, low or marginal social value, or even those which are neutral in value terms, take their place together with species having a high positive value. The same applies to plant species.

One Groote Eylandt set of linked totems illustrates the difficulties entailed in naturalistic assumptions that the intrinsic characteristics of the totems 'explain' the social value placed upon it. In one of the Creation Time myths, the mythical creatures Dumaringenduma and Neribuwa occur, together with Parrot, Central Hill and four or five sea-creatures: usually Sea-fish, Sting-ray, Comb-fish and Shark-ray.

From a utilitarian point of view, parrots are by no means important, except periodically as a source of feathers for decorating the body. Central Hill, however, is the highest hill not only on Groote Eylandt, but also in the whole Gulf of Carpentaria – an obvious naturalistic explanation of its central importance in this myth. Again, Sting-ray's importance might well be said to derive, not so much from its considerable importance as a food, but from the striking resemblance in shape of Lake Hubert (the largest lake on the island), seen from a distance, to a sting-ray. Yet the latter is only an inference – Central Hill *is* a totem itself; Lake Hubert is not, but (to the observer, under certain conditions) looks like a sting-ray, and in the myth, Sting-ray ends his journey in this lake (but so do Saw-fish, Comb-fish, and Shark-ray!). One major topographical feature – Central Hill – clearly has high place in the totemic collection; so does Lake Hubert (though only if we assume that Lake Hubert = Sting-ray). But quite as important, to the aborigine, are two utterly insignificant rocks, in physical terms, which 'are' Neribuwa and Dumaringenduma (so insignificant, among dozens of others in the same hilly outcrop, that I was never sure which two the aborigines were pointing to). In this myth, then, anthropomorphic Dream Time Beings, topo-graphical features possessed of a human-like volition and motility (Central Hill) and animals all occur together and have similar status. But Neribuwa and Dumaringenduma *became* natural features; Central Hill is always depicted as a *hill* (in bark-paintings, Neribuwa and Dumaringenduma are shown as *people*). There is really little that is systematic here. It may well be that the four sea-creatures are selected for their sharp 'noses', for these four 'cut open' the Jinuma (Anggurgwa) River, the major river of Groote Eylandt. There appears to be no good utilitarian reason why a cottonwood tree should be connected with these other totems in the myth.

This myth thus 'explains' the largest hill, the largest lake and the largest river on the island. (Other quite large lakes have no such myths attached to them.) The path of the journeys of the Dream Time creatures probably reflects something quite distinct: the major routes by which, historically, people have always moved from the mainland into Groote Eylandt.

All this makes some kind of systematic sense, much of it in utilitarian terms. Similarly, another myth 'explains', not topographical features, but the gulf between men and animals: it tells how man came to use fire in cooking fish (the word for fish — *augwalja*, — interestingly enough, is extended to mean flesh-food in general), while the sea-eagle came to eat fish raw. To say this is to analyse the myth in terms of behaviours; not, simply, to assume that animals occurring in myths are of high utilitarian value (sea-eagles, garfish and grasshopers — all of which occur in the myth — are not so valued). Similarly, the Ship totemic myth-complex 'explains' not merely the technological item, ship, but also the division of humankind into aborgines and Makassarese (smoke from a fire turned the aborigines black; the Whites, however, are not totemically 'explained' at all).

As I have described elsewhere (1955, pp. 851-61, and 1956, pp. 47-62, though the latter article suffers from a far too naturalistic interpretation, which internal evidence does not support), other important aspects of aboriginal life — topographical features such as the major hill on neighbouring Bickerton Island (also inhabited by the Wanindiljaugwa), the winds which mark the seasons, the Ship totem — represent mythological celebration of key features of Groote Eylandt life. But there is no myth to celebrate, say, the spear-thrower or the axe, the grey mullet (an important fish-food), the dugout canoe, tobacco, night and day, the differential behaviours of men and women, or a hundred and one equally significant elements in the natural and cultural worlds. And a further myth (of another clan) celebrates a whole series of utterly insignificant places: it does include four practically important items (bark canoe, barbed spears, Southeast wind and stringy-bark); lesser-valued items (casuarina tree); and various 'useless' items (caterpillar, praying mantis); and one that is, to me, inexplicable — 'place'.

To pursue systematics as far as one can, one may further observe one binary discrimination that appears an almost triumphant demonstration of mythological order: the largest clan in one moiety has the Northwest wind (wet season) as its key (most-frequently-mentioned) totem, and the largest clan in the other moiety the Southeast wind (dry season). The North wind, which blows for a short time between the major seasons, is allotted to a smaller clan in the moiety which has the Northwest wind. Each moiety contains six clans. In moiety A, four clans share the same totemic complex; in moiety B, another four clans again share another complex.

This is all very orderly, until we examine how this order comes about. It would appear likely (conjectural history) that the two totemic myth complexes mentioned (the myth shared by four clans, involving Central Hill, Sting-ray, Dumaringenduma, etc., and the Ship myth of four clans in the other moiety) embody actual migration-routes, as does the Southeast wind myth complex of the Wanindiljaugwa clan (Wanindiljaugwa being the name both of the tribe as a whole and of a clan within the tribe). We do, however, have some probably historical material to hand. Two clans – the WanungAmadada and the WurEngiljangba – are said, quite specifically, by the aborigines to be new formations, notably the former, much the larger of the two. This clan was 'produced' only one generation ago by one, still living, ritual expert from the Nunggubuju tribe on the mainland opposite, who immigrated to Groote Eylandt and adopted the totems of the WuraGwaugwa clan. He also became a Groote Eylandt ritual leader and introduced mainland rituals into Wanindiljaugwa practice. Totems and whole rituals have probably always been borrowed or introduced from the mainland and vice versa; today, the Wanindiljaugwa seem to experience a distinct sense of ritual ignorance and inferiority vis-à-vis the mainlanders, whose flourishing and rich ritual life they envy; they are therefore accustomed to 'borrow' mainland rituals.

By the creation of two new clans, entirely – it appears – contingent upon a quite recent specific immigration (even allowing for possible 'telescoping', 'fusing', etc.), a spuriously neat balance of six clans in each moiety is achieved.

This mainland contact, recorded even in eighteenth-century exploration literature, has constantly fed new totems into Groote Eylandt. A present-day Balamumu immigrant, married uxorilocally, has brought his mainland totems with him. But whether they will become adopted more widely or

211

not depends upon his influence. If a man has numerous followers — either by marrying many wives and producing many children, or by exerting himself as a community leader, e.g. as a ritual specialist, an active figure in the settlement of disputes, etc.— his totems may 'take on'. People wish to identify with him. There is thus an important personal element in totemic innovation. This also takes the form of innovation via aesthetic creation. One single man has personally produced more new 'totemic' songs than the rest of the tribe put together, including new songs relating to military forces on Groote Eylandt in the Second World War ('Army'), a song about 'Airbase', and a song about 'Catalina' flying boats. He *likes* singing, and though he belongs to a clan with only one other adult married male member, he has contributed vastly and disproportionately to the totemic repertoire of the Groote Eylandters. This gives us an important clue: the myth and song are the essential ingredients of the totemic system. *Alauwudawara* means totem, song, myth, story, work of art, painting, string figure, and even small objects that the aborigines find attractive or intriguing: a mole on the body, or a little medical phial. Totems exist, then, primarily in a mythological context, not a logical context, let alone a sociological one. They develop very largely through the self-development of myth and song, and although items important in a utilitarian sense may well be portrayed in myth and song, this is by no means always the case, as we have seen. Perhaps only an ethnomusicologist steeped in the musical culture of Groote Eylandt could estimate how far the intrinsic *musical* appeal of a particular song is a significant factor in effecting wider social acceptance of a new song, but I do not think this should be forgotten — 'Army', 'Airbase' and 'Catalina' were greatly enjoyed, and, moreover, had the attraction of novelty (though 'written' in quite traditional style).

But songs are not created by culture-free men; the innovatory songman belongs to a particular clan. His song is therefore his clan's song. But the totems do *not* neatly discriminate one clan from another. Since all clans in a moiety share each other's songs and dances, and co-operate in ritual, totems are also shared (Elkin, 1933, p 121). There are no 'diacritical' subsidiary totems discriminating clans bearing

212

Central Hill totemic myth-complex from each other; but of the clans sharing Ship in common, one clan has the further totems Conch Shell and Bailer Shell; another, the further totem, Coconut; another, the Catalina set, plus Dove and Turtle; and the fourth (on Woodah Island, near Balamumu territory), no further totems other than mainland ones (this clan is even reported, wrongly, in the literature, as being a Balamumu, not a Wanindilaugwa, clan).

Among the Wanindiljaugwa, the clan, in fact, is largely significant only at the ritual level, though, in the light of the advanced breakdown of Groote Eylandt religion, I cannot speak too confidently here. Otherwise its functions seem singularly limited; the moiety is far more important, notably in regulating marriage, and even, to a great extent, in ritual (cf. the parallel Dua and Jiridja moiety ritual divisions on the mainland). It is probably for this reason that the 'diacritical' competences of totemism remain unfulfilled on Groote Eylandt; totems are shared and borrowed, and the exact status of minor totems is unclear, even whether they are to be regarded as totems at all. Some people recognise more totems than others (hence minor discrepancies — omissions or additions — in my two lists in the different articles cited above).

For many clans, there is no 'main' totem. For others, people normally refer to one particular totem first, e.g. the Southeast wind for the Wanindiljaugwa clan, though they do not conceptualise or verbalise this as any kind of 'principal' or 'main' totem. (But since they have no word for 'clan', 'moiety' or 'tribe', either, this linguistic evidence is not conclusive.)

The allocation of totems to particular social groups is not, therefore, an intellectual attempt to order the universe according to some assumed immanent logic visible in Nature itself. The social framework of clan and moiety is the matrix within which totems are distributed. The social order structures the totemic distribution. But totems rise (and probably fall) in unpredictable ways: men immigrate, create songs, assert leadership. (In genealogies, a handful only of the 'great men' of two, rarely three, generations ago, actually remembered by living men, are recorded. Further back than that, no genealogical extensions or connections exist.)

213

The appearance of compendious systematisation can be 'substantiated' only by selective and unscientific concentration upon the more systematic parts of the totemic compendium to the exclusion of all the contingent parts I have touched upon. I have therefore tried to avoid speaking of a 'totemic system', but rather of a 'collection', for the process by which the totemic compendium develops is not via a logical ordering of the aborigines' world according to binary or any other discriminations (though this may be an *element*, e.g. the Southeast/Northwest wind division, empirically large or small according to the culture in question): the totemic 'collection' accretes, cumulates, forms agglomerations of items unconnected in systematic logic or in Nature, according to a variety of principles of association. Instead, therefore, of conceiving of the totemic schema as an ordered totality, I have called it 'agglomerative, arbitrary, and fortuitous'. Even such large totemic compendia as that of the Aranda and Loritja (containing 442 recorded 'totems') seems to be still of the same type, and not more 'systematic', despite the abundance of items represented (Spencer and Gillen, 1904, appendix B, pp. 767-73).

As far as the validation of behaviours is concerned, we find only very limited segments of aboriginal cultures expressly 'covered' in totemic mythology: man *v.* animals, and aborigines *v.* Makassarese. The 'explanation' of major topographical features is slightly more exhaustive of the major features, and therefore more satisfactory to those who expect to find system (though, for example, there is no myth to account for the separate existence of Bickerton Island, or Woodah, Chasm, Winchelsea, and other islands, or for Groote's relationship to the mainland).

These radical differences in principle of association must not be obscured. They are well expressed as an analytical distinction in a quite different substantive area, in Vygotsky's scientific dialogue with Piaget on the language and thought of the child (1962).

Vygotsky distinguishes, first, as a phase-type in the development of childhood thinking, the *unorganised congeries* or 'heap' where:

The heap, consisting of disparate objects grouped together without any basis, reveals a diffuse undirected extension of the meaning of the sign (artificial word) to inherently unrelated objects linked by chance in the child's perception.

At that stage, word meaning denotes nothing more to the child than a *vague syncretic conglomeration of individual objects* that have somehow or other coalesced into an image in his mind. (pp. 59-60)

The only order provided here, connecting the objects linked together in reality as well as in the child's mind, is the order provided by social cadres — just as the clans provide a framework for the ordering of totems.

Congeries are sharply distinguished from *complexes*, where:

In a complex, individual objects are united in the child's mind not only by his subjective impressions but also by *bonds actually existing between these objects*... In a complex, the bonds between its components are *concrete and factual* rather than abstract and logical.... (p. 61)

Finally, both congeries and complexes (within both of which classes he distinguishes sub-classes) are distinguished from *concepts*:

Since a complex is not formed on the plane of abstract logical thinking, the bonds that create it, as well as the bonds it helps to create, lack logical unity; they may be of many different kinds. *Any factually present* connection may lead to the inclusion of a given element into a complex. That is the main difference between a complex and a concept. While a concept groups objects according to one attribute, the bonds relating the elements of a complex to the whole and to one another may be as diverse as the contacts and relationships of the elements are in reality. (p. 62)

The advanced concept presupposes more than unification. To form such a concept it is necessary to *abstract,* to *single out* elements, and to view the abstracted elements apart from the totality of concrete experience in which they are embedded. In genuine concept formation, it is equally important to unite and to separate: synthesis must be combined with analysis. Complex thinking cannot do both. Its very essence is overabundance, overproduction of connections, and weakness in abstraction. (p. 76)

... A concept emerges only when the abstracted traits are synthesized anew and the resulting abstract synthesis becomes the main instrument of thought. (p. 78)

Which brings us back to Evans-Pritchard. The totemic distribution we have examined is founded either upon 'congeries thinking' or 'complex thinking', not upon 'thinking in concepts'. I am not saying that the aborigines are incapable of thinking conceptually, however. Indeed, they exhibit no mean capacity in this direction when we examine a quite separate ordering of the natural environment which they have developed, independently of the totemic 'ordering', that is, in their ethnobotanical and ethnozoological schemas. Elsewhere (Worsley, 1961, pp. 153-90) I have listed the hundreds of species of plants and animals which the aborigines not merely know of, but also classify broadly together into such taxa as *jinungwangba* (large land-animals), *wuradjidja* (flying things, including birds), *augwalja* (fish and other sea-animals), etc. — and which they also cross-associate (complex-wise) into ecologically interconnected elements. It is for this reason, no doubt, that Donald Thomson (trained as a natural scientist) described a similar ethnobotanical-zoological system of the Wik-Monkan of Northern Queensland as having 'some resemblance to a simple Linnaean classification' (Thomson, 1946, p. 167).

It is only *proto*-Linnaean not merely because the aborigines fail to develop any more adequate criteria of classification than rather gross, and largely external, indicators such as shape, size, habitat, etc., but because they limit their inspection to species of utilitarian value, for the most part (here, in the secular order, utilitarian selection *is* important, whereas in the totemic ordering it not crucial). They have a social interest, particularly, in edible species of animal, which are more finely discriminated than non-edible or non-usable species. (Leach (1964) has recently applied this

216

insight, in a much more extended way, in a fascinating analysis of animal categories embedded in ordinary English speech.)

Granted this social motivation and selection (and, thereby, the absence of 'useless' species in the system, which a more value-free scientific classification would necessarily entail), the classification thereafter proceeds along proto-scientific lines. But this system of classification is not only a parallel, and quite separate, system from the totemic compendium; it is organised on quite different principles, and involves conceptual thinking, not thinking primarily in congeries or complexes. So we have two systems of classification, not one, and it is illegitimate to conceive of the totemic distribution as representing the only (let alone the major) way in which cultural ordering of the environment is achieved by the aborigines, let alone to construct (or assume) a unitary, overall, master synthesis, or to assume that Order I = Order II.

We have, in fact, discerned three separable areas:

1. The totemic elements themselves, which are congeries-like in that the associations between totems are of mythological derivation, and are therefore random, fortuitous or haphazard (unless we start making assumptions about subconscious levels of association), though established along quite discernible, multiple lines of association (connections in Nature, connections in myth, connections effected in historical cultural experience, etc.)
2. The order introduced into this totemic collection from without, i.e. the framework provided by the association of totem and clan/moiety.
3. The proto-scientific classification.

Like Burridge, rather than assume that the totemic logic reposes upon universal traits of human thought, we have examined Groote Eylandt totemism within the context of a specific cultural idiom, and particularly 'within the context of a corpus of myths'. As he remarks, 'the approach suggested emphasizes content, regarding form as simply a convenient if revealing mode of ordering the content in a particular cultural context'. This, we should emphasise, is not

217

mere empiricism, since it is itself a mode of analysis that traces the principles of totemic association and does not merely describe.

Lévi-Strauss, Burridge remarks, 'goes to form rather than content', producing a 'spurious uniformity'. He tends to assume an overall closeness of fit between classificatory systems within the same culture and the framework of the social order that simply is not necessarily always, or often, the case. What he sometimes produces, therefore, is the anthropological equivalent of formalism in sociology, explicitly so in his formulation of totemism as

> ... an original logic, a direct expression of the structure of the mind (and behind the mind, probably, of the brain), ... not an inert product of the action of the environment on an amorphous consciousness. (Lévi-Strauss, 1962a, p. 130; 1964a, p. 90.)[4]

This logic, he says is built into 'the laws of language and even of thought'.

The Australians, are indeed victims of order, what Lévi-Strauss himself refers to as the 'ravages' of 'l'esprit de système'. Of course, the 'laws of language' might seriously mislead us, if, without going to Australia, we tried to erect a logical scheme which seriously attributed some inner conceptual and social meaning to the French classification of all things into masculine and feminine. A similar Procrustean tendency to that which appears in this treatment of totemism is visible in the treatment of Australian marriage, which has long been dealt with as if the reality coincided with the ideology expressed in the form of an algebraically representable set of rules, yielding a marriage system in which there is overall interlocking consistency, arising from a neat and rational exchange of women. In fact, the analytical problem lies in the reconciliation of prescriptive marriage rules with the normal condition of massive divergence from these rules: the problem of delineating the principles according to which the re-ordering of relationships is effected. Here, the major breakthrough has been Hart and Pilling's study of the Tiwi (1961),[5] where marriage is set within the context of struggles for power and status. What one might call 'political adultery'

218

throws out any possibility of overall system, since women change hands faster than they do in Hollywood. There *is* no overall order, only areas of consistency inconsistently linked together, on the basis of the structural primacy of the two basic groups originally, and correctly, highlighted by Radcliffe-Brown (1931): the nuclear family and the sibling group.

Aboriginal marriage is not an internally consistent system of self-reciprocating equilibrium. Mechanical analogies, as usual, are of dubious value for the study of human cultural activity, since deviation and manipulation are omnipresent, both because people have differential interests and because they innovate.

As a further instance of the overstructuring in the analysis of Australian society. Hiatt has demonstrated how the close nomadic association between the patrilineal horde and its local territory, postulated by Radcliffe-Brown, just is not the case (Hiatt, 1962).

'Only disconnect' would surely be sage advice to the systematiser faced with the temptations of Australia.

Totemism is, of course, not merely a cognitive ordering, it also has affectual and evaluative meaning. Totemism, in fact, to the aborigine, expresses symbolically the totality of his society and its relationship to the wider order of Nature and the supernatural. It also has institutional implications. It deals with the relatively fixed basic units of clan and moiety, and provides a super-empirical rationale for the order of earthly life. But other classifications, e.g. that involved in the terminological and social ordering of marriage and kinship, deal with much more fluid and manipulable matters. Kinship classification is not just an ordering; it is a set of claims and manipulations (not just — neutrally — 'exchanges'.) So there is a fundamental difference between these two types of classification, and they must be kept analytically distinct. Further, one might observe that there is yet another system of classification — a linguistic one — contained in the Groote Eylandt system of noun classification that is quite unconnected with totemic classification, proto-scientific classification, or any other (and is largely congeries-like rather than conceptual; see Worsley, 1954).

Finally, on binary discrimination. Undoubtedly, as Simmel

219

long ago demonstrated, similarity and difference lend themselves to expression within a two-cell matrix. Indeed, other, more complex multiple combinations are likely to be finally subsumable within such a framework also. Out of dozens of political parties, for example, alliances of government and opposition are formed. The binary form is thus extremely widespread. But it is by no means universal. In some political systems — as in Indonesia today — the several parties just remain several. Indeed, not the binary form, but *unity* is the ultimate residual. There are one-party states, and governments which give representation to *all* parties.

One should, therefore, not be too bemused by the binary fashion. Once upon a time (from Vico to Hegel and beyond) it was triads. Now numerological fashion has changed — binary analysis is illuminating, but if erected into an absolute and universal metaphysic, instead of being used heuristically, it becomes numerology and fashion, not science.

REFERENCES

Bergson, H. 1958 (88th ed.). 'Les Deux Sources de la morale et de la religion.' Paris: Bibliothèque de Philosophie Contemporaine.

Durkheim, E. 1950 (8th ed.). 'Rules of Sociological Method'. Glencoe, Ill.: The Free Press.

—— 1957. 'The Elementary Forms of the Religious Life.' London: Allen & Unwin.

Elkin, A. P. 1933. 'Studies in Australian Totemism'. Sydney: Australian National Research Council. Oceania Monographs no. 2.

Evans-Pritchard, E. E. 1934. 'Lévy-Bruhl's Theory of Primitive Mentality' (extract from the 'Bulletin of the Faculty of Arts', ii (1). Cairo: Imprimerie de l'Institut Francais d'Archéologie Orientale.

Fortes, M. 1945. 'The Dynamics of Clanship among the Tallensi'. London: Oxford University Press (International African Institute).

Hart, C. W. M. and Pilling, A. R. 1961. 'The Tiwi of North Australia'. New York: Holt, Rinehart & Wilson.

Hiatt, L. R. 1962 'Local Organization among the Australian Aborigines', 'Oceania', xxxii 267-86.

Leach, E. R. 1964. 'Anthropological Aspects of Language: Animal Categories and Verbal Abuse', in Eric H. Lenneberg (ed.), 'New Directions in the Study of Language'. Cambridge, Mass.: M.I.T. Press. pp. 23-63.

Lévi-Strauss, C. 1962a. 'Le Totémisme aujourd'hui'. Paris: Presses Universitaires de France (English translation, 1964a. 'Totemism'. London: Merlin Press).

—— 1962b. 'La pensée sauvage'. Paris: Plon.

—— 1963a. 'Structural Anthropology'. New York: Basic Books.

Lockwood, D. 1956. 'Some Remarks on "The Social System" ', 'British Journal of Sociology', vii 134-46.

MacBeath, A. 1952. 'Experiments in Living'. London: Macmillan.

Miller, Henry. 1936. 'Black Spring'. Paris: Obelisk Press.

Mills, C. Wright. 1963. 'The Marxists'. Harmondsworth: Pelican Books.

Nadel, S. F. 1954 'Nupe Religion'. London: Routledge & Kegan Paul.

Radcliffe-Brown, A. R. 1931. 'The Social Organization of Australian Tribes'. Melbourne: Macmillan.

Spencer, B. and Gillen, F. J. 1904. 'The Northern Tribes of Central Australia'. London: Macmillan.

Thomson, D. F. 1946. 'Names and Naming in the Wik Monkan Tribe'. 'Journal of the Royal Anthropological Institute', lxxvi (2) 157-67.

Worsley, P. 1954. 'Noun-Classification in Australian & Bantu: Formal or Semantic?', 'Oceania', xxiv 275-88.

—— 1955. 'Totemism in a Changing Society', 'American Anthropologist', lvii 851-61.

—— 1956. 'Emile Durkheim's Theory of Knowledge', 'Sociological Review', iv 47-62.

—— 1961. 'The Utilization of Food Resources by an Australian Aboriginal Tribe', 'Acta Ethnographica', x 153-90. Budapest: Academiae Scientiarum Hungaricae.

Vygotsky, L. S. 1962. 'Thought and Language' (ed. and trans. E. Hanfmann and G. Vankar). Studies in Communication. Cambridge, Mas.: M.I.T. Press.

1. Again, though I share similar (not the same) misgivings as to the value of Marxist 'laws of dialectics' as a whole to those expressed by Mills (1963, footnotes to pp. 129, 130), in so far as there might conceivably be any 'dialectical principles', they could not be 'Dialectics of Nature', *pace* Engels, or even 'in Nature'; dialectics are of the mind (which is itself, to be sure, 'in' Nature).

2. Durkheim was therefore wrong to insist that social facts are *things*; apart from their being abstractions from *process*, they are also not 'thing-like' in being exterior, as Durkheim insisted, but have to be subjectively 'understood' as Weber showed (Durkheim, 1950). They are all mediated via consciousness, and are evaluated. They are not likely even to be perceived at all unless they have 'social value', to use Radcliffe-Brown's term.

3. It is purely an empirical matter whether such closeness exists or not. As a parallel, Macbeath (1952) shows how legal and moral codes, in some societies, are closely sustained by religious validations, and are 'legitimated', or derive their rationale, by reference to beliefs about the supernatural. Other societies, however, do not connect legal, moral or 'jural' systems closely to the religious system. It is interesting that Nadel (1954), who studied the religion of a society where religious beliefs and practices only very slightly obtruded into everyday life, is careful to talk about the 'competences' and not the 'functions' of religion. Potentially religion 'can', say, provide a rationale for a work ethic; this is – in the permissive mode of speech – possible, even likely or common. But not always; so 'function' has too many deterministic and universalistic overtones, too many biological-organic holistic associations, to satisfy.

4. Cf. Lévi-Strauss (1963a), p. 65: 'Time and space modalities of the universal laws which make up the unconscious activity of the mind'.

5. Cf. David Lockwood's critique of another 'powerless' reciprocity-model, that of Talcott Parsons, in Lockwood (1956).

Contributors

Alfred Schutz left Austria during the Nazi persecution and taught at the New School of Social Research, New York, until his death. His work has been translated in three volumes of Collected Papers and as 'The Phenomenology of the Social World'.

Sidney Morgenbesser is Professor of Philosophy in Columbia University, New York City, and edited with Arthur Danto 'Philosophy of Science' (Meridian Books) and 'Philosophy of Science Today'.

Jürgen Habermas is Professor in the Goethe University, Frankfurt am Main, and is the author of 'Technik und Wissenschaft als Ideologie'.

Tom Burns is Professor of Sociology in the University of Edinburgh and is the author (with G. M. Stalker) of 'The Management of Innovation'.

Steven Lukes is a Fellow of Balliol College, Oxford, and is the author of a forthcoming book on Durkheim.

Ernest Gellner is Professor in the Department of Sociology in the University of London, at the London School of Economics and Political Science, and the author of 'Words and Things' and 'Thought and Change'.

Victor Turner is Professor of Social Anthropology in the University of Chicago. He has done field-work in Zambia and is author of 'Schism and Continuity in an African Society', 'The Forest of Symbols: aspects of Ndembu Ritual', and 'The Drums of Affliction: a Study of Religious Processes among the Ndembu of Zambia'.

Edmund Leach is Provost of King's College, Cambridge, and Reader in Anthropology in the University of Cambridge. He did field-work in Burma and Ceylon, and is author of 'The Political Systems of Highland Burma', 'Pul Eliya: A Village in Ceylon' and 'Rethinking Anthropology'.

Peter Worsley is Professor of Sociology in the University of Manchester. He did field-work in Melanesia and is author of 'The Trumpet shall Sound: A Study of Cargo Cults in Melanesia' and 'The Third World'.

Bibliography

This bibliography does not include all works cited in the text; it provides a basic guide to background reading that may be found useful in relation to the essays. Items with a special relevance to one particular essay are indicated by the number of the essay.

Agassi, J. 'Methodological Individualism', 'British Journal of Sociology', 1960 (5).

Arrow, K. 'Social Choice and Individual Values', London, 1951 (5).

Ayer, A. J. 'Man as Subject for Science', London, 1964 (3).

Becker, H. and Boskoff, A. (eds) 'Modern Sociological Theory', New York, 1957.

Bell, D. R. 'The Idea of a Social Science,' 'Proceedings of the Aristotelian Society', Supp. Vol. 1967 (9), (10).

Bennett, J. 'Rationality', London, 1964 (6).

Black, M. (ed.) 'The Social Theories of Talcott Parsons', Englewood Cliffs, 1961.

Blalock, H. 'Causal Inferences in Nonexperimental Research', Chapel Hill, 1964 (3).

Braithwaite, R. B. 'Scientific Exploration', London, 1953.

Braybrooke, D. (ed.) 'Philosophical Problems of the Social Sciences', London, 1965.

Brodbeck, M. (ed.) 'Readings in the Philosophy of the Social Sciences', London, 1965.

Brown, R. 'Explanation in Social Science', London, 1963.

Cicourel, A. V. 'Method and Measurement in Sociology', Glencoe, 1964 (2), (3).

Danto, A. 'Analytical Philosophy of History', Cambridge, 1968.

Danto, A. and Morgenbesser, S. (eds) 'Philosophy of Science', New York, 1960.

Davis, K. 'The Myth of Functional Analysis as a Special

Method in Sociology and Anthropology' 'American Sociological Review', 1959.

Donagan, A. and G., (eds) Philosophy of History', New York, 1965.

Dray, W. 'Laws and Explanation in History', London, 1957.

Dray, W. (ed.) 'Philosophical Analysis and History', New York, 1966.

Durkheim, E. 'Rules of Sociological Method', New York, 1950.

Emmet, D. M. 'Function, Purpose and Powers', London, 1957 (1), (8).

—— 'Rules, Roles and Relations', London, 1966 (1).

Evans-Pritchard, E. E. 'Social Anthropology', New York, 1954.

Feigl, H. and Brodbeck M. (eds) 'Readings in the Philosophy of Science', New York, 1953.

Feigl, H. *et al.* (eds) 'Minnesota Studies in the Philosophy of Science', i, ii, iii, Minneapolis, 1956, 1958, 1962.

Gallie, W. B. 'Philosophy and the Historical Understanding', London, 1964.

Galtung, J. 'Theory and Methods of Social Research', London, 1967.

Gardiner, P. (ed) 'Theories of History', New York, 1959.

Gellner, E. A. 'Holism versus Individualism in History and Sociology', 'Proceedings of the Aristotelian Society', 1956 (5).

—— 'Time and Theory in Social Anthropology', 'Mind', 1958.

—— 'Thought and Change', London, 1964.

Gibson, Q. 'The Logic of Social Enquiry', London and New York, 1960.

Gluckman, M. (ed.) 'Closed Systems and Open Minds', Edinburgh (8).

Goffman, E. 'Encounters', Indianapolis, 1961 (1), (6).

Goldstein, L. J. 'The Logic of Exploration in Malinowskian Anthropology', 'Philosophy of Science', 1957.

Gross, L. (ed.) 'Symposium on Sociological Theory', Evanston, 1959.

Gruner, R. 'Teleological and Functional Explanations', 'Mind', 1966.

Habermas, J. 'Zur Logik der Sozialwissenschaften' 'Philosophische Rundschau', 1967, (1), (3).
226

—— 'Technik und Wissenschaft als "Ideologie" ', Frankfurt am Main, 1968 (4).

Hampshire, S. 'Thought and Action', London, 1959 (7).

Hart, H. L. A. and Honoré, A. M. 'Causation in the Law', London 1959.

Hempel, C. G. 'Aspects of Scientific Explanation', New York, 1965 (1), (3), (6).

—— 'Philosophy of Natural Science', Englewood Cliffs, 1966.

Hodges, H. A. 'The Philosophy of Wilhelm Dilthey', London and New York, 1952 (1).

Laslett, P. *et al.* (eds) 'Philosophy, Politics and Society', 1st, 2nd and 3rd series, Oxford, 1957, 1962 and 1967.

Leach, E. R. 'The Political Systems of Highland Burma', London, 1954.

—— 'Pul Eliya', London, 1961.

—— 'Rethinking Anthropology', London, 1962.

—— 'Lévi-Strauss', 'Fontana Modern Masters', London, 1970.

MacIntyre, A. 'The Idea of a Social Science', 'Proceedings of Aristotelian Society', Supp. Vol. 1967 (2), (3).

Madden, E. H. (ed.) 'The Structure of Scientific Thought', Boston, 1960.

Merton, R. K. 'Social Theory and Social Structure', New York, 1957.

Morgenbesser, S. (ed.) 'Philosophy of Science Today', New York, 1967.

Nagel, E. 'Concept and Theory Formation in the Social Sciences', in 'Contemporary Philosophy', ed. J. L. Jarret and S. M. McMurrin, New York, 1954 (1).

—— 'A Formalization of Functionalism', in 'Logic Without Metaphysics', New York, 1957.

—— 'The Structure of Science', New York, 1961.

Natanson, M. (ed.) 'Philosophy of the Social Sciences: A Reader', New York, 1963.

Needham, R. 'Structure and Sentiment', Chicago, 1962 (9) (10).

Parsons, T. 'The Structure of Social Action', New York, 1949.

—— 'Essays in Sociological Theory', New York, 1941.

Popper, K. 'The Open Society and its Enemies', London, 1948.

—— 'The Poverty of Historicism', London, 1957.

—— 'The Logic of Scientific Discovery', London, 1959.

227

—— 'Conjectures and Refutations', London, 1963.

Rudner, R. 'Philosophy of Social Science', Englewood Cliffs, 1966 (1), (3).

Runciman, W. G. 'Social Science and Political Theory', London and New York, 1963.

Schutz, A. 'The Phenomenology of the Social World', Evanston, 1967.

—— 'Collected Papers', vols i-iii, The Hague, 1967.

Stammer, O. (ed.) 'Max Weber und die Soziologie heute', Tübingen, 1965.

Stinchcombe, J. 'Constructing Social Theories', New York, 1968.

Taylor, C. 'The Explanation of Behaviour', London, 1964.

Watkins, J. W. N. 'Holism versus Individualism', 'Proceedings of the Aristotelian Society', 1956.

Weber, M. 'On the Methodology of the Social Sciences', New York, 1949.

White, A. (ed.) 'The Philosophy of Action', London, 1968.

Winch, P. 'The Idea of a Social Science', London, 1958 (7).

Zetterberg, H. L. 'On Theory and Verification in Sociology', Totowa, 1968.

Index